Chas. B. Cushing
C/o Dunfey Hotels
500 Lafayette
Hampton, N.H.
03842

603-926-8911

May 82

FUNDAMENTALS OF QUANTITY FOOD PREPARATION

APPETIZERS,
SALAD DRESSINGS,
AND SALADS

FUNDAMENTALS OF QUANTITY FOOD PREPARATION

APPETIZERS, SALAD DRESSINGS, AND SALADS

GERALINE B. HARDWICK and ROBERT L. KENNEDY

CBI PUBLISHING COMPANY, INC.
51 Sleeper Street
Boston, Massachusetts 02210

Production Editor: Patricia Cronin
Text Designer: Debrah Welling
Compositor: Waldman
Copyright © 1982 by CBI Publishing Company, Inc.
51 Sleeper Street, Boston, MA 02210

Library of Congress Cataloging in Publication Data

Hardwick, Geraline B.
    Fundamentals of quantity food preparation—appetizers, salad dressings, & salads.

    Bibliography: p.
    Includes index.
    1. Quantity cookery. 2. Cookery (Appetizers)
3. Salad dressing. 4. Salads. I. Kennedy,
Robert L. II. Title. III. Title: Appetizers,
salad dressings, & salads.
TX820.H355   641.8′6   81–12240
ISBN 0–8436–2207–5   AACR2

Printed in the United States of America
Printing (*last digit*): 987654321

CONTENTS

ACKNOWLEDGMENTS

It would be impossible to list all of those to whom we owe a debt of gratitude for their advice and assistance in the preparation of this and the two previous volumes in the *Fundamentals of Quantity Food Preparation* series, *Desserts and Beverages* (1975) and *Breads, Soups and Sandwiches* (1978). Special thanks must go to Ann Arrington of Neptune, New Jersey, for reviewing the material in this and the earlier books. To Sonya Gaskins, Koleen Hassey, and Gloria Mitchell we extend our appreciation for their secretarial assistance and attention to detail. And for their work, patience, and cooperation we thank Philip W. Mason and all of his associates at CBI Publishing Company, Inc.

PREFACE

Appetizers, Salad Dressings, and Salads, the third volume in the *Fundamentals of Quantity Food Preparation* series, is designed to provide information of assistance and interest to those responsible for quantity foodservice in restaurants, schools, and other institutions. As in the previous volumes, *Desserts and Beverages* (1975) and *Breads, Soups and Sandwiches* (1978), the authors have compiled background materials, detailed formulas, and thorough instructions that will provide foodservice workers and students with some of the basic information necessary for effective job performance.

Part One of this book (Appetizers) includes some minor variations in format from the earlier volumes. Because appetizers are not often prepared in substantial quantities, many of the appetizer formulas featured here will yield fewer portions than other quantity formulas. The basic approach to food formula standardization is continued in Parts Two (Salad Dressings) and Three (Salads).

It may be helpful to those unfamiliar with this approach to define a quantity food formula. In its simplest terms, the quantity formula is a basic recipe developed and expanded for use in quantity foodservice operations. The term *formula* is used because specific measures and detailed instructions—more comprehensive and more standardized than in many general-use recipes—must be provided by management if employees are to perform their jobs properly, and if quality controls are to be established and maintained. In a time of increasing personnel and product costs, the procedures and techniques of quantity food preparation must become more exact and standardized if foodservice operations are to survive in their highly complex and competitive industry. The food formula, properly used, enables the operator to:

1. purchase the proper kinds and amounts of ingredients to prepare a product;
2. precost the item within budgetary limitations and in relation to the total menu;
3. determine in advance the time, equipment, and personnel required for production;
4. prepare the product with proper attention to portion control and methods of service; and
5. maintain a consistent standard of quality.

The more detailed a quantity formula, the more effectively it can be used in training centers and in actual operations. As an example, the use of AP (As Purchased) and EP (Edible Portion) to describe certain ingredients can lead to greater accuracy in preparation procedures. The use of multiple yields permits personnel to work without excessive computation of ingredient amounts, simplifies remakes and the preparation of larger quantities, allows for more accurate production control, and aids in providing a specific and consistent quality of product. A detailed rationale for and explanation of the multiple yield quantity food formula may be found in the introduction to *Desserts and Beverages*, the first volume in this series.

The authors have been gratified by the response to their first two books and hope that this one, too, will be of interest, assistance, and very practical value to foodservice managers, employees, students, and others with an interest in quantity food production.

PART 1:

APPETIZERS

APPETIZERS

Quantity foodservice operators have traditionally placed primary emphasis on simple appetizers—those that are easy to prepare and readily accepted by guests. The standard shrimp cocktail, the fruit cup, and the glass of chilled fruit or vegetable juice have been the most commonly listed appetizers on the menu. While there is no reason to delete these basic items from the appetizer selection, today's guests seek more unusual appetizers with which to begin their meals.

By definition, an appetizer is a small portion of food served before or as the first course of a meal. It is intended to stimulate the appetite, not to dull it. Appetizers of all kinds may be served for the first course of a dinner or as individual items at a buffet table, reception, or cocktail party. Appetizers may be served hot or cold and range from the simplest canape to the most elaborate of hors d'oeuvres.

There is a trend toward the use of fresh vegetables and fruits as appetizers. The results of a recent survey published in *Institutions/Volume Feeding Magazine* indicate that fresh vegetables, fresh fruit, and melon are the most frequently selected appetizers in all types of commercial and noncommercial foodservice operations. This increased preference for fresh fruits and vegetables may have resulted, in part, from the "back-to-nature" movement that has been especially strong among young people. An increased awareness of nutrition, especially of the importance of fiber in the diet, may also have contributed to this trend.

Foodservice operators are finding that the items they once gave away or used as a garnish may now be easily prepared, successfully merchandised, and sold as appetizers. The gratis vegetable-relish dish has given way to an array of fresh vegetables served with a simple dip and profitably sold as a crudite.

Guests who dine out regularly, and some who dine all over the world, are looking for new options on the appetizer menu. While it is not uncommon to see octopus or eel listed on the menus of restaurants in large cities, variations of more familiar items have created the greatest interest. The formulas in this section emphasize these variations. The Shrimp in Tomato Half Shell, for example, or the Curried Chutney Shrimp are two possible variations on the traditional shrimp cocktail.

Several of the appetizer formulas that follow utilize the concept of *nouvelle cuisine,* in which the minimal preparation and aesthetically pleasing arrangement of fresh foods is emphasized. A perfectly cooked artichoke with vinaigrette dressing, a chilled strawberry or watercress soup, or a melon slice with blackberry brandy are examples of appetizers that satisfy the demand for variety, the need for simplicity of preparation, and the desire for fresh foods.

There are times when the simplest appetizers are best. They should be available to customers and are necessary and appropriate for banquet service. At other times, it may be appropriate to lavish time-consuming culinary artistry on the ingredients and preparation of a complicated, expensive, and elegant appetizer. Many restaurants search for something new that may become a signature or distinguishing menu item for the establishment. Guests may travel miles for an appetizer such as the Cherry-Lemon Soup or the Walnut Pate as they are served in New York's *Cafe des Artistes.* Although formulas have been included for those who wish to be exceptionally innovative, it is equally possible to establish a reputation and standard of excellence for one's operation with such easy-to-prepare items as the Specialty Cream Soups.

Recently, deep fried vegetables, such as mushrooms and zucchini dipped in a light batter, have appeared on appetizer menus. Basic preparation procedures for these items has been almost completely absorbed by the frozen food industry and the quality is so consistent that there is little need for formulas for these items.

The appetizers included in this book may be placed in eight basic categories: (1) Juices or Shrubs; (2) Fruit Appetizers; (3) Jellied Appetizers; (4) Dips, Spreads, and Pates; (5) Canapes and Hors d'oeuvres; (6) Seafood Cocktails; (7) Quiche; and (8) Specialty Soups. Formulas for some of the more unique appetizers have been developed in smaller amounts than usual for quantity foodservice operations, so that test portions may be prepared. If successful, these may be prepared in larger quantities using available kitchen equipment. The formulas included in this book have been planned to provide not only the old and familiar, but the new and exotic as well.

For restaurants wishing to utilize the latest trends in the all-important first course, the following is a sample listing of appetizers that will serve as a guide:

Fruit Juice or Jellied Cocktail
Apricot-Apple Shrub
Jellied Tomato Madrilene

Hot Potage
Shrimp Bisque
Mulligatawny

Chilled Soup
Gazpacho
Zucchini

Charcuterie
Walnut Terrine des Artistes
Assortment of Charcuterie with Cornichons

Crudite of Fresh Vegetables or Fruit
Seasonal Variety with Cucumber Yogurt
Sliced Hot House Tomato with Vinaigrette
Fresh Pear with Prosciutto
Fresh Artichoke Hot or Cold with Sauce Alsacienne
Melon with Blackberry Brandy

Additional First Courses
Avocado with Crab Ravigote
Hot Clams Casino
Herb Stuffed Mushrooms
Blue Cheese Mousse
Ambassador Seafood Cocktail
Chutney Shrimp in Pastry Shell

JUICES OR SHRUBS

Fruit or vegetable juices should be served when a light appetizer is desired and are commonly listed on the menu under the title of Cocktail. The juice should be thoroughly chilled before serving and may be acidulated or contain other seasonings for added flavor. A Tomato Juice Cocktail, for example, may include lemon juice, salt, Worcestershire sauce, or a dash of hot pepper sauce. Canapes are often served as a complement to the Tomato Juice Cocktail.

In addition to the cocktail, the term *shrub* is often used on appetizer menus. It is derived from the Arabic *sharab* meaning "drink." Shrubs were served in this country in Colonial days as a punch, usually containing alcohol. Today the word *shrub* may be used to describe virtually any nonalcoholic combination of acidulated or carbonated juices. Any of the fruit juice cocktails included in this volume could be called a shrub.

A frosted shrub is one that contains fruit juice and a scoop of sherbet. The frosted shrub provides a variation in texture and flavor and has a definite tart taste.

APPLE–LIME COCKTAIL

4 oz. or ½ cup	1 Gal. 3 Cups 36 Portions	2 Gal. 1 Qt. 2 Cups 72 Portions	4 Gal. 3 Qt. 144 Portions	9 Gal. 2 Qt. 228 Portions
Apple Juice, 46-oz. can	3 cans	6 cans	1 case	2 cases
Lime Juice	1 cup	2 cups	1 qt.	2 qts.

1. Combine juices and mix thoroughly.
2. Chill until serving time.
3. Mix juices to blend before serving.

APRICOT–APPLE SHRUB

4 oz. or ½ cup	3 Qt. 2 Cups 28 Portions	1 Gal. 3 Qt. 56 Portions	3 Gal. 2 Qt. 112 Portions	7 Gallons 224 Portions
Apple Juice, 46-oz. can	2 cans	4 cans	8 cans	16 cans
Apricot Nectar, 46-oz. can	3 cups	1 can	2 cans	4 cans
Lemon Juice	1 Tbsp.	2 Tbsp.	¼ cup	½ cup

1. Combine juices and mix thoroughly.
2. Chill until serving time.
3. Mix juices to blend before serving.

Note: This cocktail is similar in taste to Apple Cider.

CRANBERRY OR GRAPE JUICE COCKTAIL

4 oz. or ½ cup	3 Gallons 96 Portions	6 Gallons 192 Portions	12 Gallons 384 Portions	24 Gallons 768 Portions
Sugar	1 lb. 4 oz.	2 lb. 8 oz.	5 lb.	10 lb.
Water	2 qt.	1 gal.	2 gal.	4 gal.
Cranberry Juice *or* Grape Juice	1 gal. 2 qt.	3 gal.	6 gal.	12 gal.
Orange Juice	1 qt. 2 cups	3 qt.	1 gal. 2 qt.	3 gal.
Lemon Juice	3 cups	1 qt. 2 cups	3 qt.	1 gal. 2 qt.
Ginger ale	2 qt.	1 gal.	2 gal.	4 gal.

1. Bring sugar and water to a boil, stirring occasionally. Cool.
2. Combine sugar syrup and fruit juices; blend thoroughly.
3. Chill.
4. Add ginger ale and stir well just before serving.

PINEAPPLE GRAPEFRUIT COCKTAIL

4 oz. or ½ cup	3 Gallons 96 Portions	6 Gallons 192 Portions	12 Gallons 384 Portions	24 Gallons 768 Portions
Pineapple Juice, 46-oz. can	6 cans	1 case	2 cases	4 cases
Grapefruit Juice, 46-oz. can	2 cans	4 cans	8 cans	16 cans
Lemon Juice	¾ cup	1½ cups	3 cups	1 qt. 2 cups

1. Combine fruit juices and mix thoroughly.
2. Chill until serving time.
3. Mix juice to blend before serving.

TOMATO COCKTAIL

4 oz. or ½ cup	1 Gal. 2 Qt. 48 Portions	3 Gallons 96 Portions	6 Gallons 192 Portions	12 Gallons 384 Portions
Tomato Juice, 46-oz. can	4 cans	8 cans	1 case 4 cans	2 cases 8 cans
Lemon Juice	¾ cup	1½ cups	3 cups	1 qt. 2 cups
Sugar	¾ oz.	1½ oz.	3 oz.	6 oz.
Salt	1 Tbsp.	1 oz.	2 oz.	4 oz.

1. Combine all ingredients and mix thoroughly.
2. Chill until serving time.
3. Serve with 2 canapes.

TANGY TOMATO COCKTAIL

4 oz. or ½ cup	1 Gal. 2 Qt. 48 Portions	3 Gallons 96 Portions	6 Gallons 192 Portions	12 Gallons 384 Portions
Tomato Juice, 46-oz. can	4 cans	8 cans	1 case 4 cans	2 cases 8 cans
Lemon Juice	½ cup	1 cup	2 cups	1 qt.
Worcestershire Sauce	2 Tbsp.	¼ cup	½ cup	1 cup
Tabasco Sauce	½ tsp.	1 tsp.	2 tsp.	1 Tbsp. 1 tsp.
Celery Salt	2 Tbsp. or ¾ oz.	1½ oz.	3 oz.	6 oz.

1. Combine all ingredients.
2. Chill until serving time.
3. Serve with two canapes.

FRUIT APPETIZERS

The natural blend of sweetness and tartness and the high vitamin and mineral content of fresh fruit make it an ideal appetizer as a light introduction to a meal. Recent surveys of customer preferences in appetizers place fresh fruit at the top in foodservice operations of all kinds. The consumption of fresh fruit by the American public has increased in recent years. And, because the public clearly desires more fresh fruit on the menu, the trend toward its use in quantity foodservices is likely to continue. A growing concern for nutrition has contributed to the acceptance of fresh fruit as an appetizer, and the near-prohibitive price of shellfish appetizers has made fresh fruit appetizers even more widely accepted.

Fruit cups are familiar items on many appetizer menus. All too often, however, they consist of nothing more than canned fruit cocktail heaped in a sherbet dish. Whenever possible, canned fruit or fruit cocktail should be combined with one or more fresh fruits. Availability and selection may vary according to seasons, but fresh fruit of one kind or another can be found on the market throughout the year. Appetizers made entirely of fresh fruit are preferable, and should be offered whenever possible.

One of the most exciting things about the fruit cup appetizer is the almost unlimited variety of fruits that may be combined to provide contrast in taste, texture, and color. Melon may be combined with grapes, for example, or pears can be served in combination with strawberries or blueberries.

Fresh fruit is usually served with a flavored liquid that enhances the natural taste and elegance of the fruit. This liquid can be as simple as a plain syrup flavored with lime juice, or as elaborate as a medley of fruit juices combined with champagne, sparkling mineral water, or ginger ale. Although certain liqueurs harmonize exceptionally well with the natural flavors of fruit, care must be taken to select one that is not so excessively sweet that the appetizer becomes a dish better served as a dessert.

In fruit cups served as appetizers, the fruit is diced or cut in small sections and usually served in a stemmed sherbet dish. Fruit compotes contain larger pieces or whole sections served on a flat compote dish. While fruit compotes traditionally have been reserved for dessert service, there are some combinations of fruit slices or segments that make excellent appetizers. As with all other appetizers, portions should be kept small so the appetite for the balance of the meal will not be dulled.

ALOHA FRUIT WITH STRAWBERRY DIP

1. Any tropical fruit may be used for this fresh fruit appetizer. Suggestions are fresh pineapple, bananas, mangoes, and papaya.
2. Cut all fruit into chunks and arrange on a plate.
3. Garnish with strawberries, red raspberries, or Bing cherries.
4. Serve with a souffle of Strawberry Dip (see following formula).

STRAWBERRY DIP

2 Tbsp. per Portion	2 Cups 16 Portions	1 Quart 32 Portions	2 Quarts 64 Portions	1 Gallon 128 Portions
Yogurt, Vanilla	2 cups	1 qt.	2 qt.	1 gal.
Strawberries, fresh, pureed	¼ cup	½ cup	1 cup	2 cups

1. Cap and wash strawberries.
2. Puree strawberries in blender until smooth and liquid.
3. Add strawberry puree to Vanilla Yogurt.
4. Serve 2 Tbsp. per portion with any combination of fresh fruit or any combination of fresh and well-drained canned fruit.

Note: One cup of fresh strawberries yields ¾ cup of puree. One quart of strawberries yields 3 cups of puree.

FROSTED RED RASPBERRIES

½ Cup Portion	8 Portions	16 Portions	32 Portions	64 Portions
Red Raspberries	1 qt.	2 qt.	4 qt.	8 qt.
Yogurt, plain	1 cup	2 cups	1 qt.	2 qt.
Sugar, Confectioner's	3 Tbsp.	6 Tbsp.	¾ cup	1½ cups
Coconut, flaked, optional	3 Tbsp.	6 Tbsp.	¾ cup	1½ cups

1. Wash and thoroughly drain raspberries. Chill.
2. When ready to serve, put ½ cup raspberries in a glass sherbet dish.
3. Top with 2 Tbsp. plain yogurt.
4. Top with 1 tsp. confectioner's sugar.
5. Top with 1 tsp. flaked coconut if desired.

Note: Vanilla yogurt may be used in place of plain yogurt. If vanilla yogurt is used, delete the confectioner's sugar.

FRESH PINEAPPLE AND STRAWBERRIES WITH COCONUT DIP

	18 Portions	36 Portions	72 Portions
Pineapple, large, ripe	1	2	4
Strawberries, large, ripe	2 qt.	4 qt.	8 qt.
Sugar, Confectioner's	2 oz.	4 oz.	8 oz.
Coconut, flaked, optional	2 oz.	4 oz.	8 oz.

1. Cut pineapple into 6 slices. Peel each slice and remove any brown nodules. Remove the hard center section of each slice.
2. Cut each slice into approximately 18 pieces. Chill.
3. Cap and wash strawberries. Drain thoroughly and chill.
4. When ready to serve put 1 tsp. confectioner's sugar in the center of a 7″ serving plate.

5. Alternate six pieces of pineapple and six strawberries per plate, so that a circle of fruit is formed around the confectioner's sugar.
6. When eating, each piece of fruit is dipped into the confectioner's sugar, which may be sprinkled with flaked coconut if desired.

KIWI FRUIT AND STRAWBERRIES WITH COCONUT DIP

	18 Portions	36 Portions	72 Portions
Kiwi Fruit	18	36	72
Strawberries	2 qt.	4 qt.	8 qt.
Sugar, Confectioner's	2 oz.	4 oz.	8 oz.
Coconut, flaked, optional	2 oz.	4 oz.	8 oz.

1. Peel Kiwi. Slice each Kiwi into 6 slices ¼" thick.
2. Cap and wash strawberries. Chill.
3. Put 1 tsp. confectioner's sugar in center of a 7" serving plate.
4. Surround confectioner's sugar with 6 slices of Kiwi.
5. Place a strawberry on top of each Kiwi slice. Confectioner's sugar may be sprinkled with flaked coconut if desired.

MINTED PINK GRAPEFRUIT CUP
Christmas Fruit Cup

½ Cup Portion	6 Portions	12 Portions	24 Portions	48 Portions
Grapefruit, pink, sectioned with juice	3 *or* 3 cups	6 *or* 1 qt. 2 cups	12 *or* 3 qt.	24 *or* 1 gal. 2 qt.
Mint Jelly, melted	3 Tbsp.	6 Tbsp.	¾ cup	1½ cups

1. Section grapefruit by peeling outside rind. Cut into sections. No white membrane should be visible after sectioning.
2. Melt mint jelly and add to grapefruit sections and juice.
3. Allow to chill several hours for flavors to blend.
4. Serve ½ cup sections and juice in a stemmed, glass sherbet dish.
5. Garnish with a mint leaf.

SPRING FRUIT CUP

¾ Cup Portion	6 Portions	12 Portions	24 Portions	48 Portions
Strawberries, fresh	1½ cups	3 cups	1 qt. 2 cups	3 qt.
Pineapple, fresh, diced	1½ cups	3 cups	1 qt. 2 cups	3 qt.
Honeydew Melon, ripe, cut in balls or cubes	1½ cups	3 cups	1 qt. 2 cups	3 qt.
Orange Juice, freshly squeezed and strained	1½ cups	3 cups	1 qt. 2 cups	3 qt.
Lime Juice	3 Tbsp.	6 Tbsp.	¾ cup	1½ cups
Honey	1½ Tbsp.	3 Tbsp.	6 Tbsp.	¾ cup

1. Cap and wash strawberries. Chill.
2. Peel pineapple. Remove the hard center core and chop coarsely. Chill.
3. Cut honeydew melon into balls or coarsely cut into cubes. Chill.
4. Combine orange juice, lime juice, and honey. Mix well and chill.
5. To serve, put ½ to ¾ cup of fruit into each sherbet dish.
6. Pour ¼ cup of the orange, lime, and honey mixture over each fruit cup.
7. Serve thoroughly chilled. Garnish with fresh mint sprig if desired.

Note: Green grapes may be substituted for honeydew melon.

SUMMER FRUIT CUP

1. Follow the formula for Spring Fruit Cup, substituting equal amounts of watermelon, cantaloupe, and green grapes.
2. Cover with fruit juice mixture given above.

MELON IN CHAMPAGNE

¾ Cup Portion	6 Portions	12 Portions	24 Portions	48 Portions
Honeydew, ripe	1	2	4	8
Cantaloupe, ripe	1	2	4	8
Orange Juice, fresh	1 cup	2 cups	1 qt.	2 qt.
Lime Juice, fresh	2 Tbsp. 2 tsp.	⅓ cup	⅔ cup	1⅓ cups
Honey	1½ Tbsp.	3 Tbsp.	6 Tbsp.	¾ cup
Honeydew Melon, coarsely chopped	¾ cup	1½ cups	3 cups	1 qt. 2 cups
Cantaloupe, coarsely chopped	¾ cup	1½ cups	3 cups	1 qt. 2 cups
Champagne, Brut	1 cup	2 cups	1 qt.	2 qt.

1. Using medium-sized melons, cut first amount of honeydew and cantaloupe into melon balls or cubes. Chill.
2. Squeeze fresh oranges and limes. Add honey to juices.
3. Coarsely chop second amount of honeydew and cantaloupe. Any part of melon left from cutting melon balls at beginning may be used for pureeing.
4. Puree orange juice, lime juice, honey, and coarsely chopped melon in blender.
5. Pour mixture into large container and add champagne. Stir to mix.
6. Serve 9 to 12 melon balls or cubes in a glass sherbet dish.
7. Pour ¼ to ½ cup champagne mixture over melon balls.
8. Garnish with mint sprig and serve thoroughly chilled.

Note: Dry white wine may be substituted for champagne.

SPARKLING FRUIT CUP

¾ Cup Portion	6 Portions	12 Portions	24 Portions	48 Portions
Lime Rind, grated	2 tsp.	1 Tbsp. 1 tsp.	2 Tbsp. 2 tsp.	¼ cup 1 Tbsp. 1 tsp.
Lime Juice, fresh	⅓ cup	⅔ cup	1⅓ cups	2⅔ cups
Honey	⅓ cup	⅔ cup	1⅓ cups	2⅔ cups
Ginger, ground	½ tsp.	1 tsp.	2 tsp.	1 Tbsp. 1 tsp.
Fruit, diced	1 qt. 2 cups	3 qt.	1 gal. 2 qt.	3 gal.

Chilled Sparkling Mineral Water as needed to fill each portion.

1. Combine lime rind, juice, honey, and ginger.
2. Add fruits and toss. Cover and refrigerate 3 to 5 hours, tossing occasionally.
3. Portion fruits and liquid into tall stemmed glasses.
4. Fill each portion with sparkling water. Serve with straws and spoons.

Note: Fruits may consist of mango, pineapple, papaya, orange sections, plums, peaches, white grapes, honeydew or other melon, and apples. If bananas are used they should be added just before serving in order to prevent being waterlogged.

RHUBARB PINEAPPLE CUP

¾ Cup Portion	12 Portions	24 Portions	48 Portions	96 Portions
Rhubarb, cut in ½" pieces	1 qt.	2 qt.	1 gal.	2 gal.
Water	1 qt.	2 qt.	1 gal.	2 gal.
Sugar	1 cup	2 cups	1 qt.	2 qt.
Pineapple, fresh, cut in ½" pieces	1 qt.	2 qt.	1 gal.	2 gal.

Note: Rhubarb should be pink for this appetizer.

1. Clean and cut rhubarb.
2. Cover with water, add sugar, and stir to mix.

3. Bake in a 350° oven until tender (when baked in oven, rhubarb pieces do not lose their form).
4. Chill covered in the refrigerator.
5. Cut pineapple in slices. Peel each slice and remove any brown nodules. Cut into ½″ pieces.
6. Combine rhubarb with fresh pineapple. Stir to mix.
7. Serve in a stemmed sherbet dish.

PEARS WITH PROSCIUTTO

	6 Portions	12 Portions	24 Portions
Pears, ripe	6	12	24
Prosciutto	6 slices	12 slices	24 slices

1. Peel pears and remove cores. Slice pears into 6 sections, 3 sections per half-pear.
2. Dip pear sections into orange juice to coat. This prevents darkening of pears.
3. Wrap each pear section with prosciutto.
4. Arrange sections of pear in a circle on a 7″ plate.
5. Put a small mound of raspberries or several strawberries in center for garnish. Sprinkle berries with confectioner's sugar.

Note: Pears must be ripe for this appetizer. Melon may be substituted for pears.

MELON WITH BLACKBERRY BRANDY

1. Use honeydew or crenshaw melon. Melon *must* be ripe.
2. Cut melon into large cubes and put ½ to ¾ cup in a glass compote dish.
3. Add 2 Tbsp. Blackberry Brandy. Serve chilled.

Note: Black or red raspberry liqueur may be substituted for the Brandy.

SIMPLE SYRUP

	1 Gallon	2 Gallons	3 Gallons	4 Gallons
Sugar	6 lb.	12 lb.	18 lb.	24 lb.
Water, hot	3 qt.	1 gal. 2 qt.	2 gal. 1 qt.	3 gal.
Lime Juice	½ cup	1 cup	1½ cups	2 cups

1. Combine sugar and hot water in steam kettle.
2. Stir to dissolve sugar.
3. Heat to boiling and simmer slowly for 10 minutes.
4. Remove from heat and cool.
5. Store in refrigerator in covered jars or other containers.
6. Add lime juice to the cold syrup before combining with fruit.

SIMPLE SYRUP WITH CANNED FRUIT JUICE

	1 Gallon	2 Gallons	3 Gallons	4 Gallons
Canned Fruit Juice, light colored	1 gal.	2 gal.	3 gal.	4 gal.
Lime Juice	½ cup	1 cup	1½ cups	2 cups

1. Combine lime juice with chilled, canned fruit juice before adding to fruit.

PEAR FRUIT CUP

½ Cup Portion	48 Portions	96 Portions	192 Portions	384 Portions
Pears, canned, halves or diced	2 #10 cans	4 #10 cans	1 case	2 cases
			2 cans	4 cans
Lime Juice	¾ cup	1½ cups	3 cups	1 qt.
				2 cups

1. Combine lime juice with pears (do not drain fruit). Chill thoroughly in refrigerator.
2. Garnish with blueberries, watermelon cubes or orange sections.

Note: In order to prepare lime juice using lime crystals, use the following amounts of lime crystals and water.

Lime Crystals	½ oz.	1 oz.	2 oz.	4 oz.
Water	¾ cup	1½ cups	3 cups	1 qt. 2 cups

DICED PEAR AND PINEAPPLE CUP

½ Cup Portion	48 Portions	96 Portions	192 Portions	384 Portions
Pears, diced	1½ #10 cans	½ case	1 case	2 cases
Pineapple, crushed	½ #10 can	1 #10 can	2 #10 cans	4 #10 cans
Lime Juice	¾ cup	1½ cups	3 cups	1 qt. 2 cups

1. Combine fruits and lime juice (do not drain fruit).
2. Chill thoroughly in refrigerator.

Note: Mandarin oranges or pineapple tidbits may be substituted for crushed pineapple.

DICED PEAR AND WATERMELON CUP

1. Follow the formula for Diced Pear and Pineapple Cup, substituting watermelon for crushed pineapple in the following amounts.

Watermelon, cubed ¼″ to ½″	1 qt. 2 cups	3 qt.	1 gal. 2 qt	3 gal.

MINTED PEAR AND PINEAPPLE CUP

½ Cup Portion	48 Portions	96 Portions	192 Portions	384 Portions
Pears, diced	1½ #10 cans	3 #10 cans	1 case	2 cases
Pineapple Tidbits	½ #10 can	1 #10 can	2 #10 cans	4 #10 cans
Essence of Peppermint	⅛ tsp.	¼ tsp.	½ tsp.	1 tsp.

1. Do not drain fruit. Combine fruits and peppermint flavoring.
2. Chill thoroughly in refrigerator.

JELLIED APPETIZERS

There are two common categories of jellied appetizers. The first is jellied soup, such as Jellied Bouillon or Jellied Tomato Madrilene. The second category includes the various jellied fish appetizers, such as the Jellied Tuna Cocktail. A third category, seen less often, is the jellied appetizer in which a fruit or vegetable is used as a base. The Avocado Mousse, with its base of avocado, is one such example.

Jellied appetizers are served most frequently in warm weather. Although a welcome addition to the summer menu, this appetizer poses a problem for the foodservice operator because it must be served thoroughly chilled. Jellied appetizers may be preportioned or set up ahead of time, refrigerated, and served directly from the refrigerator. Under no circumstances should they be permitted to stand on a serving line for any length of time.

An unflavored gelatin of excellent quality is essential to the preparation of a quality jellied appetizer. The use of a less than quality product or failure to make certain that the gelatin is completely dissolved during preparation may result in a tough, rubbery product.

The Jellied Tomato Madrilene is among the most frequently served of all jellied appetizers and is excellent when served with a

KNOX GELATIN COMPANY

Figure 1   This easy-to-prepare Jellied Tomato Madrilene may be served as an appetizer in clear glass serving dishes, topped with sour cream and bits of tomato or bell pepper.

dollop of sour cream. The Tomato Aspic is another product that lends itself to preparation as a jellied appetizer. It may be cut into squares or cubes, served with shrimp, flaked fish, or avocado cubes, and topped with a dressing. (The Tomato Aspic formula can be found in Part Three under Jellied Salads.)

JELLIED TOMATO MADRILENE

½ Cup Portion	1 Gal. 2 Qt. 48 Portions	3 Gallons 96 Portions	6 Gallons 192 Portions	12 Gallons 384 Portions
Gelatin, unflavored	3 oz.	6 oz.	12 oz.	1 lb. 8 oz.
Tomato Juice, cold, 46-oz. can	1 can	2 cans	4 cans	8 cans
Bouillon, granulated	⅜ oz.	¾ oz.	1½ oz.	3 oz.
Tomato Juice, cold, 46 oz. can	3 cans	6 cans	1 case	2 cases
Tabasco Sauce	1½ tsp.	1 Tbsp.	2 Tbsp.	¼ cup
Worcestershire Sauce	2 Tbsp.	¼ cup	½ cup	1 cup
Lemon Juice	1½ cups	3 cups	1 qt. 2 cups	3 qt.
Salt	1 Tbsp.	1 oz.	2 oz.	4 oz.
Sugar	2 Tbsp.	1¾ oz.	3½ oz.	7 oz.

1. Sprinkle gelatin over first amount of cold tomato juice. Add granulated bouillon.
2. Heat, stirring constantly, until gelatin and bouillon are dissolved.
3. Remove from heat. Add second amount of cold tomato juice, Tabasco, Worcestershire, lemon juice, salt, and sugar.
4. Pour into pans to a depth of ½". Chill in refrigerator until set.
5. To serve, cut in ½" cubes and put in bouillon cups. Garnish with parsley or watercress and lemon wedge.

Note: Mixture may also be spooned into bouillon cups and served with Sour Cream Topping (see following formula).

Note: In warm weather, the gelatin amounts may need to be increased.

SOUR CREAM TOPPING

2 Tbsp. per Portion	2 Quarts	1 Gallon	2 Gallons	4 Gallons
Sour Cream	1 qt. 2 cups	3 qt.	1 gal. 2 qt.	3 gal.
Cucumber, unpeeled, cubed ¼", EP	3 cups	1 qt. 2 cups	3 qt.	1 gal. 2 qt.

1. Combine sour cream and cucumber.
2. Serve 2 Tbsp. Sour Cream Topping on Jellied Tomato Madrilene.

OTHER SERVING SUGGESTIONS
(Tomato Madrilene)

1. Cut Tomato Madrilene in cubes and serve topped with Shrimp en Coquille (see p. 69).
2. Cut Tomato Madrilene in cubes and serve with avocado cubes. Top with Coquille Sauce, Sour Cream Topping, or topping used for Shrimp in Tomato Half-Shell (see p. 59).
3. Cut Tomato Madrilene in cubes and place a deviled egg half on top. Serve with Coquille Sauce, Sour Cream Topping, or Thousand Island Dressing (see p. 145).
4. Cut Tomato Madrilene in 2" × 2" squares and serve topped with mixed cooked seafood. Coquille Sauce, Sour Cream Topping, or Thousand Island Dressing may be used.

SHRIMP CHILI MOLD

4 oz.—½ Cup Portion	20 Portions	40 Portions	80 Portions	160 Portions
Gelatin, unflavored	1¼ oz.	2½ oz.	5 oz.	10 oz.
Water, cold	1 cup	2 cups	1 qt.	2 qt.
Water, hot	1 qt.	2 qt.	1 gal.	2 gal.
Sugar	2½ oz.	5 oz.	10 oz.	1 lb. 4 oz.
Salt	2 tsp.	1 Tbsp. 1 tsp.	1¼ oz.	2½ oz.
Lemon Juice	1 cup	2 cups	1 qt.	2 qt.
Chili Sauce	1 cup	2 cups	1 qt.	2 qt.
Shrimp, cooked, ¼″ pieces	1 qt. *or* 1 lb. 4 oz.	2 qt. *or* 2 lb. 8 oz.	1 gal. *or* 5 lb.	2 gal. *or* 10 lb.
Pickle Relish	½ cup	1 cup	2 cups	1 qt.

1. Soften gelatin in cold water.
2. Add sugar and salt to hot water. Heat to boiling.
3. Add boiling mixture to softened gelatin and stir until gelatin is dissolved.
4. Add lemon juice and chili sauce and chill until slightly thickened.
5. Stir in the shrimp and pickle relish.
6. Put ½ cup in fluted molds. Chill overnight in the refrigerator.
7. Serve on a flat plate surrounded by watercress and with any of the dressings suggested for Tomato Madrilene.

JELLIED TUNA COCKTAIL

4 oz. Molds— ½ Cup Portion	20 Portions	40 Portions	60 Portions	80 Portions
Tomato Juice, hot	1 qt. 2 cups	3 qt.	1 gal. 2 cups	1 gal. 2 qt.
Gelatin, lemon flavored	12 oz.	1 lb. 8 oz.	2 lb. 4 oz.	3 lb.
Salt	1 Tbsp.	1 oz.	1½ oz.	2 oz.
Lemon Juice	2 Tbsp.	¼ cup	¼ cup 2 Tbsp.	½ cup
Horseradish	1 Tbsp.	2 Tbsp.	3 Tbsp.	¼ cup
Onion, grated	1 Tbsp.	2 Tbsp.	3 Tbsp.	¼ cup
Tuna Fish, flaked and drained	1 lb. 4 oz. *or* 2½ cups	2 lb. 8 oz. *or* 1 qt. 1 cup	3 lb. 12 oz. *or* 1 qt. 3½ cups	5 lb. *or* 2 qt. 2 cups
Celery, EP, cubed, ¼″	2 cups *or* 8 oz.	1 qt. *or* 1 lb.	1 qt. 2 cups *or* 1 lb. 8 oz.	2 qt. *or* 2 lb.

1. Heat tomato juice to boiling.
2. Add lemon gelatin and salt, and stir until completely dissolved.
3. Add lemon juice and chill until slightly thickened.
4. Add horseradish, grated onion, flaked tuna, and celery.
5. Pour into individual 4 oz. molds or 12 × 20 × 2 pans (cut 5 × 4).

Note: Lobster, shrimp, crabmeat, or seafood (flaked fish) may be substituted for the tuna.

Note: This is a tart-sweet cocktail. If desired, the sweetness may be reduced by serving with a garlic dressing or adding cayenne using the following amounts:

Cayenne	⅛ tsp.	¼ tsp.	½ tsp.	1 tsp.

AVOCADO MOUSSE

¼ Cup Portion	6 Portions	12 Portions	24 Portions
Avocadoes, ripe, peeled	2	4	8
Gelatin, unflavored	1½ tsp.	1 Tbsp.	2 Tbsp.
Lemon Juice, fresh	1½ tsp.	1 Tbsp.	2 Tbsp.
Mayonnaise	¼ cup	½ cup	1 cup
Onion, grated	2 tsp.	1 Tbsp. 1 tsp.	2 Tbsp. 2 tsp.
Worcestershire Sauce	½ tsp.	1 tsp.	2 tsp.
Salt	½ tsp.	1 tsp.	2 tsp.
Pepper, freshly ground	¼ tsp.	½ tsp.	1 tsp.
Paprika	¼ tsp.	½ tsp.	1 tsp.
Hot Pepper Sauce	4 drops	8 drops	16 drops
Sour Cream	6 Tbsp.	¾ cup	1½ cups
Cucumber Slices, to garnish			

1. Puree avocadoes in blender until smooth.
2. Soften gelatin in lemon juice.
3. Add all ingredients, except sour cream and cucumbers, to pureed avocadoes. Mix well.
4. Put ¼ cup mixture into individual souffle dishes.
5. Whip sour cream with wire whip until smooth.
6. Spread 1 Tbsp. sour cream over each mousse (the sour cream prevents discoloration).
7. Refrigerate for several hours or until set.
8. Serve cold, garnished with 1 slice of cucumber, a small piece of pimiento in center of cucumber, and a sprig of fresh dill.

DIPS, SPREADS, AND PATES

Dips, spreads and, to some extent, pates have long been associated with informal entertaining in the home. In recent years they have gained wide acceptance as appetizers in the quantity foodservice industry, and many restaurants now include one or more dips, spreads, or pates among the selection of appetizers on their menus. The Guacamole served in individual souffle dishes or bowls surrounded by a selection of crackers or seasoned breads is often served in both specialty restaurants and in the more traditional foodservice operations.

Dips are defined as mixtures soft enough to be scooped with crackers, potato or corn chips, or crisp and freshly cut vegetables. Spreads may include many of the same ingredients, but are more firm in consistency and are prepared to be spread with a knife on toast points or strips, crackers, or breads.

A mixed bouquet of freshly cut vegetables served with a dip, such as the Spinach-Yogurt or Cucumber-Yogurt combinations, provides a light and refreshing appetizer. An array of uncooked fresh vegetables arranged on a plate or platter is called a crudite, and may include cauliflowerets, carrot sticks, celery, green pepper strips, cherry tomatoes, green onions, or sliced turnips. Whole fresh mushrooms, zucchini or yellow squash, cucumber slices or strips, and other fresh vegetables may be added to the crudite. It is important that the vegetables be fresh, thoroughly washed, drained, and chilled before serving.

The trend toward low calorie foods has increased the desirability of using yogurt, cottage cheese or a mixture of both as the base of a dip which is then seasoned with the appropriate herbs and spices. Spreads, because of their firmness, usually consist of a cream cheese base. Mayonnaise and sour cream may be used as a base for either a dip or a spread, but both of these ingredients produce high calorie products.

Pate can be served as a spread with toast rounds or other breads, or it may be baked in a loaf and served in thin slices on a plate. While there are many possible combinations of pate ingredients, the version that most often comes to mind is the famed *pate de foie gras*—the rich mixture made of livers from specially fattened geese and usually studded with truffles. Pates may also be prepared in slices encased in an aspic or baked in a pastry crust. These items are listed on menus as 'pate in aspic' or 'pate en croute.'

Many foodservice operations prepare a form of pate less exotic than the foie gras and serve it as a *pate maison,* a special pate of the house, or as a *terrine,* named for the covered dish in which it is made and from which it usually is served. The foundation for a basic pate is nothing more than well-seasoned ground meat, often layered with strips or cubes of meat to provide a variation in texture and taste when the pate is sliced and served. The basic ingredient for many baked pates is called *forcemeat*—a thick, smooth paste usually made

Figure 2   A bowl of seasoned dip may be surrounded by fried fish wedges (as shown) or by fresh shrimp or vegetables. This may be used for either buffet or table service.

of finely chopped or ground pork, pork fat, veal or other meats, eggs, onions, garlic, salt, and such spices as ginger, nutmeg, cloves, and pepper. There are many possible variations of this basic mixture. The Walnut Pate des Artistes, for example, is an interesting combination of livers enhanced with walnuts and garnished with cornichons and cocktail onions because it is so rich.

Not all pates are baked. The Curried Liver Pate and the Chicken Liver Pate with Cognac and Lemon Snow may be prepared with cooked ingredients, blended, molded, thoroughly chilled, and then sliced. The Smoked Salmon and Caviar Pate is uncooked and may be served as a spread. It should be noted that this is an extremely high food cost item, included as an example of one of the more exotic pates that may be found on the menus of some restaurants.

Most dips, spreads, and pates will hold for a week to ten days if they are covered and properly refrigerated. Baked pates may be frozen if wrapped tightly in foil, but the quality and texture deteriorate if the pate is held in the freezer for any length of time beyond two to three weeks.

AVOCADO YOGURT DIP

2 Tbsp. per Portion	1½ Cups 12 Portions	3 Cups 24 Portions	1 Qt. 2 Cups 48 Portions
Yogurt, plain	1 cup	2 cups	1 qt.
Avocado, peeled, seeded, and coarsely chopped	1	2	4
Shallots, EP, chopped	2	4	8
Onion, green, EP, chopped	1	2	4
Tarragon, dried	dash	⅛ tsp.	¼ tsp.
Oregano, dried	dash	⅛ tsp.	¼ tsp.
Lemon Juice	2 tsp.	1 Tbsp. 1 tsp.	2 Tbsp. 2 tsp.
Salt	½ tsp.	1 tsp.	2 tsp.
Pepper, white	dash	⅛ tsp.	¼ tsp.

1. Combine all ingredients in a blender.
2. Blend until smooth.
3. Serve with raw vegetable relishes.

Note: This dip can be prepared one day ahead.

CUCUMBER YOGURT DIP

2 Tbsp. per Portion	1½ Cups 12 Portions	3 Cups 24 Portions	1 Qt. 2 Cups 48 Portions	3 Quarts 96 Portions
Cucumber, large or	1 *or*	2 *or*	4 *or*	8 *or*
Cucumber, grated	1 cup	2 cups	1 qt.	2 qt.
Yogurt, plain	1 cup	2 cups	1 qt.	2 qt.
Oil, salad	1 Tbsp.	2 Tbsp.	¼ cup	½ cup
Salt	⅛ tsp.	¼ tsp.	½ tsp.	1 tsp.
Garlic Powder	⅛ tsp.	¼ tsp.	½ tsp.	1 tsp.
Dill Weed, dry	⅛ tsp.	¼ tsp.	½ tsp.	1 tsp.

Note: Prepare several hours ahead of serving time. Chill covered in the refrigerator.

1. Peel large cucumber, cut in half, and remove seeds.
2. Grate cucumber (one very large cucumber will yield 1 cup grated cucumber).
3. Drain cucumber well by pressing through a sieve.
4. Combine yogurt and oil. Stir until creamy and no yogurt lumps remain.
5. Add cucumber, salt, garlic powder, and dill weed.
6. Stir to combine thoroughly.
7. Refrigerate for about 2 hours before serving.
8. Serve with assorted vegetable dippers or with sesame chips.

SPINACH-YOGURT DIP FOR VEGETABLES

2 Tbsp. per Portion	3 Cups 24 Portions	1 Qt. 2 Cups 48 Portions	3 Qt. 96 Portions
Spinach, frozen, chopped, thawed, and drained	10 oz.	1 lb. 4 oz.	2 lb. 8 oz.
Yogurt	1 lb.	2 lb.	4 lb.
Mayonnaise	½ cup	1 cup	2 cups
Onion, finely chopped, EP	¼ cup	½ cup	1 cup
Sugar	¾ tsp.	1½ tsp.	1 Tbsp.
Salt	¾ tsp.	1½ tsp.	1 Tbsp.
Lemon Juice	¾ tsp.	1½ tsp.	1 Tbsp.
Dill Weed, fresh	½ tsp.	1 tsp.	2 tsp.

1. Drain spinach thoroughly and chop very fine.
2. Combine spinach with all other ingredients.
3. Mix well. Cover and chill until ready to serve.
4. Dip may be put in dish and surrounded by a combination of cooked, chilled vegetables and garnished with cherry tomatoes and black olives.
5. Several cooked or raw vegetables (or a combination of cooked and raw) may be arranged on a shallow pool of sauce for an individual nouvelle cuisine appetizer.

ARTICHOKES WITH PIQUANT DIP

Portions	8 Portions	16 Portions	32 Portions	64 Portions
Artichokes, cooked	8	16	32	64
Mayonnaise	1 cup	2 cups	1 qt.	2 qt.
Garlic Powder	1 tsp.	2 tsp.	1 Tbsp. 1 tsp.	2 Tbsp. 2 tsp.
Pepper, black	1 tsp.	2 tsp.	1 Tbsp. 1 tsp.	2 Tbsp. 2 tsp.
Chili Sauce	1 tsp.	2 tsp.	1 Tbsp. 1 tsp.	2 Tbsp. 2 tsp.
White Rum	1 Tbsp.	2 Tbsp.	¼ cup	½ cup

1. Cook artichokes by boiling uncovered for 15 to 20 minutes.
2. Drain artichokes and thoroughly chill in refrigerator.
3. Combine all ingredients for sauce and stir with a French whip to combine well.
4. Chill sauce covered in refrigerator.
5. To serve put one whole artichoke on a flat salad plate.
6. Put 2 Tbsp. sauce in a souffle cup and serve on the same plate with artichoke. Leaves and heart of artichoke are dipped into sauce.

Note: Do not make substitutions for ingredients in the dip.

Note: This dip may be used with other vegetables such as celery, carrots, cucumbers, mushrooms, zucchini, broccoli, cauliflower, cherry tomatoes or any other combination of raw or cooked vegetables.

ARTICHOKES WITH SAUCE ALSACIENNE

Portions	8 Portions	16 Portions	32 Portions	64 Portions
Artichokes, cooked	8	16	32	64
Egg Yolk	1	2	4	8
Mustard, prepared, imported	1½ tsp.	1 Tbsp.	2 Tbsp.	¼ cup
Salt	¼ tsp.	½ tsp.	1 tsp.	2 tsp.
Lemon Juice	1½ tsp.	1 Tbsp.	2 Tbsp.	¼ cup
Oil, salad	½ cup	1 cup	2 cups	1 qt.
Cream, heavy	2 Tbsp.	¼ cup	½ cup	1 cup
Shallots, or Scallions, minced	¾ Tbsp.	1½ Tbsp.	3 Tbsp.	6 Tbsp.
Parsley, chopped	2 Tbsp.	¼ cup	½ cup	1 cup

Note: All ingredients for sauce should be at room temperature. Sauce should be prepared a day ahead, covered, and chilled in refrigerator.

1. Using mixer, beat egg yolks for 1 or 2 minutes, until thick and sticky.
2. Add mustard, salt, and lemon juice and beat for 30 seconds.
3. Begin adding oil, drop by drop at first, while beating continuously until sauce has thickened.
4. Stop pouring and continue beating every 10 seconds or so. After ⅓ or ½ of oil has been incorporated, the sauce will thicken to a consistency of a very heavy cream.
5. Add the remaining oil, blending thoroughly after each addition.
6. Gradually beat in the heavy cream.
7. Add shallots and parsley. Refrigerate covered overnight in order to allow flavors to blend.

Note: Fresh tarragon, basil, or herbs of your choice may be substituted for the parsley. For a variation, whole eggs may be used. Simmer the eggs for three minutes until the whites are barely set and the yolks still runny. Prepare sauce with egg yolks, chop the whites and add them to the sauce with shallots and parsley.

Note: Cook artichokes by boiling uncovered for 15 to 20 minutes. Drain and thoroughly chill in refrigerator.

CURRIED DIP

2 Tbsp. per Portion	1 Cup 8 Portions	2 Cups 16 Portions	1 Quart 32 Portions	2 Quarts 64 Portions
Mayonnaise	1 cup	2 cups	1 qt.	2 qt.
Curry Powder	2 tsp.	1 Tbsp. 1 tsp.	2 Tbsp. 2 tsp.	¼ cup 1 Tbsp. 1 tsp.
Soy Sauce	2 tsp.	1 Tbsp. 1 tsp.	2 Tbsp. 2 tsp.	¼ cup 1 Tbsp. 1 tsp.
Lemon Juice	2 tsp.	1 Tbsp. 1 tsp.	2 Tbsp. 2 tsp.	¼ cup 1 Tbsp. 1 tsp.
Onion, grated, EP	1 tsp.	2 tsp.	1 Tbsp. 1 tsp.	2 Tbsp. 2 tsp.

1. Combine all ingredients and mix to blend thoroughly.
2. Serve with fresh vegetables such as cauliflower flowerets, cherry tomatoes, cucumber or zucchini slices, radishes, whole or sliced mushrooms, and turnip slices.
3. Or serve with chilled, partially cooked broccoli flowerets, Brussels sprouts, or cooked artichokes.

GUACAMOLE WITH TOMATO

2 Tbsp. per Portion	1½ Cups 12 Portions	3 Cups 24 Portions	1 Qt. 2 Cups 48 Portions	3 Quarts 96 Portions
Avocado, large, ripe, peeled and seeded	½	1	2	4
Tomato, peeled and chopped	½ cup	1 cup	2 cups	1 qt.
Green Pepper, EP, chopped	⅜ cup	¾ cup	1½ cups	3 cups
Chili Powder	½ tsp.	1 tsp.	2 tsp.	1 Tbsp. 1 tsp.
Onion Salt	½ tsp.	1 tsp.	2 tsp.	1 Tbsp. 1 tsp.
Lime Juice	½ Tbsp.	1 Tbsp.	2 Tbsp.	¼ cup
Oil, olive	½ Tbsp.	1 Tbsp.	2 Tbsp.	¼ cup
Yogurt, plain	½ cup	1 cup	2 cups	1 qt.

1. Mash peeled avocado with fork.
2. Add tomato, green pepper, chili powder, onion salt, lime juice, and oil.
3. Spread yogurt over surface to prevent darkening.
4. Just before serving, blend in yogurt.
5. Serve with corn chips, toast points, wheat thins, or assorted crackers and chips.

BOURSIN

2 Tbsp. per Portion	1 Cup 8 Portions	2 Cups 16 Portions	1 Quart 32 Portions	2 Quarts 64 Portions
Cream Cheese	8 oz.	1 lb.	2 lb.	4 lb.
Sour Cream	3 Tbsp.	6 Tbsp.	¾ cup	1½ cups
Cream, heavy	3 Tbsp.	6 Tbsp.	¾ cup	1½ cups
Parsley, EP, finely chopped	3 Tbsp.	6 Tbsp.	¾ cup	1½ cups
Scallion, EP, finely sliced, use green tops also	1	2	4	8
Garlic Cloves, large, minced	1	2	4	8
Tarragon, dried, finely crumbled	¼ tsp.	½ tsp.	1 tsp.	2 tsp.
Salt	¼ tsp.	½ tsp.	1 tsp.	2 tsp.
Pepper, white	¹⁄₁₆ tsp.	⅛ tsp.	¼ tsp.	½ tsp.
Tabasco	dash	2 drops	4 drops	8 drops

1. Place cheese (at room temperature) in bowl of mixer.
2. Using flat beater, mix cheese with both kinds of cream, beating until smooth.
3. Add remaining ingredients and mix lightly to combine.
4. Cover and chill 1 hour or overnight for flavors to blend.
5. Serve with Crudite (see following formula).

CRUDITE

1. Place Boursin spread in an individual small bowl.
2. Place bowl in center of a large glass or stainless steel plate.
3. Surround bowl of Boursin with cauliflower flowerets, cherry tomatoes, zucchini slices, and carrot slices or sticks. Crackers may be used to surround the Boursin. Fresh mushrooms may be substituted for cauliflower.
4. Garnish with sprigs of chicory or watercress.

BLUE CHEESE MOUSSE

4 Tbsp. per Portion	2 Cups 8 Portions	1 Quart 16 Portions	2 Quarts 32 Portions	1 Gallon 64 Portions
Cream, heavy	½ cup	1 cup	2 cups	1 qt.
Blue Cheese	4 oz.	8 oz.	1 lb.	2 lb.
Butter	4 oz.	8 oz.	1 lb.	2 lb.
Walnuts, chopped	1 oz.	2 oz.	4 oz.	8 oz.
Pepper, white	dash	dash	$\frac{1}{16}$ tsp.	$\frac{1}{8}$ tsp.
Pepper, Cayenne	dash	dash	$\frac{1}{16}$ tsp.	$\frac{1}{8}$ tsp.
Walnuts, whole halves	1 oz.	2 oz.	4 oz.	8 oz.
French Bread	1 loaf	2 loaves	4 loaves	8 loaves

1. Using a cold bowl and beater, whip very cold heavy cream until stiff. Chill in refrigerator until needed.
2. Cut the blue cheese and butter in small pieces and cream them together in a mixer until smooth. Add white and cayenne peppers and mix.
3. Add chopped nuts and gently fold together the cheese mixture and whipped cream.
4. Spoon the mousse into individual ramekins or individual china souffle dishes (4 Tbsp. per portion).
5. Mousse may also be put into a bowl or earthenware crock and chilled.
6. Garnish with whole walnut halves. Tomato pieces or pimiento strips may also be used for a garnish.
7. Serve with thinly sliced toasted pieces of French Bread.

Note: This mousse may also be served with fruit for dessert. Apples and pears are especially good as accompaniments.

LIPTAUER CHEESE SPREAD

2 Tbsp. per Portion	2 Cups 16 Portions	1 Quart 32 Portions	2 Quarts 64 Portions	1 Gallon 128 Portions
Butter, unsalted, softened	4 oz.	8 oz.	1 lb.	2 lb.
Cottage Cheese	8 oz.	1 lb.	2 lb.	4 lb.
Hungarian Paprika, sweet	1 Tbsp.	2 Tbsp.	¼ cup	½ cup
Pepper, black, freshly ground	⅛ tsp.	¼ tsp.	½ tsp.	1 tsp.
Salt	¼ tsp.	½ tsp.	1 tsp.	2 tsp.
Caraway Seeds	2 tsp.	1 Tbsp. 1 tsp.	2 Tbsp. 2 tsp.	¼ cup 1 Tbsp. 1 tsp.
Mustard, dry	1 tsp.	2 tsp.	1 Tbsp. 1 tsp.	2 Tbsp. 2 tsp.
Capers, chopped	1 tsp.	2 tsp.	1 Tbsp. 1 tsp.	2 Tbsp. 2 tsp.
Onion, finely chopped, EP	1 Tbsp.	2 Tbsp.	¼ cup	½ cup
Sour Cream	½ cup	1 cup	2 cups	1 qt.
Chives, chopped, EP	¼ cup	½ cup	1 cup	2 cups

1. Cream butter in the mixer using the flat beater. For small amounts, butter may be creamed by beating it against the side of a mixing bowl with a wooden spoon.
2. Rub cottage cheese through a sieve into the bowl of mixer.
3. To the cottage cheese and butter mixture add the paprika, pepper, salt, caraway seeds, mustard, capers, onion, and sour cream.
4. Mix until blended well.
5. Continue to cream mixture in the mixer at medium speed until it forms a smooth paste.
6. Chill covered in the refrigerator until solid.
7. When hard, the Liptauer cheese may be formed into a ball or mound and covered with chopped chives.

LIPTAUER DIP

1. To prepare a dip, add an additional amount of sour cream by stirring in the following amounts:

   Sour Cream   ¼ cup   ½ cup   1 cup   2 cups

2. Sprinkle the chives over the dip after it has been poured into a serving bowl.

Note: This spread or dip is especially good when served with drinks or used for service at a bar.

HERBED CHEESE DIP

2 Tbsp. per Portion	2 Cups 16 Portions	1 Quart 32 portions	2 Quarts 64 Portions	1 Gallon 128 Portions
Cottage Cheese, small curd	1 cup	2 cups	1 qt.	2 qt.
Cream Cheese, softened	4 oz.	8 oz.	1 lb.	2 lb.
Parsley, coarsely chopped	1 cup	2 cups	1 qt.	2 qt.
Chives, fresh	4	8	16	32
Garlic cloves, minced	½	1	2	4
Thyme	½ tsp.	1 tsp.	2 tsp.	1 Tbsp. 1 tsp.
Basil	¼ tsp.	½ tsp.	1 tsp.	2 tsp.

1. Combine all ingredients in blender.
2. Blend until creamy and smooth.
3. Chill covered overnight in the refrigerator.

Note: This mixture may be used as a canape spread or as a dip with fresh vegetables. It also may be used to stuff cherry tomatoes as a perfect appetizer for a Christmas buffet table.

STUFFED CHERRY TOMATOES

6 per Portion	60 Tomatoes 10 Portions	120 Tomatoes 20 Portions	240 Tomatoes 40 Portions	480 Tomatoes 80 Portions
Cherry Tomatoes	2 pints	4 pints	8 pints	16 pints

Note: The Herbed Cheese Dip must be soft enough to be used in a pastry tube or to be spooned into tomatoes.

1. Scoop out cherry tomatoes and allow to drain.
2. Using a pastry bag or small spoon, fill each cherry tomato with Herbed Cheese Dip. This can be done up to 8 hours ahead of time.
3. Serve garnished with sprigs of watercress.

SMOKED SALMON SPREAD

2 Tbsp. per Portion	2 Cups 16 Portions	1 Quart 32 Portions	2 Quarts 64 Portions	1 Gallon 128 Portions
Cream Cheese, softened	6 oz.	12 oz.	1 lb. 8 oz.	3 lb.
Sour Cream	¼ cup	½ cup	1 cup	2 cups
Salmon, canned, with skin and bones removed	3 oz.	6 oz.	12 oz.	1 lb. 8 oz.
Smoked Salmon, chopped ¼"	3 oz.	6 oz.	12 oz.	1 lb. 8 oz.
Scallions, sliced thinly, EP	¼ cup	½ cup	1 cup	2 cups
Dill, fresh, chopped	2 Tbsp.	¼ cup	½ cup	1 cup
or				
Dill, dried	2 tsp.	1 Tbsp. 1 tsp.	2 Tbsp. 2 tsp.	¼ cup 1 Tbsp. 1 tsp.
Lemon Juice	1 Tbsp.	2 Tbsp.	¼ cup	½ cup
Pepper, white	¼ tsp.	½ tsp.	1 tsp.	2 tsp.

1. Mix the cream cheese and sour cream in mixer.
2. Add salmon, scallions, dill, lemon juice, and white pepper.
3. Mix only until no flecks of cream cheese remain.
4. Chill thoroughly.

Note: This spread is good on crackers or thinly sliced pumpernickel. To use as a canape, spread 1 Tbsp. mixture on dark bread rounds. Garnish with red caviar or with a thin slice of cucumber topped with a small piece of pimiento.

CREAMY NUTTY TUNA SPREAD

2 Tbsp. per Portion	1 Cup 8 Portions	2 Cups 16 Portions	1 Quart 32 Portions	2 Quarts 64 Portions
Cream Cheese, softened	4 oz.	8 oz.	1 lb.	2 lb.
Tuna, drained	4 oz.	8 oz.	1 lb.	2 lb.
Walnuts or Pecans, chopped ⅛"	2 oz.	4 oz.	8 oz.	1 lb.
Lemon Juice	1 Tbsp.	2 Tbsp.	¼ cup	½ cup

1. Combine cheese and tuna and mix until smooth.
2. Add chopped nuts and lemon juice. Mix only until combined.
3. When served in a bowl, garnish with whole walnuts or pecans.

CURRIED LIVER PATE

2 Tbsp. per Portion	1 Cup 8 Portions	2 Cups 16 Portions	1 Quart 32 Portions	2 Quarts 64 Portions
Chicken Livers	8 oz.	1 lb.	2 lb.	4 lb.
Green Onions, chopped, EP	3	6	12	24
Bacon, cooked crisp and drained	2 slices	4 slices	8 slices	16 slices
Sour Cream	¼ cup	½ cup	1 cup	2 cups
Butter or Margarine, softened	2 Tbsp.	¼ cup	½ cup	1 cup
Lemon Juice	1 tsp.	2 tsp.	1 Tbsp. 1 tsp.	2 Tbsp. 2 tsp.
Curry Powder	1 tsp.	2 tsp.	1 Tbsp. 1 tsp.	2 Tbsp. 2 tsp.
Salt	⅛ tsp.	¼ tsp.	½ tsp.	1 tsp.
Pepper	⅛ tsp.	¼ tsp.	½ tsp.	1 tsp.

1. Cook chicken livers in a small amount of boiling salted water (to cover) about 5 minutes or until tender.
2. Drain and cool.
3. In a blender, process the onion and bacon until chopped.
4. Add remaining ingredients, including chicken livers, and blend until smooth.
5. Remove from blender, cover, and chill several hours or overnight.
6. To serve, garnish with chopped green onion and chopped hard-cooked egg.
7. Serve with crackers.

CHICKEN LIVER PATE WITH PARSLEY LEMON SNOW

2 Cup Mold	1 Mold	2 Molds	4 Molds	8 Molds
Liver Pate				
Chicken Livers	1 lb.	2 lb.	4 lb.	8 lb.
Water, cold	3 cups	1 qt. 2 cups	3 qt.	1 gal. 2 qt.
Broth, chicken	1 qt.	2 qt.	1 gal.	2 gal.
Onion, finely minced	¼ cup	½ cup	1 cup	2 cups
Bacon Drippings	2 Tbsp.	¼ cup	1 cup	2 cups
Butter, melted	8 oz.	1 lb.	2 lb.	4 lb.
Pepper, black	¼ tsp.	½ tsp.	1 tsp.	2 tsp.
Mustard, dry	½ tsp.	1 tsp.	2 tsp.	1 Tbsp. 1 tsp.
Salt	½ tsp.	1 tsp.	2 tsp.	1 Tbsp. 1 tsp.
Paprika	1 tsp.	2 tsp.	1 Tbsp. 1 tsp.	2 Tbsp. 2 tsp.
Sugar	1 tsp.	2 tsp.	1 Tbsp. 1 tsp.	2 Tbsp. 2 tsp.
Sherry *or* Cognac	2 Tbsp.	¼ cup	1 cup	2 cups
Parsley Lemon Snow				
Cream Cheese	8 oz.	1 lb.	2 lb.	4 lb.
Lemon Juice	3 Tbsp.	6 Tbsp.	¾ cup	1½ cups
Parsley and/or Olives, to garnish				

Liver Pate

1. Clean livers. Cover with cold water and bring to a simmer. Drain.
2. Cover livers with chicken broth and simmer gently for about 15 minutes, until tender. Drain.
3. Saute onion in bacon drippings until tender but not browned.
4. Chop livers into ½" pieces.
5. Add onion, melted butter, and seasonings to liver. Add sherry or cognac.
6. Blend mixture in blender until very smooth.
7. Pack into oiled 2-cup mold or crock. Cheesecloth may be used to line mold (this facilitates removal).
8. Cover and chill for several hours until firm.

Parsley Lemon Snow

9. While molds are chilling, bring cream cheese to room temperature.
10. Add lemon juice and combine thoroughly until no lumps remain.
11. Unmold pate and carefully spread cream cheese and lemon mixture over sides and top of pate.
12. Garnish with parsley and/or olives.

WALNUT PATE des ARTISTES

4 to 5 lb. Mold	3 Molds	6 Molds	12 Molds
Pork Liver	1 lb. 8 oz.	3 lb.	6 lb.
Chicken and Duck Livers	8 oz.	1 lb.	2 lb.
Onions, large, EP	1½	3	6
Shallots, peeled	6 to 7	12 to 14	24 to 28
Pork Butts, boneless	6 lb.	12 lb.	24 lb.
Fat Back	2 lb. 4 oz.	4 lb. 8 oz.	9 lb.
Garlic, chopped	⅓ cup	⅔ cup	1⅓ cups
Thyme, scant measure	1½ tsp.	1 Tbsp.	2 Tbsp.
Walnuts, roughly crushed	2 cups	1 qt.	2 qt.
Salt	2 Tbsp. 2 tsp.	⅓ cup	⅔ cup
Pepper, black, freshly ground	2 Tbsp.	¼ cup	½ cup
Monosodium Glutamate, optional	1 Tbsp.	2 Tbsp.	¼ cup
Chablis	1¼ cups	2½ cups	5 cups

1. Push livers, onion, and shallots through the fine blade of the meat grinder.
2. Change to the coarse blade and push through the pork butts and fat back.
3. Add the remaining ingredients and blend thoroughly.
4. Place into bake oven pate molds.
5. Place 3 or 4 bay leaves on top.
6. Cover each prepared mold with foil.
7. Bake in a slow oven for 2 to 2½ hours in a bain marie (water bath).
8. One-half hour before fully cooked, remove the foil and allow the top to brown.
9. Chill thoroughly in the refrigerator before serving.
10. Serve a slice on a flat plate. Garnish with chopped cornichons and small cocktail onions.

CAVIAR AND SMOKED SALMON PATE

2 Tbsp. per Portion	1½ Cups 12 Portions	3 Cups 24 Portions	1 Qt. 2 Cups 48 Portions	3 Quarts 96 Portions
Butter, sweet	2 Tbsp.	¼ cup	½ cup	1 cup
Cream Cheese	4 oz.	8 oz.	1 lb.	2 lb.
Smoked Salmon	2 oz.	4 oz.	8 oz.	1 lb.
Red Caviar	2 oz.	4 oz.	8 oz.	1 lb.
Onion, finely diced, EP	1 Tbsp.	2 Tbsp.	¼ cup	½ cup
Sour Cream	2 Tbsp.	¼ cup	½ cup	1 cup
Lemon Juice	2 tsp.	1 Tbsp. 1 tsp.	2 Tbsp. 2 tsp.	¼ cup 1 Tbsp. 1 tsp.
Celery Salt	¼ tsp.	½ tsp.	1 tsp.	2 tsp.
Pepper, white	⅛ tsp.	¼ tsp.	½ tsp.	1 tsp.
Parsley Sprigs, large	1	2	4	8

Note: Butter and cream cheese should be at room temperature, soft enough to spread before preparation.

1. Cut salmon into small squares.
2. Put all ingredients into blender and blend until mixture is smooth. Scrape ingredients from side of blender with machine in off position. Then blend again to incorporate all ingredients. Chill, preferably overnight.
3. Serve mixture well-chilled.
4. Serve in a glass bowl. Garnish with additional red caviar in the center of pate.

Note: This pate is a beautiful pink color and would be especially appropriate as an appetizer for a wedding buffet.

CHEESABUTTER
(Spread or Roll)

2 Tbsp. per Portion	1 Cup 8 Portions	2 Cups 16 Portions	1 Quart 32 Portions	2 Quarts 64 Portions
Butter, softened	½ cup	8 oz.	1 lb.	2 lb.
Seasoning, Italian Herb	¾ tsp.	1½ tsp.	1 Tbsp.	2 Tbsp.
Garlic Powder	⅛ tsp.	¼ tsp.	½ tsp.	1 tsp.
Pepper	⅛ tsp.	¼ tsp.	½ tsp.	1 tsp.
Cheese, Cheddar, sharp, shredded	1 cup	8 oz.	1 lb.	2 lb.
Lemon Juice	1 tsp.	2 tsp.	1 Tbsp.	2 Tbsp.
			1 tsp.	2 tsp.

1. In a mixer bowl, beat together butter and seasonings with whip or flat beater at medium speed until fluffy, or 3 to 5 minutes.
2. Thoroughly blend shredded cheese and lemon juice into butter mixture.
3. Store covered in refrigerator.
4. Portion as desired using #30 or #60 scoop, or shape into a log using 2 cups mixture for log approximately 12″ long and 1½″ in diameter. Wrap in plastic wrap. To serve, cut in slices ½″ thick.
5. Mixture may also be put in crocks and served as a spread.

Figure 3   The cheesabutter may be served as a dip or formed into a cheesabutter log and served in slices with assorted breads and crackers.

CANAPES AND HORS D'OEUVRES

The literal translation of the French word *canape* is "couch." The term is used for small pieces of bread, toast, crackers or pastry topped with bits of tasty food. Canapes may range from plain pieces of bread spread with something as simple as a savory butter to small pastry shells topped with a filling. Most canapes may be served either hot or cold, but in order to qualify as a true canape they must be served open-faced. They are not intended to still hunger, but are served to whet the appetite.

Canapes require a substantial amount of labor for proper preparation. Many of the basic preparatory tasks have been absorbed by the frozen food industry because most canapes freeze well and lend themselves to assembly line production. For large receptions and parties, many quantity foodservice operators simply purchase frozen canapes and either defrost or heat them before serving. In some operations, however, the preparation of canapes represents an opportunity to make productive use of leftover foods such as sandwich spreads, for example. Leftover foods used in this way must be properly refrigerated before and after preparation.

Canapes are sometimes defined as "any edible tidbit that can be picked up without utensils." This definition widens the range of possibilities to include cheese cubes rolled in parsley, dill, or walnuts; shrimp or ham rolls on a toothpick; and countless other foods that can be easily handled with the fingers.

The literal translation of the French *hors d'oeuvres* is "outside of the main work." Hors d'oeuvres are usually served as appetizers, as a part of the dinner menu, to introduce the meal. They differ from canapes in that they usually are eaten at the table with knife and fork. A great variety of foods—including oysters, shrimp, canned fish, meat, crisp vegetables, cold cuts, and cheeses—lend themselves to service as hors d'oeuvres. All of the foods commonly served on a Scandinavian smorgasbord or an Italian antipasto table are acceptable for use as hors d'oeuvres. In addition, some of the formulas included in the salad section of this text can also be served as hors d'oeuvres. Three excellent examples are the Marinated Green Beans, the German Cucumbers, and the Marinated Garden Tomatoes contained in Part Three under Small Vegetable Salads.

Many canapes and hors d'oeuvres may be prepared well in advance, frozen, and then reheated just before serving. Of course, these and other foods must not be permitted to stand at room temperature for a cumulative total of more than four hours because of the potential danger of bacterial contamination.

In American culinary language, the terms *appetizer*, *hors d'oeuvre*, and *canape* are used interchangeably for any number of foods served with cocktails or as a first course of the meal. In this text, however, canapes and hors d'oeuvres are separate items within the overall appetizer category, which includes many other types of food.

HOME ECONOMICS DEPARTMENT
AMERICAN DAIRY ASSOCIATION

Figure 3A   A cheese tray is a simple and effective appetizer that may be used for buffet table or cocktail service. Swiss, gouda, cheddar (sliced, wedged), cottage cheese, blue cheese, and ham and cheese rolls and cubes offer the advantage of simple preparation.

TUNA CHEESIES
(Canape)

2 Canapes per Portion	48 Canapes 24 Portions	96 Canapes 48 Portions	192 Canapes 96 Portions	384 Canapes 192 Portions
Tuna, drained	6 oz.	12 oz.	1 lb. 8 oz.	3 lb.
Cheese, shredded	4 oz.	8 oz.	1 lb.	2 lb.
Butter or Margarine, softened	2 oz.	4 oz.	8 oz.	1 lb.
Onion, finely chopped or grated	1⅓ Tbsp.	2⅔ Tbsp.	⅓ cup	⅔ cup
Lemon Juice	2 Tbsp.	¼ cup	½ cup	1 cup
Worcestershire Sauce	1 tsp.	2 tsp.	1 Tbsp. 1 tsp.	2 Tbsp. 2 tsp.
Paprika	½ tsp.	1 tsp.	2 tsp.	1 Tbsp. 1 tsp.
Pepper Sauce, Hot	3 drops	6 drops	12 drops	⅛ tsp.
Melba Toast Rounds	48	96	192	384

1. Drain and flake tuna.
2. Cream the cheese with the butter or margarine.
3. Add seasonings, onion, and tuna. Mix thoroughly.
4. Spread each toast round with 1 heaping tsp. of the tuna mixture.
5. Broil about 4″ from flame for 3 to 5 minutes or until lightly browned.
6. Serve 2 canapes per portion.

Note: This canape may also be served cold.

U.S. DEPARTMENT OF THE INTERIOR
BUREAU OF FISHERIES

Figure 4   These are taste-tempting Tuna Cheesies for cocktail
parties and receptions. A simple combination of tuna, shredded
cheese, margarine, lemon juice, grated onion, Worcestershire
Sauce, paprika, and hot pepper sauce is spread on melba toast
rounds and broiled for three to five minutes.

SHRIMP CANAPE WITH CUCUMBER AND DILL

	12 Canapes	24 Canapes	48 Canapes	96 Canapes
Shrimp, cooked and chilled	8 oz.	1 lb.	2 lb.	4 lb.
Cucumber, peeled and chopped ⅛″	½ cup	1 cup	2 cups	1 qt.
Cream Cheese, softened	4 oz.	8 oz.	1 lb.	2 lb.
Onion, finely chopped, EP	2 Tbsp.	¼ cup	½ cup	1 cup
Mayonnaise	2 Tbsp.	¼ cup	½ cup	1 cup
Garlic Salt	⅛ tsp.	¼ tsp.	½ tsp.	1 tsp.
Green Food Coloring, optional				
Whole Wheat Bread	12 circles	24 circles	48 circles	96 circles
Sprigs of Fresh Dill to garnish				
Pimiento, chopped ¼″, to garnish, optional				

1. Pare and chop cucumbers. Cucumbers must be dry before adding to cheese.
2. Combine cream cheese, onion, mayonnaise, garlic salt, and cucumbers.
3. Tint with a few drops of green food coloring if desired. Tint only to a delicate, light green color.
4. Cut bread into rounds (or squares) and spread bread with approximately 1 Tbsp. cream cheese mixture.
5. Top with 1 large or medium-sized shrimp or with 3 or 4 small shrimp.
6. Garnish with a small sprig of fresh dill.
7. A small piece of pimiento added to the sprig of dill will provide color contrast, and make this canape especially appropriate for Christmas or New Year buffet tables.

SEAFOOD, CHICKEN, OR TURKEY PUFFS

1 Tbsp. per Puff	40 Portions	80 Portions	160 Portions	320 Portions
Seafood, drained, Chicken *or* Turkey	12 oz.	1 lb. 8 oz.	3 lb.	6 lb.
Celery, EP, chopped fine	1 cup *or* 4 oz.	2 cups *or* 8 oz.	1 qt. *or* 1 lb.	2 qt. *or* 2 lb.
Mayonnaise	½ cup	1 cup	2 cups	1 qt.
Onion, EP, chopped	2 Tbsp.	¼ cup	½ cup	1 cup
Sweet Pickle, chopped	2 Tbsp.	¼ cup	½ cup	1 cup
Puff Shells, petite	40	80	160	320

1. Drain and flake tuna or other seafood, or dice chicken or turkey.
2. Combine all ingredients except puff shells.
3. Mix thoroughly.
4. Cut tops from puff shells.
5. Fill each shell with approximately 1 Tbsp. of seafood or poultry mixture.
6. Replace tops of shells.

Note: To prepare puff shells, use the formula for Choux Paste. Prepare small-sized shells for these puffs. Shells may become too dry if held more than one day, so bake shells and fill with mixture on the same day they are to be served.

U.S. DEPARTMENT OF THE INTERIOR
BUREAU OF FISHERIES

Figure 5   These small Tuna Puffs are a light, flaky pastry
filled with tuna and spices. They provide an ideal canape for
receptions or as appetizers.

PASTRY PUFF SHELLS

½ #50 Scoop 18 × 26 × 1 Pan	80 Portions 2 Pans	160 Portions 4 Pans	320 Portions 8 Pans
Water, hot	2½ cups	1 qt. 1 cup	2 qt. 2 cups
Butter *or* margarine	10 oz.	1 lb. 4 oz.	2 lb. 8 oz.
Flour, cake	10 oz.	1 lb. 4 oz.	2 lb. 8 oz.
Salt	¼ tsp.	½ tsp.	1 tsp.

Eggs, whole,
  Grade B,
  medium
	9	18	36

1. Add butter or margarine to hot water. Bring to the boiling point.
2. Weigh and sift flour and salt.
3. When water and butter mixture are boiling, add sifted flour and salt all at once.
4. Stir vigorously and continuously with a wire whip for approximately 2 minutes, or until mixture pulls away from sides of pan or steam kettle and forms one large ball.
5. Remove mixture from heat and empty into bowl of mixer. Cool 5 minutes.
6. Break eggs into a measure which has a pouring lip. Using a flat beater, add the eggs, singly or a few at a time, beating on #2 speed. After each egg is added, beat just until batter becomes smooth again. Scrape down sides and bottom of bowl occasionally.
7. Using half of a #50 scoop, drop cream puffs on a lightly greased 18 × 26 × 1 pan—7 × 6. If a #50 scoop is not available, drop batter into pan from a heaping teaspoon.
8. Bake at 475°F to 500°F for 10 minutes, then lower temperature to 400°F or just under. Allow puffs to continue baking for 30 minutes or until inside of cream puff is dry. Leave puffs in oven with door open for 10 minutes to ensure that puffs are completely dry on the inside and will not collapse when removed from the oven.

Note: This is a small cream puff and actual count may vary.

CURRIED INDIAN CHICKEN COCONUT BALLS

1 oz. Balls	12 Balls	24 Balls	48 Balls	96 Balls
Cream Cheese	4 oz.	8 oz.	1 lb.	2 lb.
Mayonnaise	1 Tbsp.	2 Tbsp.	¼ cup	½ cup
Chicken, cooked and chopped fine	½ cup	1 cup	2 cups	1 qt.
Pecans, unsalted and chopped fine	½ cup	1 cup	2 cups	1 qt.
Curry Powder	1½ tsp.	1 Tbsp.	2 Tbsp.	¼ cup
Chutney, chopped	1½ tsp.	1 Tbsp.	2 Tbsp.	¼ cup
Coconut, Angel Flake	⅜ cup	¾ cup	1½ cups	3 cups
Salt	¼ tsp.	½ tsp.	1 tsp.	2 tsp.

1. Cream cheese must be room temperature. Blend cream cheese and mayonnaise on #1 speed in mixer. Blend until smooth.
2. Add chopped chicken, nuts, curry powder, chutney, and salt. Mix only until blended.
3. Shape mixture into balls of approximately 1 oz. each. Balls will be about 1″ across, and may be scooped with a scoop.
4. Roll all balls in coconut and chill until stiff. This will require several hours covered in the refrigerator.

Note: Chicken and pecans should be chopped fine but should be in distinct pieces.

HERB-STUFFED MUSHROOMS

4 Mushrooms per Portion	3 Portions	6 Portions	12 Portions	24 Portions
Mushrooms, large	1 lb.	2 lb.	4 lb.	8 lb.
Oil, olive	1 Tbsp.	2 Tbsp.	¼ cup	½ cup
Pork Sausage	4 oz.	8 oz.	1 lb.	2 lb.
Shallot, minced	1	2	4	8
Garlic, large cloves, minced	½	1	2	4
Parsley, chopped	⅓ cup	⅔ cup	1⅓ cups	2⅔ cups
Thyme, dried	½ tsp.	1 tsp.	2 tsp.	1 Tbsp. 1 tsp.
Bay Leaf, finely crumbled	1	2	4	8
Tarragon, dried	pinch	⅛ tsp.	¼ tsp.	½ tsp.
Salt	½ tsp.	1 tsp.	2 tsp.	1 Tbsp. 1 tsp.
Pepper	¼ tsp.	½ tsp.	1 tsp.	2 tsp.

Topping

	3 Portions	6 Portions	12 Portions	24 Portions
Bread Crumbs, fine, dry	⅓ cup	⅔ cup	1⅓ cup	2⅔ cup
Parsley, chopped	1 Tbsp.	2 Tbsp.	¼ cup	½ cup
Oil	2 Tbsp.	¼ cup	½ cup	1 cup

1. Wash mushrooms and dry thoroughly.
2. Pull stem ends out carefully to avoid breaking caps. Put first amount of oil in a heavy pan.
3. Chop stem ends finely. Put stem ends into oil.
4. Add sausage meat, shallots, garlic, parsley, herbs, salt, and pepper.
5. Cook over moderate heat for about 5 minutes, crumbling and blending with a spoon until lightly browned. Cool.
6. Divide stuffing among mushroom caps, smoothing and rounding it neatly.
7. Sprinkle with a mixture of bread crumbs and chopped parsley.
8. Heat oil in a large heavy skillet. Since about 12 large mushrooms can be heated in a large skillet, use 2 Tbsp. oil per skillet.
9. Heat mushrooms in oil for 2 minutes or until bottoms are lightly browned.
10. Transfer to a 375°F oven for 15 minutes or until mushrooms are tender.
11. To serve, arrange 4 mushrooms on a buttered slice of toasted bread with crusts removed.

CRAB-STUFFED MUSHROOMS

3 to 4 Mushrooms per Portion	18 Mushrooms 6 Portions	36 Mushrooms 12 Portions	72 Mushrooms 24 Portions
Mushrooms, medium 1 to 1½″	1 lb. 8 oz.	3 lb.	6 lb.
Butter or Margarine	3 Tbsp.	6 Tbsp.	¾ cup
Onion, chopped fine, EP	⅓ cup	⅔ cup	1⅓ cups
Celery, chopped fine, EP	¼ cup	½ cup	1 cup
Green Pepper, chopped fine, EP	¼ cup	½ cup	1 cup
Bread Crumbs, soft	1 cup	2 cups	1 qt.
Crabmeat, flaked	½ cup	1 cup	2 cups
Cheddar Cheese, grated	2 Tbsp.	¼ cup	½ cup
Sherry, dry	2 Tbsp.	¼ cup	½ cup
Marjoram, crumbled	¼ tsp.	½ tsp.	1 tsp.
Salt	¼ tsp.	½ tsp.	1 tsp.
Pepper, black	1/16 tsp.	⅛ tsp.	¼ tsp.
Hollandaise Sauce, optional	½ cup	1 cup	2 cups

1. Rinse, pat dry, and remove stems from mushrooms; reserve stems for later use.
2. Blanch mushroom caps in boiling water for 3 minutes. Remove, drain, and place cup side up; set aside.
3. Finely chop mushroom stems.
4. Melt butter or margarine. Add chopped mushroom stems, onion, celery, and green pepper. Saute for 5 minutes.
5. Remove from heat. Add bread crumbs, crab meat, cheese, sherry, marjoram, salt, and pepper. Blend well.
6. Fill each mushroom cap with crab mixture. Heat in a 450°F oven for 5 minutes. Serve 3 or 4 mushrooms per portion.

Note: Each mushroom may be topped with Hollandaise sauce.

WALNUT-STUFFED MUSHROOMS

2 Mushrooms per Portion	12 Mushrooms 6 Portions	24 Mushrooms 12 Portions	48 Mushrooms 24 Portions
Mushrooms, large, 1½" to 2"	1 lb.	2 lb.	4 lb.
Butter or Margarine	½ cup	1 cup	1 lb.
Onions, chopped fine, EP	¼ cup	½ cup	1 cup
Bread Crumbs, soft	½ cup	1 cup	2 cups
Walnuts, English, chopped	½ cup	1 cup	2 cups
Parsley, chopped fine, EP	3 Tbsp.	6 Tbsp.	¾ cup
Salt	¾ tsp.	1½ tsp.	1 Tbsp.
Pepper, black	¹⁄₁₆ tsp.	⅛ tsp.	¼ tsp.

1. Rinse, pat dry, and remove stems from mushrooms.
2. Chop stems. Reserve caps for later use.
3. Melt butter or margarine. Brush outside caps with some of the melted butter or margarine. Place in a greased baking pan.
4. To remaining butter add onions and chopped mushroom stems.
5. Saute for 10 minutes.
6. Add bread crumbs, walnuts, parsley, salt, and pepper. Mix well.
7. Spoon about 1 Tbsp. stuffing into each mushroom cap.
8. Bake in a 350°F oven about 20 minutes. Serve 2 mushrooms per portion.

Note: There are 12 large mushrooms (1½" to 2") to 1 lb. and 16 medium mushrooms (1" to 1½") to 1 lb.

STUFFED MUSHROOMS TOLSTOY

3 Mushrooms per Portion	48 Mushrooms 16 Portions	96 Mushrooms 32 Portions	192 Mushrooms 64 Portions
Mushrooms, large, 1½" to 2"	3 lb.	6 lb.	12 lb.
Salad Oil, divided	1½ cups	3 cups	1 qt. 2 cups
Bread Crumbs, soft	3 cups	1 qt. 2 cups	3 qt.
Parsley, chopped	¼ cup	½ cup	1 cup
Oregano Leaves, crushed	2½ tsp.	1 Tbsp. 2 tsp.	3 Tbsp. 1 tsp.
Salt	1½ tsp.	1 Tbsp.	2 Tbsp.
Garlic, minced	1½ tsp.	1 Tbsp.	2 Tbsp.
Pepper, black, ground	½ tsp.	1 tsp.	2 tsp.
Eggs, whole, lightly beaten	3	6	12
Paprika, to garnish			
Lemon Wedges, to garnish			

1. Rinse, pat dry, and remove stems from mushrooms.
2. Divide oil into half and brush outside of caps with half of oil.
3. Place cavity-side down in a shallow baking pan.
4. Bake until almost tender, for about 5 minutes, in a 400°F oven. Remove from oven; invert caps.
5. Chop stems very fine and mix with bread crumbs, parsley, oregano, salt, garlic, and black pepper. Stir in eggs.
6. Spoon into baked mushroom caps. Dribble with remaining oil.
7. Bake until tender, for about 5 to 10 minutes.
8. Serve hot. Garnish with paprika and lemon wedges if desired. Serve 3 mushrooms per portion.

SHRIMP IN TOMATO HALF-SHELL

	12 Portions	24 Portions	48 Portions	96 Portions
Sour Cream	1 cup	2 cups	1 qt.	2 qt.
Onion Salt	1 tsp.	2 tsp.	1 Tbsp. 1 tsp.	2 Tbsp. 2 tsp.
Tomatoes, medium, halved	2 lb.	4 lb.	8 lb.	16 lb.
Shrimp, cooked and cleaned, EP	1 lb. 4 oz.	2 lb. 8 oz.	5 lb.	10 lb.
Chives *or* Scallion tops, chopped	2 tsp.	1 Tbsp. 1 tsp.	2 Tbsp. 2 tsp.	¼ cup

1. Combine sour cream and onion salt. Chill.
2. Peel, core, and cut tomatoes in half. Chill.
3. Fill tomato half with 1 heaping Tbsp. of the onion and sour cream mixture.
4. Sprinkle ⅛ tsp. chopped chives or chopped scallion tops in center.
5. Place on lettuce leaf or surround with chicory.
6. Arrange 3 to 4 shrimp or a 2 oz. portion over edge of tomato.

Figure 6   Shrimp in Tomato Half-Shell is simply a cored tomato half on a bed of lettuce or escarole, filled with sour cream. Place three or more shrimp at intervals around the edge, and garnish with chopped parsley or green onions.

RAVIGOTE SAUCE

	1¼ Cups	2½ Cups	1 Qt. 1 Cup	2 Qts. 2 Cups
Butter *or* Margarine	2 Tbsp.	¼ cup	½ cup	1 cup
Flour, all-purpose	1 Tbsp.	2 Tbsp.	¼ cup	½ cup
Light Cream *or* Half-and-Half	1 cup	2 cups	1 qt.	2 qt.
Lemon Juice, fresh	¼ cup	½ cup	1 cup	2 cups
Shallot, minced	1 Tbsp.	2 Tbsp.	¼ cup	½ cup
Chervil, dried, minced	1 Tbsp.	2 Tbsp.	¼ cup	½ cup
Tarragon, dried, minced	1 Tbsp.	2 Tbsp.	¼ cup	½ cup
Chives *or* Scallions, minced	1 Tbsp.	2 Tbsp.	¼ cup	½ cup
Salt	⅛ tsp.	¼ tsp.	½ tsp.	1 tsp.
Pepper, white	⅛ tsp.	¼ tsp.	½ tsp.	1 tsp.

1. Melt butter or margarine.
2. Add flour and blend until smooth.
3. Add cream or half-and-half gradually and cook, stirring constantly with a French whip, until mixture has slightly thickened.
4. Add all remaining ingredients, stir to combine, and let stand for 5 to 10 minutes.
5. Strain through cheesecloth and chill covered in the refrigerator.

CRAB RAVIGOTE IN AVOCADO

	2 Portions	4 Portions	8 Portions	16 Portions
Ravigote Sauce	¼ cup	½ cup	1 cup	2 cups
Crabmeat, drained	1 cup	2 cups	1 qt.	2 qt.
Avocadoes, ripe, medium	1	2	4	8

1. If crabmeat has been frozen, be sure it is well-drained.
2. Combine crabmeat with sauce until all pieces of crabmeat are covered with sauce. Keep under refrigeration until ready to use.
3. Cut avocado in half, remove seed, and loosen avocado meat from the skin.
4. Place avocado half on a bed of lettuce or other greens.
5. Fill center of avocado with ½ cup crab ravigote mixture.
6. Garnish with ½ Tbsp. additional sauce.

SHRIMP OR SEAFOOD RAVIGOTE IN AVOCADO

1. Follow the formula for Crab Ravigote in Avocado, substituting seafood for crabmeat.
2. Serve ½ cup of the ravigote mixture in an avocado half.
3. Garnish with ½ Tbsp. of additional sauce.

CURRIED CHUTNEY SHRIMP

½ Cup Portion	6 Portions	12 Portions	24 Portions	48 Portions
Butter *or* Margarine	¼ cup	½ cup	8 oz.	1 lb.
Onion, chopped, EP	½ cup	1 cup	2 cups	1 qt.
Curry Powder	2½ tsp.	1 Tbsp. 2 tsp.	3 Tbsp. 1 tsp.	6 Tbsp. 2 tsp.
Chutney, preferably Mango, chopped	½ cup	1 cup	2 cups	1 qt.
Shrimp, small, cooked	3 cups	1 qt. 2 cups	3 qt.	1 gal. 2 qt.
Eggs, hard-cooked, finely chopped	1	2	4	8
Parsley, minced, EP	3 Tbsp.	6 Tbsp.	¾ cup	1½ cups

1. Saute onion in butter or margarine until golden.
2. Stir in curry and chutney. Mix well.
3. Add shrimp, tossing until well-coated with sauce, and heat thoroughly. Do not allow to boil.
4. Serve in pastry shells, ½ cup per portion.
5. Sprinkle with chopped egg and parsley.

Note: The Curried Chutney Shrimp is also delicious on rice or toast rounds.

ARTICHOKES WITH SAUCE VINAIGRETTE

	6 Portions	**12 Portions**	**24 Portions**	**48 Portions**
Artichokes, cooked	6	12	24	48
Vinegar or Lemon Juice	2 Tbsp.	¼ cup	½ cup	1 cup
Salt	¼ tsp.	½ tsp.	1 tsp.	2 tsp.
Pepper, freshly ground	¼ tsp.	½ tsp.	1 tsp.	2 tsp.
Mustard, dry	¼ tsp.	½ tsp.	1 tsp.	2 tsp.
or Dijon	½ tsp.	1 tsp.	2 tsp.	1 Tbsp. 1 tsp.
Basil	½ tsp.	1 tsp.	2 tsp.	1 Tbsp. 1 tsp.
Oil	½ cup	1 cup	2 cups	1 qt.

1. After artichokes have completed cooking, drain and chill in refrigerator.
2. Combine all ingredients for Vinaigrette. Shake thoroughly, and always shake well before using.
3. Put 1 to 1½ Tbsp. Vinaigrette in a pool in a compote-type dish.
4. Center artichoke in the pool of Sauce Vinaigrette.

Note: Other spices—such as tarragon, dill, thyme, and marjoram—may be used for variety.

Note: For Creamy Vinaigrette, add the following amounts of sour cream, heavy cream, plain yogurt, mayonnaise or buttermilk to the dressing:

2 Tbsp.	¼ cup	½ cup	1 cup

MUSHROOMS A LA GRECQUE

¼ Cup per Portion	1 Cup 4 Portions	2 Cups 8 Portions	1 Quart 16 Portions	2 Quarts 32 Portions
Mushrooms, small, button, whole	8 oz.	1 lb.	2 lb.	4 lb.
Lemon Juice, fresh	1½ Tbsp.	3 Tbsp.	¼ cup 2 Tbsp.	¾ cup
Olive Oil	4½ Tbsp.	½ cup 1 Tbsp.	1 cup 2 Tbsp.	2¼ cups
Coriander Seeds	½ tsp.	1 tsp.	2 tsp.	1 Tbsp. 1 tsp.
Garlic Cloves, minced	1	2	4	8
Chicken Broth	2 Tbsp.	¼ cup	½ cup	1 cup
Salt	⅛ tsp.	¼ tsp.	½ tsp.	1 tsp.
Pepper, freshly ground	⅛ tsp.	¼ tsp.	½ tsp.	1 tsp.

1. Leave mushrooms whole. If large mushrooms only are available, they may be cut into quarters.
2. Put mushrooms into a pan with lemon juice and stir to coat.
3. Add all remaining ingredients.
4. Cover and cook 7 to 8 minutes, stirring occasionally.
5. Uncover and cook over high heat about 5 minutes.
6. Remove from heat and let cool.

CLAMS CASINO

4 Clams per Portion	4 Portions	8 Portions	16 Portions	32 Portions
Clams on Half-Shell	16	32	64	128
or				
Canned Shells	16	32	64	128
Clams, canned, minced, and drained	7 oz.	14 oz.	1 lb. 12 oz.	3 lb. 8 oz.
Butter, sweet	4 oz.	8 oz.	1 lb.	2 lb.
Bread Crumbs, dry	¼ cup	½ cup	1 cup	2 cups
Garlic Powder	¼ tsp.	½ tsp.	1 tsp.	2 tsp.
Oregano	½ tsp.	1 tsp.	2 tsp.	1 Tbsp. 1 tsp.
Pepper, black, freshly ground	¼ tsp.	½ tsp.	1 tsp.	2 tsp.
Bacon, diced ¼"	2 oz.	4 oz.	8 oz.	1 lb.
Green Pepper, diced, EP	2 Tbsp.	¼ cup	½ cup	1 cup
Red Pepper, EP *or* Pimiento, diced	2 Tbsp.	¼ cup	½ cup	1 cup

1. If using canned clams, distribute them among the half-shells using about 1 tsp. minced clams per half-shell.
2. Combine butter, bread crumbs, garlic powder, oregano, and black pepper.
3. Cover whole clams or canned minced clams with about 1 tsp. of the butter mixture.
4. Cook bacon bits until almost crisp. Drain.
5. Distribute bacon pieces evenly over all clams.
6. Press pieces of green and red pepper (or pimiento) on each clam.
7. Bake at 350°F for 15 minutes or until golden and very hot. Serve 4 clams per portion.

Note: These may be baked in individual ramekins, although they are hot to handle individually after baking.

Note: If clams are served as an entree, double the portion size to 8 clams per portion.

OYSTERS FLORENTINE

3 Oysters per Portion	2 Portions	4 Portions	8 Portions	16 Portions
Bacon, cooked	2 slices	4 slices	8 slices	16 slices
Spinach, cooked	½ cup	1 cup	2 cups	1 qt.
Oysters, large	6	12	24	48
White Wine	½ cup	1 cup	2 cups	1 qt.
Bechamel Sauce	½ cup	1 cup	2 cups	1 qt.
Swiss Cheese, grated	2 Tbsp.	¼ cup	½ cup	1 cup
Parmesan Cheese, grated	1 Tbsp.	2 Tbsp.	¼ cup	½ cup

1. Chop the bacon and spinach and divide evenly among the oyster shells.
2. Poach the oysters in white wine for about 30 seconds, just to set.
3. Place one oyster in each shell on top of the bacon and spinach.
4. Spoon about 1 to 2 Tbsp. Bechamel Sauce over each oyster.
5. Combine the Swiss and Parmesan Cheeses and sprinkle over the oysters.
6. Broil 3 to 5 minutes until glazed.
7. Serve 3 oysters per portion, hot and garnished with a lemon star and chopped parsley.

Note: Oysters may be served as an entree. Double the portion size to 6 oysters per portion.

FISH AND SHELLFISH COCKTAILS

The shrimp cocktail is perhaps the most familiar of all appetizers and, therefore, needs little discussion. Traditionally, shrimp and other fish cocktails are served in a footed cocktail dish. They may also be served on a plate with a lettuce cup used as a base. Chopped celery or avocado cubes can be used as filler to give height and depth to servings of shrimp. Whole shrimp are usually placed on top of the filler base, while pieces of shrimp or fish are often mixed with the celery or avocado cubes. Cocktail sauce can be spooned on top of the serving, mixed with the ingredients, or served in a separate souffle cup. In the Deep South, a remoulade sauce is often served in place of the traditional cocktail sauce.

Another variation in the fish and shellfish appetizer category is the Shrimp en Coquille, in which the shrimp is diced and combined with a sour cream sauce and served on a lettuce cup in a Coquille dish. Coquille dishes add a decorative touch and may be used for other items, such as Crab au Gratin.

Still another variation is the Ambassador Seafood Cocktail, in which a large plate is covered with a bed of ice with a souffle cup of cocktail sauce in the center. Around it are placed oysters, clams on the half-shell, crab, and other types of fish, along with watercress and lemon garnishes. A Piquant Sauce or Dressing may be used instead of the traditional cocktail sauce. The Crab and Artichoke with Piquant Dressing is an example of this variation on fish and shellfish cocktails.

SHRIMP EN COQUILLE

¼ Cup Portion	12 Portions	24 Portions	48 Portions	96 Portions
Sour Cream	1½ cups	3 cups	1 qt. 2 cups	3 qt.
Onion Salt	1½ tsp.	1 Tbsp.	2 Tbsp.	1½ oz.
Chili Sauce	¼ cup 2 Tbsp.	¾ cup	1½ cups	3 cups
Shrimp, cooked, for mixture	1 lb. 2 oz.	2 lb. 4 oz.	4 lb. 8 oz.	9 lb.
Shrimp, cooked, for garnish	6 oz.	12 oz.	1 lb. 8 oz.	3 lb.

Note: If shrimp for mixture are small, leave whole. If large, cut in ½″ pieces. Allow one whole shrimp per portion for use as a garnish.

1. Combine sour cream, onion salt, and chili sauce. Chill.
2. Add first amount of chilled, cooked shrimp to chilled sour cream mixture.
3. To serve, line chilled coquille dish or small salad plate with a small lettuce cup. Fill lettuce cup with ¼ cup shrimp mixture. Top with one whole shrimp and garnish with lemon wedge.

Note: Crabmeat, lobster, or a combination of seafood may be used in place of shrimp.

COCKTAIL SAUCE

2 Tbsp. per Portion	1 Qt. 2 Cups 48 Portions	3 Quarts 96 Portions	1 Gal. 2 Qt. 192 Portions	3 Gallons 384 Portions
Catsup	3 cups	½ #10 can	1 #10 can	2 #10 cans
Chili Sauce	3 cups	½ #10 can	1 #10 can	2 #10 cans
Lemon Juice	2 Tbsp.	¼ cup	½ cup	1 cup
Horseradish, prepared	¼ cup	½ cup	1 cup	2 cups

1. Combine all ingredients and chill.
2. Serve 2 Tbsp. per cocktail (on 2 oz. cooked shrimp, crabmeat, lobster, or seafood combination), or serve with oysters and clams on the half-shell.

REMOULADE SAUCE I

2 Tbsp. per Portion	1½ Cups 12 Portions	3 Cups 24 Portions	1 Qt. 2 Cups 48 Portions	3 Quarts 96 Portions
Mayonniase	1 cup	2 cups	1 qt.	2 qt.
Garlic Clove, medium, finely chopped	1	2	4	8
Parsley, fresh, finely chopped	1 Tbsp.	2 Tbsp.	¼ cup	½ oz.
Capers, chopped	1 Tbsp.	2 Tbsp.	¼ cup	½ cup
Eggs, hard-cooked, finely chopped	1	2	4	8
Mustard, Dijon	1 tsp.	2 tsp.	1 Tbsp. 1 tsp.	2 Tbsp. 2 tsp.
Tarragon, dry	1 tsp.	2 tsp.	1 Tbsp. 1 tsp.	2 Tbsp. 2 tsp.

1. Combine all ingredients. Chill.
2. Allow sauce to chill for 1 hour or more before serving.
3. Serve 2 Tbsp. Remoulade Sauce on 2 oz. cooked shrimp.
4. This sauce may also be served as a dressing on Hearts of Lettuce Salad (see p. 228).

REMOULADE SAUCE II

	1¼ Cups	2½ Cups	1 Qt. 1 Cup	2 Qt. 2 Cups
Egg Yolks	4	8	16	32
Garlic Salt	⅛ tsp.	¼ tsp.	½ tsp.	1 tsp.
Salt	½ tsp.	1 tsp.	2 tsp.	1 Tbsp. 1 tsp.
Pepper, white	⅛ tsp.	¼ tsp.	½ tsp.	1 tsp.
Mustard, dry	½ tsp.	1 tsp.	2 tsp.	1 Tbsp. 1 tsp.
Oil, salad	1 cup	2 cups	1 qt.	2 qt.
Vinegar, Tarragon	2 Tbsp.	¼ cup	½ cup	1 cup
Shallot, minced	1	2	4	8
Parsley, chopped fine	1 Tbsp.	2 Tbsp.	¼ cup	½ cup
Chervil, dry	1 Tbsp.	2 Tbsp.	¼ cup	½ cup
Pickles, gherkin, minced	1 Tbsp.	2 Tbsp.	¼ cup	½ cup
Capers, minced	1 Tbsp.	2 Tbsp.	¼ cup	½ cup

1. To egg yolks in mixer, add garlic salt, salt, pepper, and dry mustard.
2. While beating with balloon whip on #3 speed, add tarragon vinegar alternating with oil until an emulsion is formed.
3. Reduce speed of mixer and add shallot, parsley, chervil, gherkins, and capers. Mix only until well blended.
4. Chill covered in refrigerator overnight.

SHRIMP REMOULADE

1. Place 4 to 6 medium-sized cooked shrimp on a bed of lettuce, romaine, endive, or spinach leaves.
2. Top with 2 to 3 Tbsp. Remoulade Sauce or enough to cover.

Note: Shrimp Remoulade may also be served in a sherbet dish, in the same manner as shrimp cocktail. Shrimp and crabmeat may be combined and then covered with Remoulade.

Figure 7   One of the most popular shrimp appetizers is Shrimp Remoulade, for which we have two formulas. The sauce may be combined with the shrimp prior to serving or poured over the shrimp after they are arranged in a serving dish on a bed of escarole.

KING CRAB AND ARTICHOKES SUPREME

	12 Portions	24 Portions	48 Portions
Alaska King Crab Legs	2 lb. 8 oz.	5 lb.	10 lb.
Artichoke Hearts, marinated	24	48	96
Mousseline Dressing	**1½ cups**	**3 cups**	**1 qt. 2 cups**
Mayonnaise	1 cup	2 cups	1 qt.
Chili Sauce	2 Tbsp.	¼ cup	½ cup
Lemon Juice	1 Tbsp.	2 Tbsp.	¼ cup
Tabasco Sauce	¹⁄₁₆ tsp.	⅛ tsp.	¼ tsp.
Sugar	¾ tsp.	1½ tsp.	1 Tbsp.
Salt	¹⁄₁₆ tsp.	⅛ tsp.	¼ tsp.
Heavy Cream, whipped	¼ cup	½ cup	1 cup
Cognac, optional	¼ oz.	½ oz.	1 oz.

1. Arrange 3⅓ oz. crab leg slices and 2 artichoke hearts on a crisp, curly lettuce leaf in an iced supreme dish.
2. Combine all ingredients for dressing and fold in whipped cream.
3. Serve with 2 Tbsp. dressing and lemon wedge.

AMBASSADOR HOTEL, Chicago
and
BUREAU OF COMMERCIAL FISHERIES

Figure 8   These clam shells are filled with one raw clam, crab meat, lobster, and shrimp. The shells are placed on a bed of ice around a container of chilled seafood sauce and served with lemon wedges to form this Ambassador Seafood Platter from the Ambassador Hotel in Chicago.

QUICHE

A quiche is a combination of cheese, egg custard, and other ingredients baked in a pastry shell. It has been a staple on the menus of France and other European countries for generations. Only in the past decade, however, has quiche become a popular item on the menus of many American restaurants. Although quiche now ranks among the top ten favorite appetizers, it is served most often as a light luncheon entree. It is served so frequently in institutional foodservices that several manufacturers now offer a frozen quiche.

While the French Quiche Lorraine remains the best known and most served item, the definition of quiche has been expanded to include almost any combination of eggs, cheeses, vegetables, and meat or seafood baked and served in a pastry shell. Variations in ingredients seem limited only by seasonal or regional availability.

If personnel and time are available, standard pie crusts may be prepared with butter used as a portion of the shortening ingredient to provide added flavor and richness. Frozen pie crusts may be used, but they should be deep dish crusts that can support the weight of the filling and prevent it from boiling over in the oven during baking. Quiche that is to be served directly from the oven should be permitted to stand a few minutes before cutting. Baked quiche may be kept in the refrigerator for several days and reheated before serving.

QUICHE LORRAINE

9″ Deep Dish Quiche Cut 8 Slices per Quiche	1 Quiche 8 Portions	2 Quiche 16 Portions	4 Quiche 32 Portions
Pastry Shell, 9″ deep dish, frozen, unbaked	1	2	4
Bacon Strips, lean, cut in ¼″ slices	8	16	32
Eggs, whole	3	6	12
Egg Yolk	1	2	4
Cream, heavy	1½ cups	3 cups	1 qt. 2 cups
Salt	¼ tsp.	½ tsp.	1 tsp.
Pepper, white	⅛ tsp.	¼ tsp.	½ tsp.
Swiss Cheese, grated	1 cup	2 cups	1 qt.
Parmesan Cheese, freshly grated	½ cup	1 cup	2 cups
Butter, cut in very small pieces	2 Tbsp.	¼ cup	½ cup

1. Cook bacon until very crisp. Drain well.
2. Combine eggs, extra yolks, cream, and seasonings.
3. Stir in grated cheeses.
4. Sprinkle bacon into each deep dish pastry shell.
5. Pour egg-cheese mixture on top of bacon in shell.
6. Sprinkle the top with butter cut in small pieces.
7. Bake at 375°F for 45 to 50 minutes or until filling is puffed and light brown, and a knife inserted in the center comes out clean.

SPINACH-MUSHROOM QUICHE

9″ Deep Dish Quiche Cut 8 Slices per Quiche	1 Quiche 8 Portions	2 Quiche 16 Portions	4 Quiche 32 Portions	8 Quiche 64 Portions
Pastry Shell, 9″ deep dish, frozen, unbaked	1	2	4	8
Butter *or* Margarine	1 Tbsp.	2 Tbsp.	¼ cup	½ cup
Spinach, frozen, chopped, cooked, and drained	½ cup	1 cup	2 cups	1 qt.
Mushrooms, pieces, fresh or canned, ⅛″	½ cup	1 cup	2 cups	1 qt.
Pepper, black, freshly ground	dash	⅛ tsp.	¼ tsp.	½ tsp.
Garlic Powder	½ tsp.	1 tsp.	2 tsp.	1 Tbsp. 1 tsp.
Eggs	4	8	16	32
Flour	1 Tbsp.	2 Tbsp.	¼ cup	½ cup
Cream, Light *or* Half-and-Half	1½ cups	3 cups	1 qt. 2 cups	3 qt.
Nutmeg	¼ tsp.	½ tsp.	1 tsp.	2 tsp.
Butter *or* Margarine, melted	1 Tbsp.	2 Tbsp.	¼ cup	½ cup

1. Bake pastry shell at 375°F for 10 minutes. Set aside to cool.
2. Saute spinach and mushrooms in first amount of butter for a few minutes.
3. Add pepper and garlic powder. Cool.
4. Sprinkle spinach and mushroom mixture on partially baked pastry shell.
5. Combine eggs, flour, cream, and nutmeg.
6. Pour mixture into shell over spinach and mushrooms.
7. Pour second amount of melted butter over top of quiche.
8. Bake 45 to 50 minutes in preheated 350°F oven or until quiche is set. Spinach and mushrooms will float to the top during baking.

Note: This recipe is good served hot or cold. If served hot, allow to stand a few minutes after removing from oven in order for flavors to blend.

Note: Fresh, cooked, chopped spinach may be substituted for frozen.

HAM AND CHEESE QUICHE

9″ Deep Dish Quiche Cut 8 Slices per Quiche	1 Quiche 8 Portions	2 Quiche 16 Portions	4 Quiche 32 Portions
Pastry Shell, 9″ deep dish, frozen, unbaked	1	2	4
Pineapple, crushed, in juice	8 oz.	1 lb.	2 lb.
Ham, cooked and thinly sliced (deli-packed)	4 oz.	8 oz.	1 lb.
Cheddar Chese, sharp, sliced	4 oz.	8 oz.	1 lb.
Swiss Cheese, process, sliced	4 oz.	8 oz.	1 lb.
Butter	¼ cup	½ cup	1 cup
Onion, chopped, EP	¼ cup	½ cup	1 cup
Green Pepper, chopped, EP	¼ cup	½ cup	1 cup
Pineapple Juice	½ cup	1 cup	2 cups
Eggs, whole	4	8	16
Cream, light	½ cup	1 cup	2 cups
Mustard, Dijon	1 Tbsp. 1 tsp.	2 Tbsp. 2 tsp.	¼ cup 1 Tbsp. 1 tsp.
Pepper, white	¼ tsp.	½ tsp.	1 tsp.
Horseradish, prepared	¼ tsp.	½ tsp.	1 tsp.
Beef Base, granulated	¼ tsp.	½ tsp.	1 tsp.

1. Drain pineapple, saving juice.
2. Partially bake pastry shell in moderately hot oven at 375° for 10 minutes.
3. Cut ham and cheese in julienne strips.
4. Melt half the butter and add onion and green pepper.
5. Cook slowly 4 minutes. Add pineapple juice and cook 4 minutes or until juice is absorbed.
6. Add pineapple and ham strips and cook about 4 seconds or just long enough to blend.
7. Spread mixture over pie shells, reserving 4 Tbsp. for each shell for topping.
8. Add cheeses in separate clumps to vary color.
9. Beat together eggs and remaining ingredients.
10. Pour slowly into pie shell. Sprinkle remaining ham mixture on top. Dot with remaining butter.
11. Bake 30 to 40 minutes at 375°F or until set.

SPECIALTY SOUPS

Among the many possible classifications of soups served in quantity foodservices, the category of specialty soups must be added. Specialty soups are most often prepared for service as appetizers. They differ from the more standard stock and cream soups because they often contain unusual ingredients, are not usually prepared in large quantities, can be made "to order" if necessary, and provide the foodservice operator with an opportunity for innovation in preparation and service.

Standard soups, such as the Chicken Noodle or Cream of Tomato, have been served as appetizers in most types of foodservices for many years. The preparation and service of the basic stock and cream soups were discussed in some detail in *Fundamentals of Quantity Food Preparation: Breads, Soups and Sandwiches* (CBI Publishing Company, 1978, pp. 77–118), and they continue to constitute an important part of the institutional foodservice menu. In recent years, however, many restaurants and other foodservice operators have placed considerable emphasis on the preparation and service of specialty soups, which provide variations on the appetizer menu and offer dramatic eye and taste appeal.

The following specialty soup formulas have been divided into the categories of Cold Fruit and Cold Vegetable Soups, Stock Soups, Gourmet Vegetable Cream Soups, and Miscellaneous Soups such as cheese, bean, fish, and nut soups. There is some overlapping of categories, as in the case of certain cold fruit and vegetable soups that may also be served hot, and the Gourmet Potato Soup which may be served well-chilled as Vichyssoise.

Specialty soups have not only assumed an increasingly important place on the menus of quantity foodservices but, in many instances, they offer the advantage of reasonably low ingredient and labor costs as well. As the tastes of the American public become more sophisticated and as the search for innovation in quantity foodservice menus continues, the specialty soup will be valued all the more highly as an addition to the appetizer menu.

COLD FRUIT AND COLD VEGETABLE SOUPS

With the exception of Vichyssoise and Gazpacho, cold vegetable and cold fruit soups were long considered far too esoteric for service in all but a few specialty restaurants. Yet they have been standard fare on the menus of French, Scandinavian, and other Continental restaurants since before the days of Escoffier. As foodservice operators in restaurants and universities searched for innovative appetizers and as increasing emphasis was placed on the service of light foods, cold fruit and vegetable soups became widely accepted as refreshing, appetite-stimulating items appropriate for service in most types of operations.

The cold fruit soup formulas that follow include a variety of fruit flavors and preparation techniques ranging from the very simple to the complex. In those formulas that call for the addition of a red or rose wine, it is recommended that no substitutions be made. The specified wines contribute their own distinctive flavor to a soup and, in some instances, provide an important element of color. The minimal amounts of alcohol in each serving should not be objectionable to the vast majority of customers.

The taste and appearance of many of the fruit soups may be enhanced by the addition of a dollop of chilled yogurt or sour cream. These and other garnishes should be added just before serving. Any garnish used with a cold fruit soup should complement the basic fruit flavor or provide a sharp contrast. The yogurt and sour cream add a distinctive taste that complements the flavor of cherries, peaches, and other fruit, while a wafer-thin slice of lemon provides a decorative touch and a pleasant contrast.

The cold vegetable soups may be garnished with slices or finely chopped pieces of the basic ingredients. A bowl of Gazpacho, for example, gains in flavor and texture when finely chopped tomato, cucumber, bellpepper, and onions are sprinkled on top as a garnish. Because the natural flavor is so important in the cold vegetable soups, it is suggested that garnishes be held to a minimum. The Vichyssoise is one example in which the addition of anything but a sprinkling of chopped chives would be inappropriate.

The cold soups—both fruit and vegetable—should be served very cold in well-chilled soup plates or cups. Some restaurants assure the serving of a chilled soup by using an underliner filled with crushed ice. One restaurant, for example, serves the chilled Spanish Avocado Soup and the Gazpacho in a pewter soup cup or mug with an ice-filled pewter soup plate underliner. Other restaurants use frosted glass bowls or freezer-chilled soup plates. Just as a hot soup loses its appeal when served lukewarm, so does a chilled soup that has been allowed to reach room temperature.

TRADITIONAL SWEDISH FRUIT SOUP

¾ Cup Portion	1 Qt. 1 Cup 6 Portions	2 Qt. 2 Cups 12 Portions	1 Gal. 1 Qt. 24 Portions	2 Gal. 2 Qt. 48 Portions
Apricots, dried, ¼″ pieces	½ cup	1 cup	2 cups	1 qt.
Apple Slices, dried, cut in half	½ cup	1 cup	2 cups	1 qt.
Peaches, dried, ¼″ pieces	¼ cup	½ cup	1 cup	2 cups
Raisins, dark, optional	1 Tbsp.	2 Tbsp.	¼ cup	½ cup
Water	1 qt.	2 qt.	1 gal.	2 gal.
Sugar	2 Tbsp. 2 tsp.	⅓ cup	⅔ cup	1⅓ cups
Cinnamon Stick	½	1	2	4
Lemon Rind, grated	1½ tsp.	1 Tbsp.	2 Tbsp.	¼ cup
Strawberry Syrup, bottled	½ cup	1 cup	2 cups	1 qt.
Yogurt				

1. Combine chopped fruits with water. Let stand 1 hour.
2. Add sugar, cinnamon stick, and lemon rind to fruit mixture. Cover.
3. Heat to boiling. Reduce heat and simmer for 30 minutes or until fruits are tender.
4. Remove and discard cinnamon stick.
5. Stir in strawberry syrup.

6. Cool to lukewarm.
7. Refrigerate covered overnight.
8. Serve with a dollop of yogurt in center.

Note: A combination of dried pears and dried apples may be used. Chopped dried prunes may be substituted for dried peaches.

SWEDISH FRUIT SOUP

¾ Cup Portion	1 Qt. 6 Portions	2 Qt. 12 Portions	1 Gal. 24 Portions	2 Gal. 48 Portions
Apricots, dried, ¼" pieces	½ cup	1 cup	2 cups	1 qt.
Apple Slices, dried, cut in half	½ cup	1 cup	2 cups	1 qt.
Peaches, dried, ¼" pieces	½ cup	1 cup	2 cups	1 qt.
Raisins	1 Tbsp.	2 Tbsp.	¼ cup	½ cup
Water	2 cups	1 qt.	2 qt.	1 gal.
Wine, red	1 cup	2 cups	1 qt.	2 qt.
Sugar	¼ cup	½ cup	1 cup	2 cups
Cinnamon Stick	½	1	2	4
Lemon Slices	3	6	12	24
Lemon Juice	2 Tbsp.	¼ cup	½ cup	1 cup
Orange Juice	2 Tbsp.	¼ cup	½ cup	1 cup

1. Cover dried fruits with water and wine. Allow to stand 1 hour.
2. Add sugar, cinnamon, lemon slices, and juices.
3. Heat to boiling and simmer until fruits are tender—about 15 to 20 minutes.
4. Remove from heat. Remove and discard the cinnamon stick and lemon slices.
5. Cool to lukewarm temperature, cover, and refrigerate overnight.
6. Serve in ¾ cup portions with a dollop of yogurt in center.

Note: Dried pears may be substituted for apples, or a combination of pears and apples may be used.

Note: As a variation, after fruits have been cooled they may be drained. Blend fruits with some of the liquid until smooth and return pureed fruits to liquid. Chill and serve.

SPANISH AVOCADO SOUP

¾ Cup Portion	1 Qt. ½ Cup 6 Portions	2 Qt. 1 Cup 12 Portions	1 Gal. 2 Cups 24 Portions	2 Gal. 1 Qt. 48 Portions
Butter *or* Margarine	2 Tbsp.	¼ cup	½ cup	1 cup
Onion, medium, chopped	1	2	4	8
Chicken Stock, canned	1 qt.	2 qt.	1 gal.	2 gal.
Garlic Cloves, large	6	12	24	48
Avocado, ripe, medium, cut in ½" pieces	1	2	4	8

1. Remove fat from chicken stock before using.
2. Melt butter or margarine.
3. Add chopped onion and saute until soft. Do not brown.
4. Add stock and garlic. Cover and barely simmer for 15 minutes.
5. Strain onion and garlic and put in blender.
6. Add avocado pieces to onion and garlic, along with enough of the hot stock to cover.
7. Blend until very smooth.
8. Add pureed avocado mixture to remaining hot stock and bring back to a boil. Do not boil.
9. Serve hot and garnished with watercress leaves, minced green onion tops, or chopped chives.

FROSTY APRICOT-MELON SOUP

¾ Cup Portion	1 Qt. 6 Portions	2 Qts. 12 Portions	1 Gal. 24 Portions	2 Gals. 48 Portions
Cantaloupe *or* Honeydew Melon, chopped	2 cups	1 qt.	2 qt.	1 gal.
Apricot Nectar	2 cups	1 qt.	2 qt.	1 gal.
Lemon Juice	2 Tbsp.	¼ cup	½ cup	1 cup
Salt	dash	dash	1/16 tsp.	⅛ tsp.
Lemon Sherbet				

1. Combine well-chilled melon, apricot nectar, lemon juice, and salt.
2. Blend in a blender for a few seconds. Chill. After chilling, it may be necessary to blend again for a smooth texture.
3. Float a scoop of sherbet on each ¾-cup serving.

Note: This may be prepared without blending. Just combine finely chopped melon with other ingredients. This soup can be made to order if both melon and apricot nectar are chilled. Use one 5½-oz. can of chilled nectar, 1 cup of chopped melon, 1 Tbsp. lemon juice, and a dash of salt. Blend until melon is in small bits (a few seconds) and then serve. Serves two.

COLD APPLE SOUP

¾ Cup Portion	1 Qt. 2 Cups 8 Portions	3 Qt. 16 Portions	1 Gal. 2 Qt. 32 Portions	3 Gal. 64 Portions
Apples, tart	3	6	12	24
Apple Juice	1 cup	2 cups	1 qt.	2 qt.
Lemon Juice	2 Tbsp.	¼ cup	½ cup	1 cup
Sugar	1 Tbsp.	2 Tbsp.	¼ cup	½ cup
Cinnamon Stick	½	1	2	4
Vanilla	¼ tsp.	½ tsp.	1 tsp.	2 tsp.
Orange Juice, cold	1 cup	2 cups	1 qt.	2 qt.
Cream, heavy, cold	1 cup	2 cups	1 qt.	2 qt.
Triple Sec or Cointreau	1½ Tbsp.	3 Tbsp.	6 Tbsp.	¾ cup
Apples, tart, optional	1	2	4	8

1. Peel, core, and quarter first amount of apples.
2. Combine peeled apples with apple juice, lemon juice, sugar, cinnamon stick, and vanilla.
3. Cover and cook over medium heat until apples are very soft, about 20 minutes.
4. Let cool, then cover and refrigerate 24 hours.
5. Remove cinnamon stick.
6. Add orange juice and heavy cream to apples and puree in batches in blender until smooth.
7. Add Triple Sec or Cointreau and serve at this point in a stemmed sherbet dish.
8. For a different texture, shred second amount of apples (unpeeled) into soup and serve.

COLD CHERRY LEMON SOUP

¾ Cup Portion	1 Quart 6 Portions	2 Quarts 12 Portions	1 Gallon 24 Portions	2 Gallons 48 Portions
Cherries, dark, sweet, pitted, canned with juice	2 cups	1 qt.	2 qt.	1 gal.
Cloves, whole	2	4	8	16
Cinnamon Stick	½	1	2	4
Water	1½ cups	3 cups	1 qt. 2 cups	3 qt.
Red Wine	1 cup	2 cups	1 qt.	2 qt.
Lemon Juice	2 Tbsp.	¼ cup	½ cup	1 cup
Lemon Slices, thin	3	6	12	24
Orange Juice	2 Tbsp.	¼ cup	½ cup	1 cup
Sugar	¼ cup	½ cup	1 cup	2 cups
Cornstarch	1 tsp.	2 tsp.	1 Tbsp. 1 tsp.	2 Tbsp. 2 tsp.
Water, cold	1 tsp.	2 tsp.	1 Tbsp. 1 tsp.	2 Tbsp. 2 tsp.

1. Open cherries. Tie cloves and cinnamon stick in cheesecloth.
2. Combine cherries and juice with spices, first amount of water, wine, lemon juice and slices, orange juice, and sugar.
3. Bring to a boil. Reduce heat and simmer for 5 minutes.
4. Mix cornstarch with second amount of cold water and a little of the simmering juice. Add to the simmering soup and stir well.
5. Bring soup back to a boil and simmer another 3 to 5 minutes.
6. Remove lemon slices and bag of spices. Put mixture through a sieve.
7. Put cherries in a blender with a small amount of the cherry juice mixture and blend until cherries are in small pieces, about ⅛" in size.
8. Add blended cherries to hot juice mixture and mix to combine.
9. Chill for 4 hours in the refrigerator.
10. Serve in a stemmed glass sherbet dish with a thin lemon slice floating on the top.

Note: Two to 4 whole cherries may be added to each individual portion of soup when served, if desired.

AMERICAN DAIRY ASSOCIATION
FOODSERVICE DIVISION, ROSEMONT, ILLINOIS.

Figure 8A   A touch of glamour may be added to chilled fruit soups by serving them in transparent glassware and adding a fruit garnish. For example, the chilled strawberry soup may be garnished with a whole strawberry and mint leaves.

CHERRY SOUP

¾ Cup Portion	2 Quarts 10 Portions	1 Gallon 20 Portions	2 Gallons 40 Portions	4 Gallons 80 Portions
Water, cold	3 cups	1 qt. 2 cups	3 qt.	1 gal. 2 qt.
Sugar	1 cup	2 cups	1 qt.	2 qt.
Cinnamon Stick	1	2	4	8
Sour Cherries, pitted, canned with juice	1 qt.	2 qt.	1 gal.	2 gal.
Cornstarch	2 Tbsp.	¼ cup	½ cup	1 cup
Water, cold	2 Tbsp.	¼ cup	½ cup	1 cup
Burgundy Wine	¾ cup	1½ cups	3 cups	1 qt. 2 cups
Cream, heavy, optional	¼ cup	½ cup	1 cup	2 cups

1. Combine first amount of water, sugar, and cinnamon stick.
2. Bring to a boil, then add the cherries and juice.
3. Partially cover and simmer over low heat for 10 minutes. Remove the cinnamon stick.
4. Mix the cornstarch with the second amount of cold water into a paste.
5. Add to soup, stirring constantly.
6. Bring the soup to a boil, reduce heat, and simmer about 2 minutes, or until clear and slightly thickened.
7. Refrigerate until chilled.
8. Add Burgundy just before serving and serve chilled.

Note: Heavy cream may be added for variation if desired.

PEACH AND PLUM SOUP

¾ Cup Portion	1 Qt. 2 Cups 8 Portions	3 Quarts 16 Portions	1 Gal. 2 Qts. 32 Portions	3 Gallons 64 Portions
Plums, fresh, diced	2 cups	1 qt.	2 qt.	1 gal.
Peaches, fresh, diced	2 cups	1 qt.	2 qt.	1 gal.
Red Wine, dry	1½ cups	3 cups	1 qt. 2 cups	3 qt.
Water	1½ cups	3 cups	1 qt. 2 cups	3 qt.
Sugar	⅔ cup	1⅓ cups	2⅔ cups	1 qt. 1⅓ cups
Lemon Slices	1	2	4	8
Cinnamon Stick, 4″	1	2	4	8
Cognac, optional	2 Tbsp.	¼ cup	½ cup	1 cup

1. Cook plums, peaches, wine, water, sugar, lemon, and cinnamon stick in a covered pot until fruits are soft.
2. Discard lemon and cinnamon stick. Cool.
3. Blend in blender until almost smooth. The soup is a light plum color after blending.
4. Add cognac, if desired, and chill. Stir well before serving.

Note: This soup is good served hot. Always cool before blending, then reheat.

LEMON CLOUD SOUP
(Lemon Meringue Soup)

¾ Cup Portion	1 Quart 6 Portions	2 Quarts 12 Portions	1 Gallon 24 Portions	2 Gallons 48 Portions
Water, cold	¼ cup	½ cup	1 cup	2 cups
Cornstarch	2 Tbsp.	¼ cup	½ cup	1 cup
Water	1¾ cup	3½ cups	1 qt. 3 cups	3 qt. 2 cups
Lemon Juice	¼ cup	½ cup	1 cup	2 cups
Sugar	2 Tbsp.	¼ cup	½ cup	1 cup
Lemon Rind, grated	1½ Tbsp.	3 Tbsp.	6 Tbsp.	¾ cup
Vanilla	½ tsp.	1 tsp.	2 tsp.	1 Tbsp. 1 tsp.
Egg Yolks, lightly beaten	2	4	8	16
Egg Whites	2	4	8	16
Sugar	¼ cup	½ cup	1 cup	2 cups
Lemon Peel Slices, to garnish				

1. Combine and mix first amount of water and cornstarch.
2. Add second amount of water, lemon juice, first amount of sugar, lemon rind, and vanilla.
3. Cook over medium heat, stirring constantly, until mixture thickens and bubbles for 3 minutes.
4. Add some of the hot mixture to the egg yolks. Stir to mix. Add egg yolk mixture to remaining hot lemon mixture.
5. Cook over low heat, stirring constantly, for 1 minute. Refrigerate covered until cold.
6. Beat egg whites until foamy. Add second amount of sugar gradually until stiff peaks form.
7. Fold ¾ of the meringue into lemon mixture until smooth.
8. Dollop each portion with remaining meringue.
9. Garnish with lemon peel slices.

FRUIT GAZPACHO
(Cold Peach Soup with Fresh Mint)

½ Cup Portion	6 Portions	12 Portions	24 Portions	48 Portions
Sugar	⅓ cup	⅔ cup	1⅓ cups	2⅔ cups
Water	2 Tbsp.	¼ cup	½ cup	1 cup
Cinnamon, ground	½ tsp.	1 tsp.	2 tsp.	1 Tbsp. 1 tsp.
Lemon Juice	2 Tbsp.	¼ cup	½ cup	1 cup
Peaches, fresh, very ripe	3	6	12	24
Peaches, ripe	3	6	12	24
Mint Sprigs, to garnish				

1. Combine sugar, water, and cinnamon.
2. Heat until thoroughly dissolved, stirring constantly with a wire whip. Remove from heat.
3. Add lemon juice and set aside.
4. Peel first amount of peaches by dipping in very hot water, then cooling in cold water. Slip off skins, halve, and pit; or peel peaches with a knife.
5. Cut peaches into cubes directly into blender.
6. Blend until pureed.
7. Combine pureed fruit with cinnamon and sugar mixture. Stir to combine thoroughly.
8. Chill covered until very cold.
9. When ready to serve, cut ½ peach into small cubes and put in bottom of a stemmed sherbet dish.
10. Put ¼ to ⅓ cup peach puree over the peaches and serve with a sprig of mint.

Note: Volume yields are not included because the soup is a combination of puree and fresh peaches.

PEACH, MELON, AND ORANGE SOUP

½ Cup Portion	6 Portions	12 Portions	24 Portions	48 Portions
Sugar	⅓ cup	⅔ cup	1⅓ cups	2⅔ cups
Water	2 Tbsp.	¼ cup	½ cup	1 cup
Cinnamon, ground	½ tsp.	1 tsp.	2 tsp.	1 Tbsp. 1 tsp.
Lemon Juice *or* Lime Juice	2 Tbsp.	¼ cup	½ cup	1 cup
Peaches, medium, fresh, ripe, cubed	2	4	8	16
Cantaloupe, small cubes	¼ melon	½ melon	1 melon	2 melons
Orange Juice, strained	¼ cup	1 cup	2 cups	1 qt.
Peaches, medium	2	4	8	16
Mint Sprigs, to garnish				

1. Combine sugar, water, and cinnamon.
2. Heat until thoroughly dissolved and smooth, stirring constantly with wire whip. Remove from heat.
3. Add lemon or lime juice. A combination of lemon and lime juice may be used. Set aside.
4. Peel first amount of peaches by dipping in very hot water and then removing skins and pits. Peaches may be peeled with a knife instead.
5. Cut peaches in cubes into blender.
6. Cut rind from cantaloupe and remove seeds.
7. Cube into blender along with peaches.
8. Blend peaches and cantaloupe until pureed.
9. Squeeze orange juice, strain, and add to pureed fruits.
10. Combine fruit with cinnamon and sugar mixture. Stir to combine thoroughly. Chill covered until very cold.
11. When ready to serve, cut ⅓ peach (peeled) into small cubes and put in bottom of stemmed sherbet dish.
12. Put ½ cup of the fruit puree over the peaches and serve with a sprig of mint.

Note: Volume yields are not included because the soup is a combination of puree and fresh peaches.

STRAWBERRY SOUP

¾ Cup Portion	3 Cups 4 Portions	1 Qt. 2 Cups 8 Portions	3 Quarts 16 Portions	1 Gal. 2 Qt. 32 Portions
Water	¾ cup	1½ cups	3 cups	1 qt. 2 cups
Red Wine, light bodied	⅜ cup	¾ cup	1½ cups	3 cups
Sugar	¼ cup	½ cup	1 cup	2 cups
Lemon Juice, fresh	1 Tbsp.	2 Tbsp.	¼ cup	½ cup
Cinnamon Stick	½	1	2	4

Strawberries,
  stemmed and
  pureed
	1 pint	1 qt.	2 qt.	1 gal.

Cream, heavy	¼ cup	½ cup	1 cup	2 cups
Sour Cream	2 Tbsp.	¼ cup	½ cup	1 cup

1. Combine water, wine, sugar, lemon juice, and cinnamon and simmer uncovered for 15 minutes, stirring occasionally.
2. Add strawberry puree and simmer, stirring frequently for 10 minutes.
3. Discard cinnamon stick and cool.
4. Whip heavy cream.
5. Combine with sour cream and fold into strawberry mixture.
6. Serve at cool room temperature.

STRAWBERRY RHUBARB SOUP

¾ Cup Portion	3 Cups 4 Portions	1 Qt. 2 Cups 8 Portions	3 Qts. 16 Portions	1 Gal. 2 Qt. 32 Portions

Rhubarb, fresh,
  cut into 1″
  pieces
	1 qt.	2 qt.	1 gal.	2 gal.

Water	1 cup	2 cups	1 qt.	2 qt.
Honey	½ cup	1 cup	2 cups	1 qt.
Strawberries, fresh, hulled	2 cups	1 qt.	2 qt.	1 gal.
Nutmeg	½ tsp.	1 tsp.	2 tsp.	1 Tbsp. 1 tsp.
Salt	¼ tsp.	½ tsp.	1 tsp.	2 tsp.
Orange Juice	1½ cups	3 cups	1 qt. 2 cups	3 qt.

Note: Rhubarb should be pink and strawberries very ripe.

1. Combine rhubarb and water.
2. Bring to a boil. Lower heat.
3. Cover and simmer for about 3 minutes. Allow to cool.
4. Combine rhubarb mixture, honey, strawberries, nutmeg, and salt in blender.
5. Blend until smooth.
6. Add orange juice. Mix to combine.
7. Chill and serve cold.

PEACH SOUP

¾ **Cup Portion**	**1 Qt. 2 Cups 8 Portions**	**3 Quarts 16 Portions**	**1 Gal. 2 Qt. 32 Portions**	**3 Gallons 64 Portions**
Water	1 cup	2 cups	1 qt.	2 qt.
Sugar	¼ cup	½ cup	1 cup	2 cups
Whole Cloves	1 tsp.	2 tsp.	1 Tbsp. 1 tsp.	2 Tbsp. 2 tsp.
Cinnamon Stick	1	2	4	8
Cornstarch	1 Tbsp. 1 tsp.	2 Tbsp. 2 tsp.	¼ cup 1 Tbsp. 1 tsp.	½ cup 2 Tbsp. 2 tsp.
White Wine, dry	2 cups	1 qt.	2 qt.	1 gal.
Peaches, frozen, unsweetened, thawed, undrained, and pureed	2 lb. 8 oz.	5 lb.	10 lb.	20 lb.
Cinnamon	1 tsp.	2 tsp.	1 Tbsp. 1 tsp.	2 Tbsp. 2 tsp.
Sugar	2 Tbsp.	¼ cup	½ cup	1 cup

1. Combine water, first amount of sugar, cloves, and cinnamon stick.
2. Bring to a boil and simmer covered for 15 minutes. Strain and discard cloves and cinnamon stick.
3. Combine cornstarch with white wine and stir to blend thoroughly.
4. Add cornstarch mixture to sugar and water mixture.
5. Bring to a boil and simmer until thick, stirring occasionally.
6. Add pureed peaches.
7. Combine cinnamon with second amount of sugar. Mix thoroughly.
8. Add to peach mixture, stirring until thoroughly combined.
9. Chill and serve in a footed glass sherbet dish.

Note: If a thin soup is preferred, reduce the amount of cornstarch by half.

GAZPACHO

¾ Cup Portion	1 Quart 6 Portions	2 Quarts 12 Portions	1 Gallon 24 Portions
Green Pepper, finely chopped, EP	¼ cup	½ cup	1 cup
Pimiento, finely chopped, EP	¼ cup	½ cup	1 cup
Onion, diced fine, EP	¼ cup	½ cup	1 cup
Celery, diced fine, EP	¼ cup	½ cup	1 cup
Cucumber, peeled and chopped fine, EP	½ cup	1 cup	2 cups
Tomatoes, fresh, peeled, EP	½ cup	1 cup	2 cups
Olive Oil	1 Tbsp.	2 Tbsp.	¼ cup
Wine Vinegar	1 Tbsp.	2 Tbsp.	¼ cup
Salt	¼ tsp.	½ tsp.	1 tsp.
Pepper	⅛ tsp.	¼ tsp.	½ tsp.
Tomato Juice, as needed to fill measure			

Note: Quart or gallon jars with lids are the ideal measures to use for this formula.

1. Place all chopped ingredients in the appropriate quart or gallon containers.
2. Add the olive oil, vinegar, salt, and pepper along with enough tomato juice to fill measure.
3. Shake well. Refrigerate.
4. Serve very cold.

COLD CUCUMBER SOUP

1. Follow the formula for Cucumber Yogurt Dip (see p. 27).
2. Do not include oil when preparing soup.
3. Place cucumbers and seasonings in blender with ½ of the yogurt and blend until very smooth.
4. Remove mixture from blender and add remaining yogurt.
5. Stir to combine thoroughly and chill.
6. If desired, the following ingredients may be added.

¾ Cup Portion	1½ Cups 2 Portions	3 Cups 4 Portions	1 Qt. 2 Cups 8 Portions	3 Quarts 16 Portions
Cream, light	¼ cup	½ cup	1 cup	2 cups
Parsley, finely chopped	1 tsp.	2 tsp.	1 Tbsp. 1 tsp.	2 Tbsp. 2 tsp.

CURRIED CREAM OF CUCUMBER SOUP

1. Follow the formula for Cold Cucumber Soup, adding the following amounts of curry powder:

Curry Powder	⅛ tsp.	¼ tsp.	½ tsp.	1 tsp.

COLD WATERCRESS SOUP

1. Follow the formula for Cream of Watercress Soup on p. 107.
2. Chill and serve very cold.

COLD ZUCCHINI SOUP

¾ Cup Portion	1 Qt. 1 Cup 6 Portions	2 Qt. 2 Cups 12 Portions	1 Gal. 1 Qt. 24 Portions	2 Gal. 2 Qt. 32 Portions
Zucchini, medium, EP	3	6	12	24
Onion, medium, thinly sliced, EP	1	2	4	8
Curry Powder	¾ tsp.	1½ tsp.	1 Tbsp.	2 Tbsp.
Chicken Broth, canned	1½ cups	3 cups	1 qt. 2 cups	3 qt.
Heavy Cream	½ cup	1 cup	2 cups	1 qt.
Milk	¼ cup	½ cup	1 cup	2 cups
Salt	½ tsp.	1 tsp.	2 tsp.	1 Tbsp. 1 tsp.

Chives, chopped
to garnish

1. Wash and dry all zucchini and cut off ends. Cut the following amount of zucchini in two and slice thinly, then stack and cut into matchstick strips:

       ½ zucchini   1 zucchini   2 zucchini   4 zucchini

2. Place matchstick zucchini in a pan with cold water to cover and boil for 3 to 4 mintues. Drain, reserving both zucchini and zucchini water. Set aside.
3. Cut remaining zucchini into 1-inch pieces, then in quarters, and combine with onion in a pan. Sprinkle with curry powder and stir to coat pieces.
4. Add chicken broth and bring to a boil. Cover and simmer 15 to 20 minutes or until zucchini is tender.
5. Blend in a blender to a fine puree or use food processor. There should be the following amount when blended:

       1 qt.   2 qt.   1 gal.   2 gal.

If there is not enough for these amounts after blending, add chicken broth and zucchini water to bring up to the required amount.
6. Remove from blender and add cream, milk, and salt.
7. Add reserved zucchini strips. Chill thoroughly.
8. Serve ¾ cup portions, sprinkled with chopped chives.

Note: This soup may be made a day ahead. It improves in flavor when seasonings have had time to blend.

PURE GOLD SOUP

¾ Cup Portion	1 Qt. 2 Cups 8 Portions	3 Quarts 16 Portions	1 Gal. 2 Qt. 32 Portions	3 Gallons 64 Portions
Butter *or* Margarine, melted	2 Tbsp.	¼ cup	½ cup	1 cup
Onion, finely chopped, EP	1 cup	2 cups	1 qt.	2 qt.
Celery Stalk and Leaves, finely chopped, EP	½ cup	1 cup	2 cups	1 qt.
Carrots, ¼" rounds, EP	1 lb.	2 lb.	4 lb.	8 lb.
Potatoes, peeled and diced, EP	1 cup	2 cups	1 qt.	2 qt.
Sugar	⅔ tsp.	1⅓ tsp.	2⅔ tsp.	1 Tbsp. 2⅓ tsp.
Fresh Dill, chopped	2 tsp.	1 Tbsp. 1 tsp.	2 Tbsp. 2 tsp.	¼ cup 1 Tbsp. 1 tsp.
Chicken Stock, canned	1 qt.	2 qt.	1 gal.	2 gal.
Milk	⅔ cup	1⅓ cups	2⅔ cups	1 qt. 1⅓ cups
Cream, heavy	⅔ cup	1⅓ cups	2⅔ cups	1 qt. 1⅓ cups
Cayenne Pepper	pinch	pinch	dash	dash

Note: Remove fat from cans of chicken stock before using.

1. Saute onion and celery in melted butter or margarine until translucent.
2. Add carrots, potatoes, sugar, dill, and chicken stock.
3. Simmer covered for 20 to 25 minutes or until vegetables are just tender.
4. Cool slightly and puree in blender in batches until smooth.
5. Add pureed mixture to milk, cream, and cayenne. Stir to combine.
6. Chill covered in refrigerator.

Note: This soup may also be served hot. Do not allow to boil after adding milk and cream.

Note: Dried dill may be substituted for fresh dill. Use one-third the amount specified in this formula.

GOURMET CREAM SOUPS

Americans are especially fond of soups with a pure vegetable flavor. In addition to such traditional vegetable soups as potato, celery, and mushroom, the more unusual vegetable bases such as broccoli, watercress, zucchini, and artichoke have gained increasing acceptance. The retention of the basic vegetable flavor, the simplicity of ingredients, and ease of preparation have been the paramount considerations in developing the formulas that follow.

Many of these gourmet cream soups contain only three ingredients—canned chicken stock and the vegetable, combined in equal volume and cooked until the vegetables are tender, and a small amount of heavy cream. The cooked vegetable and enough chicken stock to cover it are blended, returned to the container of hot stock, and heated with the heavy cream. The soup should not be permitted to boil but should be heated to just below the boiling point. The preparation of this soup is so quick and simple that it could be made to order if necessary.

Canned chicken stock or broth (the terms are synonymous) is used in these soups because it is a standard and consistent product. It contains enough salt to eliminate the need for salt as an added ingredient. When using canned chicken stock or broth it is important to remove all chicken fat from the tops of the cans before use. The fat may be saved and used in soups that need to be thickened, such as the Cream of Spinach and Cream of Watercress soups. Kitchen-prepared chicken stock may be used if it is available, but it should be a rich stock and may require additional salt. Chicken stock reconstituted from bouillon granules or cubes should not be used in these soups.

When large amounts of soup are prepared it may be necessary to blend the cooked vegetables and stock in several batches, since there are no blenders larger than the one-gallon size and some splashing is inevitable. It may also be necessary to cool large batches of cooked vegetables before blending because, if the vegetable is very hot and the blender filled to capacity, the pressure may force the top from the blender. For both safety and ease of handling, it is recommended that the blender not be filled to capacity.

If a cutter-mixer (formerly called a VCM) is available it may be used as a substitute for the blender. Large strainers are available that can be used directly in the steam kettle while cooking the vegetable in the stock. Use of these strainers eliminates the need to strain the vegetables in a separate sieve and reduces the time and labor involved in preparation.

It is suggested that these soups be tested in small amounts before deciding whether or not to include them on the menu. Although a restaurateur is usually familiar with customer preferences, sample servings may determine the potential acceptance of a specialty soup. Even if guests have an established preference for Old Fashioned Chicken and Noodle Soup, they may be ready to accept a new flavor or type of soup if they are given the opportunity.

CREAM OF ARTICHOKE SOUP

¾ Cup Portion	1 Qt. ½ Cup 6 Portions	2 Qt. 1 Cup 12 Portions	1 Gal. 2 Cups 24 Portions	2 Gal. 1 Qt. 48 Portions
Chicken Stock, canned	1 qt.	2 qt.	1 gal.	2 gal.
Artichoke Hearts, frozen	1 lb. 2 oz.	2 lb. 4 oz.	4 lb. 8 oz.	9 lb.
Pepper, white	⅛ tsp.	¼ tsp.	½ tsp.	1 tsp.
Lemon Juice, freshly squeezed	1 tsp.	2 tsp.	1 Tbsp. 1 tsp.	2 Tbsp. 2 tsp.
Cream, heavy	½ cup	1 cup	2 cups	1 qt.

Note: Remove fat from chicken stock before using.

1. Bring stock to a boil.
2. Add the artichoke hearts, reduce heat, and simmer partly covered until hearts are very tender. If hearts were still frozen when added this will take about 25 minutes. If defrosted, cooking should take 12 to 15 minutes.
3. Drain the artichokes (save the stock) and puree them in a blender with a little of the stock until smooth. Then return the pureed artichokes to the reserved stock.

4. Add pepper, lemon juice, and heavy cream. Stir until smooth.
5. Reheat gently just to the boiling point if serving the soup hot; or chill it and serve in chilled cups. In either case, garnish with snipped chives or rounds of scallion greens.

Note: Artichoke hearts that are packed in oil or an acidulated dressing are not suitable.

Note: If canned chicken broth is used, no salt will be needed. If using your own kitchen prepared stock, it should be a rich stock. To the homemade stock add the following amounts of salt, taste for seasoning, and adjust if necessary.

2 tsp.	1 Tbsp.	2 Tbsp.	¼ cup
	1 tsp.	2 tsp.	1 Tbsp.
			1 tsp.

Note: If there is objection to the pieces of small artichoke fiber of ½″ (which do not puree), then the soup should be strained to remove them before serving. Strain while hot.

CREAM OF CELERY AND WATERCRESS SOUP

¾ Cup Portion	1 Qt. 2 Cups 8 Portions	3 Quarts 16 Portions	1 Gal. 2 Qt. 32 Portions	3 Gallons 64 Portions
Chicken Stock, canned	1 qt.	2 qt.	1 gal.	2 gal.
Celery, chopped ¼″, EP	1 qt.	2 qt.	1 gal.	2 gal.
Cream, heavy	½ cup	1 cup	2 cups	1 qt.
Watercress Leaves, to garnish				

Note: Remove all fat from chicken stock before using.

1. Heat chicken stock to boiling.
2. Add chopped celery and simmer covered, for 3 to 5 minutes, or until celery is just tender but still crisp.
3. Strain celery from chicken stock and puree in blender with a small amount of stock until smooth.
4. Return pureed celery to hot stock.

5. Add cream and heat until just under boiling.
6. Sprinkle a few watercress leaves on top of soup before serving. Serve hot. This soup has a light green color, with flecks of celery throughout.

CREAM OF BROCCOLI SOUP

1. Use the preceding formula for Cream of Celery and Watercress Soup.
2. Substitute broccoli for celery. Cut outside skin from stems of broccoli. Then cut stems into slices about ¼″ thick. Cut broccoli flowerets into ½″ pieces.
3. Cook broccoli in chicken broth uncovered. Simmer only until tender-crisp, for about 3 to 5 minutes.
4. Return to direction 3 in Celery and Watercress Soup and continue as directed.
5. Serve hot without garnish of watercress.

CREAM OF FRESH ASPARAGUS SOUP

1. Use the formula for Cream of Celery and Watercress Soup.
2. Substitute asparagus for celery.
3. Prepare asparagus by removing the light brown triangular pieces on the stem. Cut stems into ½″ pieces and wash asparagus thoroughly.
4. Cook asparagus in chicken stock, covered, for 3 to 5 minutes or until asparagus is tender.
5. Return to direction 3 in Celery and Watercress Soup and continue as directed.
6. Serve hot, without garnish of watercress.

CREAM OF CAULIFLOWER SOUP

1. Use the formula for Cream of Celery and Watercress Soup on p. 102.
2. Substitute cauliflower for celery. Cut cauliflower flowerets and stems into ½″ pieces.
3. Cook cauliflower in chicken broth uncovered. Simmer for 3 to 5 minutes, or until cauliflower is tender-crisp.
4. Return to direction 3 in Celery and Watercress Soup and continue as directed.
5. Sprinkle with chopped chives or parsley before serving.

CREAM OF ZUCCHINI SOUP

1. Use formula for Cream of Celery and Watercress Soup on p. 102.
2. Substitute zucchini for celery. Wash zucchini, slice into ¼″ slices, then into ¼″ matchstick pieces.
3. Cook zucchini in chicken stock, covered. Simmer for 3 to 5 minutes or until zucchini is tender-crisp.
4. Return to direction 3 in Celery and Watercress Soup and continue as directed.

Note: This is a light green color and is a lightly flavored zucchini soup. If a thicker soup is desired use amounts for thickening in the Cream of Spinach Soup on p. 106. The unthickened soup is good served cold. If a smoother soup is preferred, blend until very smooth.

CREAMY MUSHROOM SOUP

1. Use the formula for Cream of Celery and Watercress Soup on p. 102.
2. Substitute mushrooms for celery.
3. Wash mushrooms and slice. Caps and stems may be used, or stems only may be used.
4. Cook mushrooms in chicken stock, covered, for 3 to 5 minutes or until mushrooms are tender.
5. Return to direction 3 in Celery and Watercress Soup and continue as directed.
6. Serve hot, without garnish of watercress.

Note: There should be flecks of mushroom throughout this soup. Do not blend mushrooms until smooth.

CREAMY POTATO SOUP

¾ Cup Portion	1 Quart 6 Portions	2 Quarts 12 Portions	1 Gallon 24 Portions	2 Gallons 48 Portions
Chicken Stock, canned	2 cups	1 qt.	2 qt.	1 gal.
Potatoes, cubed ¼″, EP	2 cups	1 qt.	2 qt.	1 gal.

Scallions, small,
   chopped,
   including tops
	2	4	8	16

Cream, heavy	¼ cup	½ cup	1 cup	2 cups
Chicken Stock, canned	2 cups	1 qt.	2 qt.	1 gal.

Note: Remove fat from chicken stock before using.

1. Heat first amount of chicken stock.
2. Add potatoes and scallions and simmer covered for 5 minutes, or until potatoes are tender.
3. Blend in blender until very smooth.
4. Return to heat. Add cream and second amount of stock. Heat to boiling.
5. Serve hot, sprinkled with minced chives or chopped parsley.

VICHYSSOISE

1. Use the preceding formula for Creamy Potato Soup.
2. Chill for several hours or overnight in the refrigerator. Serve in chilled cups or bowls, garnished with minced chives.

CREAM OF SPINACH SOUP

¾ Cup Portion	1 Qt. 2 Cups 8 Portions	3 Quarts 16 Portions	1 Gal. 2 Qt. 32 Portions	3 Gallons 64 Portions
Chicken Stock, canned	1 qt.	2 qt.	1 gal.	2 gal.
Spinach, fresh, EP	1 qt.	2 qt.	1 gal.	2 gal.
Margarine *or* Chicken Fat	¼ cup	½ cup	1 cup	2 cups
Flour	¼ cup	½ cup	1 cup	2 cups
Cream, heavy	½ cup	1 cup	2 cups	1 qt.

Note: Remove fat from chicken stock before using. Use fat later in preparing roux.

1. Heat canned stock.
2. While stock is heating, remove spinach leaves from stems.
3. Wash spinach several times to remove all sand.
4. Add spinach leaves to hot chicken broth and simmer for 3 to 5 minutes, or until leaves are completely wilted.
5. Strain spinach leaves from broth and puree in a blender (with a small amount of stock) until smooth.
6. Melt margarine or chicken fat, or a combination of both.
7. Add flour and stir with a wire whip until smooth.
8. Add hot chicken broth to roux and heat until slightly thickened.
9. Add pureed spinach and heavy cream. Stir until well mixed.
10. Heat until just under boiling and serve hot.

Note: If canned chicken broth is used no salt or pepper is needed. If kitchen-prepared chicken stock is used, add salt and pepper to taste.

Note: This soup is also delicious served cold. If it seems too thick after cooling, thin with chicken broth to desired consistency.

CREAM OF WATERCRESS SOUP

1. Use the preceding formula for Cream of Spinach Soup.
2. Substitute watercress leaves for spinach. Use as few stems of watercress as possible. Watercress leaves should be packed when measuring.

Note: If a lighter color is desired, add more heavy cream.

SPINACH CHEESE SOUP

¾ Cup Portion	2¼ Cups 3 Portions	1 Qt. ½ Cup 6 Portions	2 Qt. 1 Cup 12 Portions	1 Gal. 2 Cups 24 Portions
Spinach, cooked	½ cup	1 cup	2 cups	1 qt.
Milk	½ cup	1 cup	2 cups	1 qt.
Butter *or* Margarine	1 Tbsp.	2 Tbsp.	¼ cup	½ cup
Flour	1 Tbsp.	2 Tbsp.	¼ cup	½ cup
Chicken Broth, canned	1 cup	2 cups	1 qt.	2 qt.
Cheddar Cheese, shredded	¼ cup	½ cup	1 cup	2 cups

1. Cut spinach leaves from stems. Discard stems.
2. Wash spinach thoroughly to remove all grains of sand.
3. Cook spinach with water that clings to the leaves. Cook, stirring until leaves are wilted completely.
4. Put the cooked spinach, milk, butter or margarine, and flour into the blender.
5. Cover and blend on high speed for 20 seconds.
6. Empty mixture into pan. Add chicken broth and cheese.
7. Heat to boiling, stirring constantly.
8. Serve hot.

Note: Frozen spinach may be substituted for fresh. Use directions on the package for cooking.

OLD-FASHIONED CREAM OF TOMATO SOUP

¾ Cup Portion	3 Cups 4 Portions	1 Qt. 2 Cups 8 Portions	3 Qt. 16 Portions	1 Gal. 2 Qt. 32 Portions
Tomatoes, AP	1 lb.	2 lb.	4 lb.	8 lb.
Sugar	1 Tbsp.	2 Tbsp.	¼ cup	½ cup
Salt	1 tsp.	2 tsp.	1 Tbsp. 1 tsp.	2 Tbsp. 2 tsp.
Pepper	pinch	dash	¹⁄₁₆ tsp.	⅛ tsp.
Butter	½ oz.	1 oz.	2 oz.	4 oz.
Soda	⅛ tsp.	¼ tsp.	½ tsp.	1 tsp.
Milk	1 cup	2 cups	1 qt.	2 qt.
Cream, light	1 cup	2 cups	1 qt.	2 qt.

1. Peel tomatoes and cut into ½″ to ¾″ pieces.
2. Simmer tomatoes slowly until they become tender, about 10 to 12 minutes.
3. Add sugar, salt, pepper, and butter to the tomatoes and mix well until all tomatoes are well-seasoned.
4. Heat milk and cream separately and heat only to scalding point.
5. Add the soda to the tomatoes and mix all tomatoes into the hot milk immediately.
6. Add the cream immediately and mix to combine.

Note: Combine in quantities that are sent to the service bar at one time. The soup should be kept in a double container at the service bar.

Note: For a smooth cream soup, the soup may be blended after cooking. If seeds are objectionable, strain the soup.

Note: This soup is excellent served cold.

STOCK AND MISCELLANEOUS SOUPS

Broth or stock-type soups are well-accepted as appetizers in quantity foodservice operations. The specialty stock soups are variations on the basic formulas that provide a distinctive flavor ideally suited for the introduction to a meal. The terms broth and stock are used interchangeably in the stock soup formula.

A stock soup is made from a highly flavored broth of beef, pork, ham, poultry, or fish. The broth itself is frequently called a bouillon and is made by simmering bones, meat, fish, or vegetables in water to extract their flavors and color. Consomme is a clear broth that results when bouillon has been clarified, or it may consist of a combination of broth and a juice, as in the Beef-Lemon Consomme.

Many of the following formulas call for the use of chicken stock; although it may be prepared in the kitchen from the meat and bones of chickens, the use of canned stock is preferred. If kitchen-prepared stocks are used, the amount of salt indicated in the formulas must be increased. Reconstituted bouillon granules or cubes are not recommended as a stock for soups. While these products have some uses, they do not provide the richness or natural flavor of kitchen-prepared or quality canned beef or chicken stock.

Soups should be stirred frequently during cooking. An agitator may be necessary when preparing some soups in a large kettle, since vegetables have a tendency to sink to the bottom. If these soups are placed on a serving line, they should be stirred often for proper distribution of ingredients.

Many of the specialty stock soups may be garnished with chopped parsley or chives; some may lend themselves to a garnish of fresh croutons. In most instances, however, the garnish should be kept as simple as possible so that it will not interfere with the natural flavor of the soups. Melba toast, assorted crackers, or bread sticks may be served as an accompaniment.

Finally, all soups should be tasted to make certain that the seasonings are properly balanced. And, of course, hot soups should be served hot because even the best soup is unappetizing if served lukewarm.

BEEF LEMON CONSOMME

¾ Cup Portion	1 Quart 6 Portions	2 Quarts 12 Portions	1 Gallon 24 Portions	2 Gallons 48 Portions
Beef Stock, freshly made	2 cups	1 qt.	2 qt.	1 gal.
Beef Stock, reconstituted	2 cups	1 qt.	2 qt.	1 gal.
Lemon Juice	1 Tbsp. 1 tsp.	2 Tbsp. 2 tsp.	¼ cup 1 Tbsp. 1 tsp.	½ cup 2 Tbsp. 2 tsp.
Salt	¼ tsp.	½ tsp.	1 tsp.	2 tsp.
Pepper	dash	1/16 tsp.	⅛ tsp.	¼ tsp.

Lemon Slices,
  thin, for
  garnish				

1. Prepare first amount of beef stock by simmering leftover steak or prime rib bones. Add water to cover.
2. Simmer 30 minutes. Strain.
3. Refrigerate covered. Fat will congeal on top.
4. When ready to prepare consomme for service, remove fat from stock.
5. Reconstitute second amount of beef stock using beef base.
6. Combine and heat fresh stock with reconstituted stock.
7. Add lemon juice, salt, and pepper.
8. Float each serving with a very thin lemon slice.

MUSHROOM CONSOMME WITH BARLEY

1 Cup Portion	3 Gallons 48 Portions	6 Gallons 96 Portions	12 Gallons 192 Portions	24 Gallons 384 Portions
Beef Stock	2 gal. 2 qt.	5 gal.	10 gal.	20 gal.
Barley	4 oz.	8 oz.	1 lb.	2 lb.
Onions, finely chopped, EP	4 oz.	8 oz.	1 lb.	2 lb.
Mushrooms, finely chopped	1 lb.	2 lb.	4 lb.	8 lb.
Green Peas, frozen, cooked	2 cups	1 qt.	2 qt.	1 gal.
Salt	1 oz.	2 oz.	4 oz.	8 oz.

1. Use beef stock made with beef bones or reconstitute beef base.
2. Simmer barley in stock for 30 minutes.
3. Add chopped onions and mushrooms. Continue to simmer for another 30 minutes.
4. Add peas and salt just before serving.

Note: Peas become discolored very quickly in the soup and, therefore, should be added in small amounts.

MULLIGATAWNY SOUP

¾ Cup Portion	3 Quarts 16 Portions	1 Gal. 2 Qt. 32 Portions	3 Gallons 64 Portions	6 Gallons 128 Portions
Chicken Fat	1 oz.	2 oz.	4 oz.	8 oz.
Onion, ½" pieces, EP	2½ oz.	5 oz.	10 oz.	1 lb. 4 oz.
Carrots, fresh, ½" cubes, EP	2½ oz.	5 oz.	10 oz.	1 lb. 4 oz.
Celery, ½" cubes, EP	2¼ oz.	4½ oz.	9 oz.	1 lb. 2 oz.
Green Pepper, ¼" pieces, EP	¾ oz.	1½ oz.	3 oz.	6 oz.
Apples, raw, peeled, cubed ½", EP	10 oz.	1 lb. 4 oz.	2 lb. 8 oz.	5 lb.
Tomatoes, canned, broken 1" pieces	2 cups	1 qt.	2 qt.	1 gal.
Salt	1 tsp.	2 tsp.	1 Tbsp. 1 tsp.	2 Tbsp. 2 tsp.
Curry Powder	⅜ tsp.	¾ tsp.	1½ tsp.	1 Tbsp.
Pepper	dash	1/16 tsp.	⅛ tsp.	¼ tsp.
Chicken Stock, canned	2 qt. 1 cup	1 gal. 2 cups	2 gal. 1 qt.	4 gal. 2 qt.
Flour	3 oz.	6 oz.	12 oz.	1 lb. 8 oz.
Water, cold	1 cup	2 cups	1 qt.	2 qt.
Chicken, cooked, ¼ to ½" pieces	8 oz.	1 lb.	2 lb.	4 lb.
Parsley, finely chopped, for garnish				

1. Use fat from cans of chicken stock to saute onion, carrots, celery, green peppers, and apples for 10 to 15 minutes until vegetables are tender and apples soft.
2. Add tomatoes, salt, curry powder, pepper and canned chicken stock. Mix to combine.
3. Combine flour and cold water. Mix until smooth. Add to stock and vegetable mixture, stirring constantly.

4. Heat to boiling point, reduce heat, and simmer for 1 hour.
5. Add the chopped chicken and simmer 5 to 10 minutes longer to heat the chicken.
6. Sprinkle ⅛ tsp. finely chopped parsley on top as served.

Note: For a less expensive soup, delete the chopped chicken; the soup will still have a good chicken flavor without it.

Note: Stir soup before each portion is removed to maintain correct proportion of solids and liquids.

POTATO AND LEEK SOUP

¾ Cup Portion	1 Qt. ½ Cup 6 Portions	2 Qt. 1 Cup 12 Portions	1 Gal. 2 Cups 24 Portions	2 Gal. 1 Qt. 48 Portions
Leeks, medium, sliced ⅛″, EP	1	2	4	8
Margarine	2 Tbsp.	¼ cup	½ cup	1 cup
Chicken Stock, canned	2 cups	1 qt.	2 qt.	1 gal.
Water	2 cups	1 qt.	2 qt.	1 gal.
Potatoes, cubed ¼″, EP	1 cup	2 cups	1 qt.	2 qt.
Salt	½ tsp.	1 tsp.	2 tsp.	1 Tbsp. 1 tsp.
Pepper, white	⅛ tsp.	¼ tsp.	½ tsp.	1 tsp.
Margarine	1 Tbsp.	2 Tbsp.	¼ cup	½ cup

Note: Remove fat from chicken stock before using.

1. Slice leeks crosswise into very thin slices. Some of the green part of the leeks may be used.
2. Rinse leeks well in water until all dirt is removed.
3. Melt first amount of margarine. Add leeks and saute for 5 minutes, stirring often. Do not brown.
4. Add stock, water, cubed potatoes, salt, and white pepper.
5. Bring to a boil and simmer for 20 minutes.
6. Add second amount of margarine.
7. Bring soup back to a boil and serve hot.

POTAGE BON FEMME

¾ Cup Portion	1 Qt. ½ Cup 6 Portions	2 Qt. 1 Cup 12 Portions	1 Gal. 2 Cups 24 Portions	2 Gal. 1 Qt. 48 Portions
Chicken Stock, canned	1 qt.	2 qt.	1 gal.	2 gal.
Scallions, sliced ⅛", including tops	1 cup	2 cups	1 qt.	2 qt.
Potatoes, peeled, diced, EP	1 cup	2 cups	1 qt.	2 qt.

Note: Remove fat from cans of chicken stock before using.

1. Heat chicken stock to boiling.
2. Add scallions and potatoes.
3. Cook covered at a simmer for 10 minutes.
4. Serve hot with Melba Toast.

CHICKEN EGG DROP SOUP

1. Use the preceding formula for Potage Bon Femme.
2. Dribble the following amount of stirred whole eggs into the hot soup just before serving.

Eggs	1	2	4	8

EGG DROP SOUP

¾ Cup Portion	1 Qt. 1 Cup 6 Portions	2 Qt. 2 Cups 12 Portions	1 Gal. 1 Qt. 24 Portions	2 Gal. 2 Qt. 48 Portions
Eggs, whole fresh	1	2	4	8
Chicken Stock, canned	1 qt. 1 cup	2 qt. 2 cups	1 gal. 1 qt.	2 gal. 2 qt.
Chives *or* Green Onion Tops, ⅛" pieces, for garnish				

Note: Remove fat from chicken stock before using.

1. Beat egg with a fork just until the white and yolk have blended to a uniform yellow color.
2. Heat the chicken stock to a rolling boil.
3. Add the egg to the chicken stock in small amounts as needed for service to avoid toughening the egg. Pour the egg into the broth moderately fast. Do not stir.
4. Let egg thicken in the soup for several seconds until it begins to coagulate. Then stir with a wire whip to break egg into shreds.
5. To serve, sprinkle each serving with ¼ tsp. chopped chives or green onion tops.

SPINACH EGG DROP SOUP

¾ Cup Portion	1 Qt. ½ Cup 6 Portions	2 Qt. 1 Cup 12 Portions	1 Gal. 2 Cups 24 Portions	2 Gal. 1 Qt. 48 Portions
Chicken Broth, canned	1 qt.	2 qt.	1 gal.	2 gal.
Scallions, sliced thin, EP	1 cup	2 cups	1 qt.	2 qt.
Potatoes, diced ¼", EP	1 cup	2 cups	1 qt.	2 qt.
Spinach, fresh, 1" pieces, EP	1 cup	2 cups	1 qt.	2 qt.
Egg, stirred	1	2	4	8

Note: Remove fat from chicken stock before using.

1. Heat chicken broth to a boil.
2. Add scallions and potatoes.
3. Simmer for 5 to 10 minutes, or until potatoes are tender. Do not boil.
4. Wash spinach until all sand is removed. Tear spinach into 1" pieces.
5. Add spinach to soup and cook until wilted.
6. Stir whole egg with a fork until it is well-combined.
7. Heat soup to a boil and then dribble egg into soup in a very thin stream until all egg has been added; do not allow soup to boil when adding egg.
8. Serve hot with Melba Toast.

SPRING SPINACH SOUP

¾ Cup Portion	3 Cups 4 Portions	1 Qt. 2 Cups 8 Portions	3 Quarts 16 Portions	1 Gal. 2 Qt. 32 Portions
Margarine	1 Tbsp.	2 Tbsp.	¼ cup	½ cup
Scallions, with tops, sliced thin, EP	1 bunch *or* 1 cup	2 bunches *or* 2 cups	4 bunches *or* 1 qt.	8 bunches *or* 2 qt.
Chicken Broth, canned	3 cups	1 qt. 2 cups	3 qt.	1 gal. 2 qt.
Potatoes, peeled and diced ¼", EP	1 cup	2 cups	1 qt.	2 qt.
Carrots, peeled and sliced thin, diagonally	½ med. *or* ¼ cup	1 med. *or* ½ cup	2 med. *or* 1 cup	4 med. *or* 2 cups
Spinach Leaves, cut in strips, EP	1 cup	2 cups	1 qt.	2 qt.

Note: Remove fat from chicken stock before using.

1. Melt margarine.
2. Clean scallions and wash. Saute scallions in melted margarine. Stir occasionally. Do not brown.
3. Add chicken broth, diced potatoes, and sliced carrots.
4. Cover and simmer for about 10 minutes, or until vegetables are tender. Do not boil rapidly.
5. Add spinach strips. Return to a boil and simmer uncovered for an additional 3 to 5 minutes, or until spinach is tender.
6. Serve hot.

Note:
1. Watercress leaves, washed, may be substituted for spinach.
2. Escarole, romaine, or lettuce may also be substituted for spinach. Wash and cut in strips.
3. Heavy cream or half-and-half may be added to soup if desired in the following amounts:

¼ cup	½ cup	1 cup	2 cups

LETTUCE AND RICE SOUP

1 Cup Portion	1 Quart 4 Portions	2 Quarts 8 Portions	1 Gallon 16 Portions	2 Gallons 32 Portions
Margarine	2 Tbsp.	¼ cup	½ cup	1 cup

Scallions, with
  tops, sliced ⅛″,
  EP
	1 cup	2 cups	1 qt.	2 qt.

Flour	1½ Tbsp.	3 Tbsp.	6 Tbsp.	¾ cup

Chicken Stock,
  canned, hot
	3 cups	1 qt.
		  2 cups
			3 qt.	1 gal.
				  2 qt.

Rice, cooked	⅜ cup	¾ cup	1½ cups	3 cups
Boston Lettuce, shredded	1 cup	2 cups	1 qt.	2 qt.

Green Peas,
  frozen, thawed
	½ cup *or*
	  ½ 10 oz.
	  pkg.
		1 cup *or* 1
		  10 oz.
		  pkg.
			2 cups *or* 1
			  lb. 4 oz.
				1 qt. *or* 2
				  lb. 8 oz.

Salt	¼ tsp.	½ tsp.	1 tsp.	2 tsp.
Pepper	⅛ tsp.	¼ tsp.	½ tsp.	1 tsp.

Note: Remove fat from chicken stock before using.

1. Saute scallions in margarine for about 3 to 5 minutes, until soft but not brown.
2. Add flour and stir until smooth.
3. Remove from heat.
4. Add chicken broth, stirring until smooth.
5. Add cooked rice and heat to boiling. Reduce heat.
6. Add lettuce and peas.
7. Simmer uncovered for about 3 minutes, or until peas are hot.
8. Add salt and pepper.

LETTUCE AND WATERCRESS SOUP

1 Cup Portion	2 Quarts 8 Portions	1 Gallon 16 Portions	2 Gallons 32 Portions	4 Gallons 64 Portions
Butter or Margarine	4 oz.	8 oz.	1 lb.	2 lb.
Flour	2 oz.	4 oz.	8 oz.	1 lb.
Chicken Stock, canned, hot	2 qt.	1 gal.	2 gal.	4 gal.
Iceberg Lettuce, coarsely chopped, EP	8 oz.	1 lb.	2 lb.	4 lb.
Celery, sliced or diced, EP	4 oz.	8 oz.	1 lb.	2 lb.
Watercress, stemmed and chopped, EP	¼ bunch	½ bunch	1 bunch	2 bunches
Salt	½ tsp.	1 tsp.	2 tsp.	1 Tbsp. 1 tsp.
Pepper	⅛ tsp.	¼ tsp.	½ tsp.	1 tsp.

Note: Remove fat from chicken stock before using.

1. Melt butter or margarine. Blend in flour.
2. Cook over low heat about 5 minutes.
3. Blend into broth. Cook and stir over low heat until thickened.
4. Add lettuce, celery, and watercress. Cook until vegetables are tender and crisp.
5. Season with salt and pepper.
6. Keep hot, but do not boil.

Note: Lettuce trimmings or any outside lettuce leaves not suitable for salad may be used in this soup.

ALMOND SOUP

¾ Cup Portion	1 Qt. 1 Cup 6 Portions	2 Qt. 2 Cups 12 Portions	1 Gal. 1 Qt. 24 Portions	2 Gal. 2 Qt. 48 Portions
Butter or Margarine	1 Tbsp.	2 Tbsp.	¼ cup	½ cup
Almonds, sliced or julienne	1 cup	2 cups	1 qt.	2 qt.
Chicken Broth, canned	1 qt.	2 qt.	1 gal.	2 gal.
Milk	1 cup	2 cups	1 qt.	2 qt.
Cream, heavy	¼ cup	½ cup	1 cup	2 cups
Sherry, very dry	3 Tbsp.	6 Tbsp.	¾ cup	1½ cups
Butter or Margarine	¼ cup	½ cup	1 cup	2 cups
Flour	¼ cup	½ cup	1 cup	2 cups
Chives, minced	1 tsp.	2 tsp.	1 Tbsp. 1 tsp.	2 Tbsp. 2 tsp.

1. Melt first amount of butter or margarine. Add almonds and cook, stirring constantly until light brown. Do not burn or scorch.
2. Blend almonds and chicken broth in the blender until smooth.
3. Combine blended almonds with milk, cream, and sherry.
4. Melt second amount of butter or margarine. Add flour and stir until smooth.
5. Add almond broth mixture.
6. Heat, stirring frequently, until thickened and smooth.
7. Serve with a garnish of minced chives and a few pieces of julienne almonds.

Note: This soup may also be served cold. If too thick after chilled, thin with chicken broth.

BLACK BEAN SOUP

1 Cup Portion	2 Quarts 8 Portions	1 Gallon 16 Portions	2 Gallons 32 Portions	4 Gallons 64 Portions
Black Beans, dried	1 lb.	2 lb.	4 lb.	8 lb.
Water	2 qt.	1 gal.	2 gal.	4 gal.
Butter *or* Margarine	¼ cup	½ cup	8 oz.	1 lb.
Onion, small, chopped, EP	1	2	4	8
Garlic Cloves, minced	2	4	8	16
Water	2 qt.	1 gal.	2 gal.	4 gal.
Celery Stalks, chopped, EP	2	4	8	16
Ham Bone *or* Hock	1	2	4	8
Bouquet Garni (few sprigs of parsley, bay leaf, pinch of thyme)	1	2	4	8
Salt	1 tsp.	2 tsp.	1 Tbsp. 1 tsp.	2 Tbsp. 2 tsp.
Pepper	¼ tsp.	½ tsp.	1 tsp.	2 tsp.
Sherry	¼ cup	½ cup	1 cup	2 cups

1. To quick-soak beans, rinse them and pick over to remove any grit.
2. Bring water to a boil in a steam kettle.
3. Add beans and boil 2 minutes.
4. Turn off heat, cover, and soak 1 hour.
5. Drain and rinse beans.
6. Melt butter or margarine. Add onion and garlic and saute until golden.
7. Add beans, second amount of water, celery, ham bone. bouquet garni, salt, and pepper.
8. Cover and bring to a boil.
9. Reduce heat and simmer about 3 hours, or until beans are very tender.
10. Discard bone and bouquet garni.
11. Put beans with remaining liquid in blender.
12. Return to soup pot, adding more water if mixture seems too thick.

13. Return to boil. Add sherry, taste, and adjust seasoning.
14. Serve hot and garnished with lemon slices or hard-cooked egg.

Note: This soup may also be served cold. Chill very well and add sherry just before serving.

SENATE BEAN SOUP

1 Cup Portion	1 Gal. 2 Qt. 24 Portions	3 Gallons 48 Portions	6 Gallons 96 Portions	12 Gallons 192 Portions
Navy Beans, white, dry	2 lb.	4 lb.	8 lb.	16 lb.
Water, cold	1 gal.	2 gal.	4 gal.	8 gal.
Ham Hocks *or* Pork Butt	3 lb.	6 lb.	12 lb.	24 lb.
Onion, chopped, EP	2 cups	1 qt.	2 qt.	1 gal.
Garlic Cloves, large, minced	4	8	16	32
Celery, chopped, EP	2 cups	1 qt.	2 qt.	1 gal.
Potato Flakes, instant, mashed	1⅓ cups	2⅔ cups	1 qt. 1⅓ cups	2 qt. 2⅔ cups
Parsley, chopped, EP	½ cup	1 cup	2 cups	1 qt.
Salt	1 Tbsp.	1 oz.	2 oz.	4 oz.
Pepper	1 tsp.	2 tsp.	1 Tbsp. 1 tsp.	2 Tbsp. 2 tsp.
Nutmeg	2 tsp.	1 Tbsp. 1 tsp.	2 Tbsp. 2 tsp.	¼ cup 1 Tbsp. 1 tsp.
Oregano	2 tsp.	1 Tbsp. 1 tsp.	2 Tbsp. 2 tsp.	¼ cup 1 Tbsp. 1 tsp.
Basil	2 tsp.	1 Tbsp. 1 tsp.	2 Tbsp. 2 tsp.	¼ cup 1 Tbsp. 1 tsp.
Bay Leaves	2	4	8	16

1. Soak beans overnight in refrigerator. Drain.

2. Add cold water and ham hocks.
3. Bring to a boil. Simmer for 1 hour.
4. Add remaining ingredients and simmer for another 20 to 30 minutes.
5. Trim ham from bones and return to soup.

Note: This soup stores well in the refrigerator for several days. When reheating, add water to thin and lemon juice to taste. Store soup in refrigerator in containers no larger than 2½ gal.

CURRIED BOMBAY LENTIL SOUP

1 Cup Portion	1 Qt. 1 Cup 5 Portions	2 Qt. 2 Cups 10 Portions	1 Gal. 1 Qt. 20 Portions	2 Gal. 2 Qt. 40 Portions
Lentils	6 oz.	12 oz.	1 lb. 8 oz.	3 lb.
Chicken Broth	2 qt.	1 gal.	2 gal.	4 gal.
Turmeric	½ tsp.	1 tsp.	2 tsp.	1 Tbsp. 1 tsp.
Butter *or* Margarine	5 Tbsp.	10 Tbsp.	1¼ cups	2½ cups
Onion, chopped fine, EP	2 oz.	4 oz.	8 oz.	1 lb.
Garlic Cloves, minced	1	2	4	8
Pepper, black	¼ tsp.	½ tsp.	1 tsp.	2 tsp.
Salt	½ tsp.	1 tsp.	2 tsp.	1 Tbsp. 1 tsp.
Curry Powder	1½ tsp.	1 Tbsp.	2 Tbsp.	¼ cup

1. Combine lentils, broth, and turmeric.
2. Bring to a boil and simmer over low heat for 1½ to 2 hours, or until the lentils are tender.
3. Melt butter or margarine. Add onions and garlic and saute for 5 minutes.
4. Add pepper, salt, and curry powder. Saute 5 minutes longer, stirring frequently.
5. Add the onion mixture to the lentils and simmer for 15 minutes longer.

Note: If canned chicken broth is used, delete salt.

Note: This is a hot curry soup. If a milder curry soup is desired, use half the amount of curry. The Curried Bombay Lentil Soup is especially good with buttered French or rye bread and served with raw vegetables.

MANHATTAN CLAM CHOWDER

1 Cup Portion	3 Gallons 48 Portions	6 Gallons 96 Portions	12 Gallons 192 Portions	24 Gallons 384 Portions
Margarine	8 oz.	1 lb.	2 lb.	4 lb.
Onions, finely chopped, EP	1 lb. 8 oz.	3 lb.	6 lb.	12 lb.
Water	1 gal. 2 qt.	3 gal.	6 gal.	12 gal.
Celery, chopped ⅛", EP	1 lb. 12 oz.	3 lb. 8 oz.	7 lb.	14 lb.
Carrots, cubed ¼", EP	1 lb. 12 oz.	3 lb. 8 oz.	7 lb.	14 lb.
Potatoes, cubed ¼ to ½", AP	4 lb.	8 lb.	16 lb.	32 lb.
Tomatoes, canned	½ #10 can	1 #10 can	2 #10 cans	4 #10 cans
Minced Clams and Juice (46 oz. can)	1 can	2 cans	4 cans	8 cans
Thyme	¼ tsp.	½ tsp.	1 tsp.	2 tsp.
Pepper	1 tsp.	2 tsp.	1 Tbsp. 1 tsp.	2 Tbsp. 2 tsp.
Salt	2 oz.	4 oz.	8 oz.	1 lb.
Flour, all-purpose	4 oz.	8 oz.	1 lb.	2 lb.
Water, cold	1 cup	2 cups	1 qt.	2 qt.

1. Saute margarine and onions together in steam kettle.
2. Add water and bring to a boil.
3. Add celery, carrots, and potatoes. Simmer.
4. Run tomatoes in power mixer on #1 speed using balloon whip for 2 minutes.
5. Add tomatoes, clams, thyme, pepper, and salt to kettle; simmer together 1 hour.
6. Mix flour with cold water and stir with a wire whip until smooth. Add to chowder.
7. Simmer until slightly thickened.
8. Taste for flavor. Serve hot.

CRABMEAT GUMBO

1 Cup Portion	3 Gallons 48 Portions	6 Gallons 96 Portions	12 Gallons 192 Portions	24 Gallons 384 Portions
Chicken *or* Turkey Stock	2 gal.	4 gal.	8 gal.	16 gal.
Rice, uncooked	8 oz.	1 lb.	2 lb.	4 lb.
Onions, chopped fine, EP	12 oz.	1 lb. 8 oz.	3 lb.	6 lb.
Green Peppers, chopped fine, EP	12 oz.	1 lb. 8 oz.	3 lb.	6 lb.
Okra, canned, sliced	1 qt.	2 qt.	1 gal.	2 gal.
Tomatoes, canned, standard	1 #10 can	2 #10 cans	4 #10 cans	8 #10 cans
Pepper, white	½ tsp.	1 tsp.	2 tsp.	1 Tbsp. 1 tsp.
Salt	1 oz.	2 oz.	4 oz.	8 oz.
Margarine, Chicken *or* Turkey Fat	6 oz.	12 oz.	1 lb. 8 oz.	3 lb.
Flour, pastry	6 oz.	12 oz.	1 lb. 8 oz.	3 lb.
Crabmeat, cubed ¼"	1 lb.	2 lb.	4 lb.	8 lb.

Note: Chicken stock may be prepared by reconstituting chicken base. Follow directions on jar or can.

1. Bring the stock to a boil in a stock pot or steam kettle. Reduce heat.
2. Add rice, onions, green peppers, okra, tomatoes (broken), white pepper, and salt. Simmer until vegetables are tender, or about 30 minutes.
3. Melt margarine or poultry fat. Add pastry flour and stir until smooth.
4. Add some of the hot stock mixture slowly to the roux, stirring with a wire whip to prevent lumping.
5. Add the roux mixture to the stock mixture. Cook until slightly thickened.
6. Add the crabmeat and simmer until served.
7. Taste for flavor. Serve hot.

Note: Shrimp may be substituted for crabmeat to prepare a Shrimp Gumbo.

OYSTER AND SPINACH BISQUE

1 Cup Portion	1 Qt. 2 Cups 6 Portions	3 Quarts 12 Portions	1 Gal. 2 Cups 18 Portions
Water	1 cup	2 cups	3 cups

Oysters,
    shucked and
    liquor
	2 cups	1 qt.	1 qt.
			    2 cups

Butter *or*
    Margarine
	2 Tbsp.
	    2 tsp.
		¼ cup
		    1 Tbsp.
		    1 tsp.
			½ cup

Onion, finely chopped, EP	1 oz.	2 oz.	3 oz.
Celery, finely chopped, EP	1 oz.	2 oz.	3 oz.

Flour, all-
    purpose
	2 Tbsp.
	    2 tsp.
		¼ cup
		    1 Tbsp.
		    1 tsp.
			½ cup

Milk, hot	1⅓ cups	2⅔ cups	1 qt.
Cream, light, hot	1⅓ cups	2⅔ cups	1 qt.
Steak sauce	1 tsp.	2 tsp.	1 Tbsp.
Salt	1 tsp.	2 tsp.	1 Tbsp.
Pepper, white	¹⁄₁₆ tsp.	⅛ tsp.	¼ tsp.
Nutmeg	dash	¹⁄₁₆ tsp.	⅛ tsp.

Spinach, frozen,
    chopped,
    thawed
	10 oz.	1 lb. 4 oz.	2 lb.

1. Bring water to full rolling boil in stockpot.
2. Add oysters and return to boil over medium heat, stirring frequently.
3. Remove from heat. Oysters should be curled and firm. Set aside to cool.
4. Melt butter or margarine in stock pot or steam kettle.
5. Saute onion and celery until tender but not brown.
6. Add flour and stir until smooth.
7. Add hot milk and cream. Cook stirring constantly until mixture comes to a simmer.
8. Reduce heat to very low and continue to cook for 15 to 20 minutes, stirring frequently.

9. Add salt, steak sauce, pepper and nutmeg stirring until well blended.
10. Puree oysters and liquid in blender or put through fine blade of grinder.
11. Puree spinach. Add oysters and spinach to soup.
12. Heat thoroughly and serve hot.

Note: Serve garnished with salted whipped cream, if desired.

SHRIMP BISQUE WITH SHERRY

1 Cup Portion	2 Gal. 3 Qt. 44 Portions	5 Gal. 2 Qt. 88 Portions	11 Gallons 176 Portions	22 Gallons 352 Portions
Butter *or* Margarine	2 lb.	4 lb.	8 lb.	16 lb.
Flour, pastry	12 oz.	1 lb. 8 oz.	3 lb.	6 lb.
Milk, hot	1 gal. 3 qt.	3 gal. 2 qt.	7 gal.	14 gal.
Cream, heavy	2 cups	1 qt.	2 qt.	1 gal.
Sherry, cooking	½ cup	1 cup	2 cups	1 qt.
Shrimp, cooked and chopped ¼″	2 lb.	4 lb.	8 lb.	16 lb.
Salt	1 oz.	2 oz.	4 oz.	8 oz.

1. Melt butter or margarine.
2. Add flour and stir until smooth.
3. Add milk and stir for about 10 minutes, or until maximum thickness is reached.
4. Add heavy cream and sherry.
5. Just before serving, add shrimp and salt and bring back to a simmer.
6. Serve hot.

Note: This soup may also be served as Shrimp Sauce Supreme over salmon or tuna loaf.

CANADIAN CHEESE CHOWDER

¾ Cup Portion	1 Qt. 2 Cups 8 Portions	3 Quarts 16 Portions	1 Gal. 2 Qt. 32 Portions	3 Gallons 64 Portions
Welsh Rarebit, frozen, heated	2 cups	1 qt.	2 qt.	1 gal.
Milk, hot	2½ cups	1 qt. 1 cup	2 qt. 2 cups	1 gal. 1 qt.
Potatoes, diced ⅜″, EP	4 oz.	8 oz.	1 lb.	2 lb.
Carrots, diced ¼″, EP	3 oz.	6 oz.	12 oz.	1 lb. 8 oz.
Celery, diced ¼″, EP	3 oz.	6 oz.	12 oz.	1 lb. 8 oz.
Onion, diced ¼″, EP	1 oz.	2 oz.	4 oz.	8 oz.
Green Pepper, diced ¼″, EP	1 oz.	2 oz.	4 oz.	8 oz.
Salt	⅜ tsp.	¾ tsp.	1½ tsp.	1 Tbsp.

1. Combine heated rarebit and hot milk.
2. Steam vegetables in steamer for 16 minutes, or until barely tender. Drain well. Add salt. Stir well.
3. Add well-drained, cooked vegetables to hot soup. Stir to combine.
4. Cover and keep hot.

To Hold on Steamtable: Place pan containing chowder into a pan containing hot water. This prevents chowder from breaking down.

DANISH CHEESE SOUP
(Solskin Suppe)

¾ Cup Portion	1 Qt. ½ Cup 6 Portions	2 Qt. 1 Cup 12 Portions	1 Gal. 2 Cups 24 Portions	2 Gal. 1 Qt. 48 Portions
Celery, diced, EP	¾ cup	1½ cups	3 cups	1 qt. 2 cups
Carrots, sliced, EP	1 cup	2 cups	1 qt.	2 qt.
Leeks, small, thinly sliced, EP	1 cup	2 cups	1 qt.	2 qt.
Water, hot	3 cups	1 qt. 2 cups	3 qt.	1 gal. 2 qt.
Salt	¾ tsp.	1½ tsp.	1 Tbsp.	2 Tbsp.
Pepper, white	⅛ tsp.	¼ tsp.	½ tsp.	1 tsp.
Half-and-Half	½ cup	1 cup	2 cups	1 qt.
Danish Cheese, shredded, firmly packed	½ cup	1 cup	2 cups	1 qt.
Chives *or* Parsley, chopped, to garnish				

Note: Tybo, Esrom, Samsoe or Havarti Danish Cheese may be used.

1. Combine celery, carrots, leeks, water, salt, and pepper.
2. Bring to a boil. Cover and simmer 20 to 25 minutes, or until vegetables are tender.
3. Put cooked vegetables with some of the liquid in a blender and blend until smooth.
4. Return pureed vegetables to hot liquid in kettle.
5. Add half-and-half and shredded cheese. (Havarti cheese is especially good in this recipe.)
6. Bring only to a boil. Serve hot and sprinkled with chopped chives or parsley.

Note: There may be tiny flecks of cheese throughout this soup.

ROQUEFORT SOUP

¾ Cup Portion	1 Qt. 2 Cups 8 Portions	3 Quarts 16 Portions	1 Gal. 2 Qt. 32 Portions	3 Gallons 64 Portions
Butter *or* Margarine	¼ cup	½ cup	1 cup	1 lb.
Cabbage, white, chopped, EP	½ head	1 head	2 heads	4 heads
Cauliflower, coarsely chopped, EP	½ head	1 head	2 heads	4 heads
Chicken Broth, canned	1 qt.	2 qt.	1 gal.	2 gal.
Heavy Cream	½ cup	1 cup	2 cups	1 qt.
Roquefort Cheese	2 Tbsp.	¼ cup	½ cup	1 cup

Note: Cabbage heads should be large and cauliflower heads should be medium.

1. Combine butter or margarine, cabbage, cauliflower and chicken broth.
2. Bring to a boil. Reduce heat and simmer for 15 to 30 minutes or until vegetables are tender.
3. Combine and mix heavy cream and roquefort cheese until smooth.
4. Stir cheese and cream mixture into soup. Mix to combine.
5. Bring to a boil and serve hot with croutons.

Note: If desired, soup may be pureed. Cool mixture slightly and puree in batches.

PART 2:
SALAD DRESSINGS

Every foodservice operator is faced with the question: "Shall I buy, or shall I make my own mayonnaise and salad dressings?" The final answer depends on several factors, including the quality required for a particular operation, the availability and skill of personnel, equipment limitations, and budget restrictions. In addition, the current cost of products on the market must be evaluated in relation to the *total* cost of preparing them. Many excellent mayonnaise and salad dressings are available, and there are times when a foodservice director can profit by developing variations of these products rather than attempting to prepare them. On the other hand, many restaurants have become famous for their house dressings, and would not consider serving a commercially-prepared salad dressing.

The dressings in this book have been divided into the categories of 1) Mayonnaise; 2) Cooked Salad Dressings, including those for vegetables and creamy fruit dressings; 3) Semipermanent French Dressings of the type used on both vegetables and fruit salads; 4) Temporary Marinating Dressings of the oil and vinegar variety; 5) Cheese Dressings; and 6) Nouvelle Cuisine Dressings. Some of the variations on the basic mayonnaise formula can be classified as sauces. Formulas for certain variations, such as Remoulade Sauce and Mousseline dressing, can be found in Part One under Fish and Shellfish Cocktails.

The preparation of salad dressings requires attention to detail and careful supervision of employees. If mayonnaise and salad dressings are to be prepared on the premises, it may be helpful for personnel to understand a few of the elementary concepts of chemistry involved in their preparation.

DISPERSIONS OR DISPERSED SYSTEMS

Dispersed systems are important elements throughout the entire cooking process; in fact, it would be difficult to find a food preparation procedure in which colloidal dispersions are not involved in some way. The importance of dispersions in food preparation warrants an examination of some of the factors involved.

Colloidal chemistry explains why eggs coagulate, why eggs and cream whip, and why salad dressings emulsify. Colloidal dispersions are involved in making cream sauces and puddings, and in the preparation of batters and doughs. A *dispersed system*, often called simply a *dispersion*, is a system composed of two or more component substances dispersed in relationship to one another. There are three types of dispersions: 1) *true solutions*, 2) *colloidal dispersions* (sometimes erroneously referred to as colloidal solutions), and 3) *suspensions*.

Dispersions vary from the simple relationship between two substances to the very complex dispersions of many substances. Simple dispersions include sugar in water (a true solution), gelatin in water (a colloidal dispersion), and starch in water (a suspension). A complex dispersion of many substances is exemplified by a cake batter that includes a true solution of sugar, salt, and baking powder in water; a colloidal dispersion of proteins in water; and a suspension of the starch (flour) in water.

Mayonnaise and salad dressings are categorized as colloidal dispersions. They are a dispersion of one liquid, such as oil, in another liquid, such as vinegar. The dispersed material (oil) is called the *dispersed* or *discontinuous phase*, while the material used to disperse the oil (water in the form of vinegar) is called the *dispersion medium* or *continuous phase*. The oil is dispersed in droplets in the vinegar; but, because the two are immiscible, they do not form a true solution. Instead, the drops remain suspended in the vinegar, neither dissolving nor settling out completely. The mixture remains in a colloidal state and is therefore neither a true solution nor a true suspension.

The particles in a colloidal dispersion are so large that they will not pass through a filter easily, and some colloidal mixtures—such as mayonnaise, gravies, and gelatins—will merely clog a filter. On the other hand, a substance such as sugar will dissolve in water because its particles are small enough for the water to diffuse. Hence, a mixture of sugar and water will pass through a filter with no problem. The size of the particles is the main characteristic of a colloidal dispersion and provides the unique appearance of salad dressings, gravies, and gelatins. There is a tendency toward separation of dispersed substances from the dispersion medium. With some colloidal dispersions, the separation may become apparent after a few minutes or hours; with others, the separation may not become visible for extended periods.

In addition to liquid-in-liquid dispersions such as salad dressings, there are also gas-in-liquid dispersions such as whipped cream and beaten egg whites, and solid-in-solid dispersions, such as hot chocolate. Colloidal dispersions are midway between true solutions and suspensions. Although they may appear at times to be a true solution and while the particles will sometimes settle as in a suspension, they are neither. Notice, for example, that cocoa mixed with milk forms a suspension (the cocoa particles will settle out). As the cocoa is cooked, however, the starch particles of cocoa swell, remain suspended, and the mixture reaches a colloidal state. Other examples of colloidal states are sols (gravies), gels (gelatin and jelly), foams (whipped egg whites), and emulsions (mayonnaise).

In summary, a true solution is made up of a solute (the substance dissolved in the solution) and a solvent (the substance used for dissolving). One example is the combination of sugar (the solute) and water (the solvent) to form a solution in which the particles are exceedingly small, invisible, and easily filtered.

A colloidal dispersion is made up of a dispersed phase and a dispersion medium. In such examples as mayonnaise and French dressing, the particles are large although not visible to the eye, and the dispersion can barely be passed through a filter, if at all.

A suspension includes a suspended material and a liquid in which the material is suspended. Starch in water and cocoa in milk are two examples of suspensions in which the dispersed particles are very large, visible to the eye, and nonfilterable.

PROTECTIVE COLLOIDS

Any salad dressing that has appreciable stability must contain a *protective colloid*, defined as any colloid that stabilizes a colloidal dispersion. Mayonnaise, for example—a colloidal dispersion of oil and water (in the form of vinegar)—requires a protective colloid in order to be permanent. Egg, a protein ingredient, serves as the protective colloid in mayonnaise and is called the *emulsifying agent*. When a colloidal dispersion uses such an agent, the dispersed colloidal state itself is called an *emulsion*.

There are protective colloids other than egg protein. In many types of French dressings, the protective colloid is a starch ingredient, such as cornstarch. The most frequently used protective colloid in fruit cream dressings is flour. It should be noted that gelatin, too, is sometimes used as an emulsifying agent or protective colloid.

EMULSOIDS

Salad dressings represent three types of emulsions: the *temporary*, the *semipermanent*, and the *permanent*. An example of the temporary emulsion is seen in the marinating French dressings. The red and white French dressings are examples of semi-permanent emulsions. The permanent emulsions are typified by mayonnaise, cooked salad dressings, and cream dressings used for fruit.

TEMPORARY EMULSIONS

A temporary emulsion is a mixture of oil, acid, and seasonings combined by mechanical agitation (beating in a mixer, blending, or simply shaking). Agitation causes the oil to break into small globules that scatter throughout the liquid. When this dressing stands for any length of time, the globules of fat run together, or coalesce, and the mixture separates. The acid ingredient, while providing some flavor, reduces the viscosity of the oil and makes it easier to form small globules. The seasonings—such as salt, sugar, paprika, and mustard—act as partial emulsifying agents, although they are included in such small quantities that their emulsifying properties are negligible.

The Clear French dressing and Clear Italian dressing are temporary emulsions best suited for marinating a salad just before serving. In many operations a salad bowl of mixed greens is brought to the table, the temporary marinating dressing added, and the salad greens and dressing tossed together and immediately served to the guests. In other types of operations, where chopped lettuce is placed in a $12 \times 20 \times 2$ pan and transported or held on a cold serving line, a marinating oil and vinegar dressing may be poured over the chopped lettuce. If the dressing is permitted to run to the bottom of the pan and is not mixed with the greens, the salad will transport or hold quite well. But when large quantities of salad greens are mixed with dressing and allowed to stand for a long serving period, the salad ingredients will lose their crispness, become "waterlogged" with dressing, and lose their appeal for service.

SEMIPERMANENT EMULSIONS

Although the marinating types of dressings separate easily and need reshaking or frequent stirring, they do have a place in some foodservice operations. Many institutions prefer to use a French-type dressing that will remain dispersed for a week or longer. In developing such semipermanent dressings, a protective colloid is used in addition to the seasonings.

In order to transform a temporary dressing into semipermanent form, one need only add cornstarch, which serves as the protective colloid or emulsifying agent. The cornstarch base is cooked until it becomes transparent, and is then strained into the mixer. The resulting paste is beaten while alternately adding oil and vinegar. The starch granules contained in the paste will swell during the cooking process, and when the oil and vinegar are added to the cooked paste, the starch will aid in emulsifying in the same way that eggs aid in the preparation of mayonnaise. The only difference between the cornstarch and egg emulsifying process is that the starch mixture will not be as permanent as the egg mixture. Consequently, dressings that contain starch as the emulsifying agent will separate after a period of time.

PERMANENT EMULSIONS

As indicated earlier, the most common examples of permanent emulsions in salad dressings are found in mayonnaise, cooked salad dressings, and cream dressings for fruit salads. In the preparation of mayonnaise, egg yolks or whole eggs may be used, although one should not be substituted for the other. The specific amounts and directions in each formula should be followed. When preparing mayonnaise, the ingredients must be combined in such a way that the oil breaks into small droplets, each coated with a liquid protein solution. The protein of the egg forms a viscous and stable film around the drops of oil and prevents them from coalescing as they do in temporary French dressings. The emulsifying agent also lowers the surface tension of the liquids.

Several other factors aid in the emulsification process of mayonnaise. Emulsification is facilitated if the egg mixture is thickened by agitation and if the egg mixture contains acid ingredients. The acid dilutes the protein solution and enables it to cover the fat globules more completely. In addition, the acid aids in keeping bacterial content low and in reducing the tendency of the oil to become rancid. The addition of seasonings to eggs also contributes to the emulsifying process, although in a negligible way. The oil combines best with the other ingredients when it is at room temperature. When oil is cold it is more difficult to break into the small globules necessary for proper emulsification.

Permanent emulsions can be broken so that the oil coalesces into a continuous phase and forms an oily layer. Failure to follow the precautions outlined in this discussion may cause demulsification. Other factors, such as considerable jarring or shaking, freezing, long storage, or agitation during shipping, can result in a broken mayonnaise.

HOW TO REFORM BROKEN (DEMULSIFIED) MAYONNAISE

When preparing mayonnaise in an institutional kitchen, a broken emulsion is not a culinary disaster. The process of recovering or reforming a demulsified (broken) mayonnaise is a complicated one that can best be explained by use of an example. It is difficult to establish a formula for this process, although one has been included in this section. The following explanation is based on the directions contained in that formula.

METHOD I

Assume that all ingredients for one gallon of mayonnaise have been assembled, and that the three-quarter cup of egg yolk and seasonings are in the mixer bowl. The correct amounts of oil and vinegar are in readiness and, after half of the vinegar and one quart of the oil have been added, the emulsion breaks.

The entire broken mixture should be removed from the mixer bowl and the preparation process begun once again with a three-quarter cup of yolks. The new yolks should be beaten on number three speed and the broken emulsion added slowly to the new yolks in the mixer. A new emulsion should form and, when it does, the oil and vinegar remaining from the first emulsion should be added. This method will yield one gallon of mayonnaise, using twice the amount of egg yolks ordinarily required. Although doubling the egg yolks will increase the cost of this particular batch, waste will be avoided.

METHOD II

Assume that one gallon of mayonnaise is being made and that it breaks at the same point as in Method I. Again, the broken mayonnaise should be emptied from the mixer bowl and the preparation process, including the addition of seasonings, should be started over with a three-quarter cup of yolks and seasonings. The yolks should be beaten on number three speed until a new emulsion is formed. Slowly, the broken mayonnaise should be incorporated into the new emulsion. When this process is satisfactorily completed, the oil and vinegar remaining from the first gallon of broken mayonnaise should be added. At this point, oil and vinegar for a second gallon should be added as well. This method will yield two gallons of mayonnaise, and the ratios of egg, seasonings, oil, and vinegar will be correct. The cost ratio will also be correct because the amount of yolk for a single gallon will not have been doubled, as it was in Method I.

While both of these methods are satisfactory, Method II is recommended, even though it will result in the preparation of an extra gallon of mayonnaise. Because mayonnaise is a standard item in foodservices, it is less expensive to prepare two gallons than to substantially increase the cost of one.

COOKED SALAD DRESSING

Cooked salad dressing is often referred to as *boiled dressing*—"boiled" because the starch and water mixture is brought to a boil before the eggs have been added, although the mixture should never be boiled afterward. Cooked salad dressings are prepared by substituting starch for part of the egg content. For this reason, they have a much lower ratio of eggs than does mayonnaise—a difference that makes them less expensive to prepare. Fruit cream dressings are also made with a starch base, but light colored fruit juices are used in place of vinegar.

Some people object to what they consider the oily flavor of mayonnaise, while others object to the tartness of a cooked salad dressing. A third basic dressing that can satisfy both tastes is achieved by combining mayonnaise and cooked salad dressing. This is the Combination dressing.

Many restaurants feature a "house dressing"—a dressing that has been developed by the staff and has become distinctive to that operation. Guests soon become accustomed to the fact that a house dressing is something unique or special. According to a recent menu census published by *Institutions/Volume Feeding Magazine*, the house dressing is the most frequently ordered of all salad dressings. The Standard House Dressing in this section is a basic formula that can be modified by the addition or deletion of ingredients, to produce a house specialty dressing. In fact, most of the dressings that follow, if well-accepted by customers, could be labeled a house dressing.

MAYONNAISE AND VARIATIONS
Mayonnaise Dressings

MAYONNAISE
(With Egg Yolks)

	1 Gallon	**2 Gallons**	**3 Gallons**	**4 Gallons**
Egg Yolks	12 *or* ¾ cups	24 *or* 1½ cups	36 *or* 2¼ cups	48 *or* 3 cups
Mustard, dry	2 Tbsp.	1 oz.	1½ oz.	2 oz.
Sugar	1 Tbsp.	1 oz.	1½ oz.	2 oz.
Salt	1 Tbsp.	1 oz.	1½ oz.	2 oz.
Paprika, Spanish, optional	½ tsp.	1 tsp.	1½ tsp.	2 tsp.
Vinegar, cider	1 cup	2 cups	3 cups	1 qt.
Oil, salad	3 qt. 1 cup	1 gal. 2 qt. 2 cups	2 gal. 1 qt. 3 cups	3 gal. 1 qt.

1. Add dry ingredients to egg yolks in bowl of mixer. Scrape down bowl.
2. Using wire balloon whip, beat egg yolks and dry ingredients on #3 speed.
3. Add ½ of the vinegar gradually, alternating with oil, and beating on #3 speed. Do not stop machine.
4. Put remainder of oil in oil dripper and allow to drip into mayonnaise, beating constantly until all salad oil has been added. If mayonnaise becomes very stiff, the machine can be slowed to #2 speed.
5. Scrape down sides and bottom of bowl.
6. Add remainder of vinegar and beat enough to blend.
7. Store covered in refrigerator.

MAYONNAISE Broken–How to Reform

1. Use 12 egg yolks (or ¾ cup) for every gallon of broken mayonnaise.
2. Beat egg yolks on #3 speed for 3 to 5 minutes, or until light. Because of the comparatively small quantity of egg yolks, it may be necessary to beat them in a small mixer, transferring them to a large mixer before adding the broken mayonnaise.
3. Add the broken mayonnaise slowly, while beating on #3 speed, until mixture begins to emulsify and appears smooth and creamy.
4. Add broken mayonnaise more rapidly until completely combined.
5. Add remaining oil and vinegar.
6. Scrape down sides of bowl and beat again until combined.
7. Refrigerate in covered containers.

MAYONNAISE
(With Whole Eggs)

	5 Gallons	10 Gallons	20 Gallons
Eggs, whole	2 qt. *or* 40	1 gal. *or* 80	2 gal. *or* 160
Mustard, prepared	6 Tbsp.	¾ cup	1½ cups
Sugar	7 oz.	14 oz.	1 lb. 12 oz.
Salt	2 oz.	4 oz.	8 oz.
Vinegar, cider	1 qt.	2 qt.	1 gal.
Oil, salad	4 gal.	8 gal.	16 gal.

1. Put eggs in bowl of mixer.
2. Add dry ingredients to eggs.
3. Add vinegar gradually on #3 speed, alternating with oil. Oil dripper may be used.
4. Store covered in refrigerator.

Note: Both the mayonnaise with egg yolks and the mayonnaise with whole eggs may be made in a cutter mixer (formerly called VCM). Put the eggs and dry ingredients into the mixer and add the vinegar and oil through the funnel at the top of machine on low speed.

Cutter Mixer MAYONNAISE
(Lemon Flavor)

	4 Gallons	8 Gallons
Eggs, whole	2 qt. 1 cup *or* 48	1 gal. 1 qt. *or* 96
Mustard, prepared	2 Tbsp.	¼ cup
Sugar	5 oz.	10 oz.
Salt	4 oz.	8 oz.
Pepper, white	1 oz.	2 oz.
Lemon Juice	¼ cup	½ cup
Vinegar, cider	1 qt. 2 cups	3 qt.
Oil, salad	3 gal.	6 gal.

1. Place all ingredients except oil in bowl of cutter mixer.
2. Mix for 2 or 3 seconds on low speed.
3. Turn machine on high speed and add oil in a stream about the size of the little finger, until emulsion is formed. Then add oil rapidly until finished.
4. Open machine and scrape down sides of bowl. Turn machine on low speed for 5 or 6 seconds until mayonnaise is complete.
5. Store covered in the refrigerator.

MAYONNAISE SUPREME

	1 Gallon	2 Gallons	4 Gallons	8 Gallons
Cornstarch	5¼ oz.	10½ oz.	1 lb. 5 oz.	2 lb. 10 oz.
Water, cold	1 cup	2 cups	1 qt.	2 qt.
Water, boiling	3 cups	1 qt. 2 cups	3 qt.	1 gal. 2 qt.
Mustard, prepared	3 Tbsp.	¼ cup 2 Tbsp.	¾ cup	1½ cups
Sugar	4 oz.	8 oz.	1 lb.	2 lb.
Salt	1½ oz.	3 oz.	6 oz.	12 oz.
Paprika	1 Tbsp.	2 Tbsp.	1 oz.	2 oz.
Eggs, whole	8 *or* 1½ cups	16 *or* 3 cups	32 *or* 1 qt. 2 cups	64 *or* 3 qt.
Vinegar, white	1 cup	2 cups	1 qt.	2 qt.
Oil, salad	2 qt. 2 cups	1 gal. 1 qt.	2 gal. 2 qt.	5 gal.

1. Combine cornstarch and cold water. Mix to form a paste.
2. Add cornstarch mixture to boiling water and cook until clear and thick.
3. Put thickened cornstarch mixture into bowl of mixer and beat, using balloon whip, at #3 speed. Whip until cool.
4. Add prepared mustard to mixture and continue beating.
5. Add enough vinegar to the dry ingredients to dissolve them; then add to the cooled cornstarch and mustard mixture and mix well.
6. Add eggs, a few at a time, beating well after each addition. Scrape down bowl.
7. Slowly and alternately add oil and remaining vinegar and beat well.
8. Store covered in the refrigerator.

RUSSIAN DRESSING

	1 Gallon	2 Gallons	3 Gallons	4 Gallons
Mayonnaise	3 qt. 2 cups	1 gal. 3 qt.	2 gal. 2 qt. 2 cups	3 gal. 2 qt.
Chili Sauce	2 cups	1 qt.	1 qt. 2 cups	2 qt.
Onion, chopped fine, EP, optional	2 oz.	4 oz.	6 oz.	8 oz.
Worcestershire Sauce, optional	2 Tbsp.	¼ cup	¼ cup 2 Tbsp.	½ cup
Pepper, Cayenne, optional	⅛ tsp.	¼ tsp.	⅜ tsp.	½ tsp.

1. Add chili sauce to mayonnaise.
2. Mix lightly, but thoroughly.
3. If desired, add the onion, Worcestershire sauce, and cayenne pepper to the mayonnaise along with the chili sauce. These ingredients give the dressing a stronger flavor, but are not absolutely necessary.
4. Chill and store covered in the refrigerator.

THOUSAND ISLAND DRESSING

	1 Gallon	2 Gallons	3 Gallons	4 Gallons
Eggs, hard-cooked	8	16	24	32
Mayonnaise	2 qt. 3 cups	1 gal. 1 qt. 2 cups	2 gal. 1 cup	2 gal. 3 qt.
Pimiento, drained, chopped	½ cup	1 cup	1½ cups	2 cups
Sweet Pickle Relish, drained	¾ cup	1½ cups	2¼ cups	3 cups
Chili Sauce	2 cups	1 qt.	1 qt. 2 cups	2 qt.
Onions, chopped fine, EP	6 oz.	12 oz.	1 lb. 2 oz.	1 lb. 8 oz.

1. Chop hard-cooked eggs.
2. Add all ingredients to mayonnaise.
3. Mix lightly but thoroughly.
4. Chill and store covered in the refrigerator.

CRAB LOUIE DRESSING

	1 Gal. 1 Qt.	2 Gal. 2 Qt.	5 Gallons	10 Gallons
Mayonnaise	2 qt.	1 gal.	2 gal.	4 gal.
Buttermilk	2 cups	1 qt.	2 qt.	1 gal.
Chili Sauce	2 cups	1 qt.	2 qt.	1 gal.
Pickle Relish	2 cups	1 qt.	2 qt.	1 gal.
Vinegar	½ cup	1 cup	2 cups	1 qt.
Green Pepper, chopped, EP	4 oz.	8 oz.	1 lb.	2 lb.
Celery, finely chopped, EP	4 oz.	8 oz.	1 lb.	2 lb.
Pimiento, chopped	2 oz.	4 oz.	8 oz.	1 lb.
Sugar	3½ oz.	7 oz.	14 oz.	1 lb. 12 oz.
Salt	1 oz.	2 oz.	4 oz.	8 oz.
Eggs, hard-cooked	6	12	24	48

1. Combine all ingredients and mix well.
2. Refrigerate covered. Serve with Crab Louie Salad.

Note: The hard-cooked eggs and pickle relish are optional ingredients.

LOUIE DRESSING

	1 Quart	2 Quarts	1 Gallon	2 Gallons
Mayonnaise	2¾ cups	1 qt. 1½ cups	2 qt. 3 cups	1 gal. 1 qt. 2 cups
Cocktail Sauce	½ cup	1 cup	2 cups	1 qt.
Lemon Juice	½ cup	1 cup	2 cups	1 qt.
Vinegar, red wine	3 Tbsp.	6 Tbsp.	¾ cup	1½ cups
Worcestershire Sauce	2 Tbsp.	¼ cup	½ cup	1 cup
Garlic Powder	1 tsp.	2 tsp.	1 Tbsp. 1 tsp.	2 Tbsp. 2 tsp.
Pepper, white	1 tsp.	2 tsp.	1 Tbsp. 1 tsp.	2 Tbsp. 2 tsp.

1. Combine all ingredients. Mix to blend.
2. Refrigerate covered.

CREAMY RED FRENCH DRESSING

	3 Quarts	**1 Gal. 2 Qt.**	**3 Gallons**	**6 Gallons**
Paprika	¾ oz.	1½ oz.	3 oz.	6 oz.
Water, hot	¼ cup	½ cup	1 cup	2 cups
Eggs, whole	3	6	12	24
Sugar	6 oz.	12 oz.	1 lb. 8 oz.	3 lb.
Salt	1½ oz.	3 oz.	6 oz.	12 oz.
Mustard, dry	1 Tbsp.	2 Tbsp.	1 oz.	2 oz.
Pepper, white	½ tsp.	1 tsp.	2 tsp.	1 Tbsp. 1 tsp.
Catsup	2 Tbsp.	¼ cup	½ cup	1 cup
Onion Juice	1 Tbsp.	2 Tbsp.	¼ cup	½ cup
Worcestershire Sauce	1½ tsp.	1 Tbsp.	2 Tbsp.	¼ cup
Tabasco Sauce	½ tsp.	1 tsp.	2 tsp.	1 Tbsp. 1 tsp.
Oil, salad	2 qt.	1 gal.	2 gal.	4 gal.
Vinegar, cider	1 cup	2 cups	1 qt.	2 qt.
Lemon Juice	½ cup	1 cup	2 cups	1 qt.
Water	½ cup	1 cup	2 cups	1 qt.

Note: Make the day before service.

1. Dissolve paprika in hot water.
2. Beat eggs well in mixer with wire whip on #3 speed. Add dissolved paprika and dry ingredients. Beat until a good emulsion is formed.
3. Add catsup, onion juice, Worcestershire sauce, and Tabasco sauce, mixing well.
4. Add small amounts of oil, alternating with vinegar and lemon juice (combined) and beating continuously. Add water in small amounts and mix well.
5. Store covered in the refrigerator.

GREEN GODDESS SALAD DRESSING I

	1 Quart	2 Quarts	1 Gallon	2 Gallons
Mayonnaise *or* Combination Dressing	2 cups	1 qt.	2 qt.	1 gal.
Sour Cream, cultured	1 cup	2 cups	1 qt.	2 qt.
Vinegar, tarragon	⅓ cup	⅔ cup	1⅓ cups	2⅔ cups
Lemon Juice	1 Tbsp.	2 Tbsp.	¼ cup	½ cup
Parsley, finely chopped	½ cup	1 cup	2 cups	1 qt.
Anchovy Paste	2 oz.	4 oz.	8 oz.	1 lb.
Garlic Cloves, finely chopped	½	1	2	4

1. Combine all ingredients thoroughly.
2. Chill before serving.
3. Serve on tossed salad, hearts of Iceberg lettuce, or Bibb lettuce.

Note: The amount of parsley may be doubled. The amount of anchovy paste may be too strong for some tastes, and may be reduced by one-half.

GREEN GODDESS SALAD DRESSING II

	1 Quart	2 Quarts	1 Gallon	2 Gallons
Mayonnaise	2 cups	1 qt.	2 qt.	1 gal.
Sour Cream	1 cup	2 cups	1 qt.	2 qt.
Parsley, finely chopped	½ oz.	1 oz.	2 oz.	4 oz.
Scallions *or* Chives, chopped	⅜ cup	¾ cup	1½ cups	3 cups
Garlic Cloves, chopped	2	4	8	16
Lemon Juice	¼ cup	½ cup	1 cup	2 cups
Vinegar, tarragon, wine, *or* cider	⅜ cup	¾ cup	1½ cups	2 cups
Curry Powder	½ tsp.	1 tsp.	2 tsp.	1 Tbsp. 1 tsp.
Pepper, black	½ tsp.	1 tsp.	2 tsp.	1 Tbsp. 1 tsp.

1. Combine all ingredients.
2. Chill until needed.
3. Serve on tossed salad, hearts of Iceberg lettuce, or Bibb lettuce.

YOGURT DRESSING

	2½ Cups	1 Qt. 1 Cup	2 Qt. 2 Cups	1 Gal. 1 Qt.
Yogurt, plain	2 cups	1 qt.	2 qt.	1 gal.
Mayonnaise	½ cup	1 cup	2 cups	1 qt.
Scallions, thinly sliced	½ cup	1 cup	2 cups	1 qt.
Parsley, chopped	½ cup	1 cup	2 cups	1 qt.
Horseradish, prepared	1 tsp.	2 tsp.	1 Tbsp. 1 tsp.	2 Tbsp. 2 tsp.
Sugar	½ tsp.	1 tsp.	2 tsp.	1 Tbsp. 1 tsp.
Worcestershire Sauce	1 tsp.	2 tsp.	1 Tbsp. 1 tsp.	2 Tbsp. 2 tsp.
Salt	½ tsp.	1 tsp.	2 tsp.	1 Tbsp. 1 tsp.

1. Combine all ingredients.
2. Mix well.
3. Cover and refrigerate until ready to serve.

EASY BLUE CHEESE DRESSING

1. Follow the preceding formula for Yogurt Dressing, deleting the parsley.
2. Add the following amount of blue cheese chopped in small pieces:

Blue Cheese	1 oz.	2 oz.	4 oz.	8 oz.

Note: This is a lightly-flavored blue cheese dressing.

Appetizers and hors d'oeuvres may take many forms in restaurants and institutional food-services. The variations and types of service are almost unlimited and may range from hot or cold specialty soups, served with attractive garnishes, to a spinach quiche or a crab quiche, served with artichoke hearts. Small pastry shells, filled with seafood salads or with tangy combinations of cheese and other ingredients, are standard buffet items or may be served as an appetizer with three or four stuffed shells to a plate.

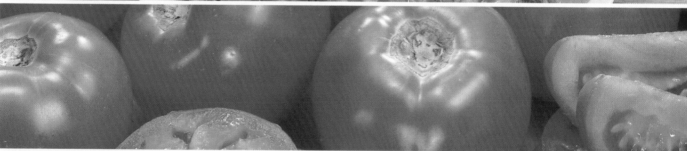

The acceptance of salads and salad-sandwich combinations depends in large part on the use of fresh ingredients, and their attractive presentation, in a form as appealing to the eye as to the taste. A simple platter of freshly-sliced red tomatoes and onions, served with a vinaigrette dressing, provides a tempting salad for service with steaks or other hearty menu items. Crisp Iceberg lettuce, as a base and as an ingredient, provides color and texture to arrangements of fresh vegetables, meat, and cheeses in salads that are high in protein. When served with freshly baked breads, these salad-sandwiches serve as a complete luncheon and add variety to the menu.

Salads, combining garden fresh vegetables and substantial portions of seafood or other high protein foods, are popular luncheon menu items. Many restaurants offer a combination of such salads and a serving of soup. The specialty soups may be served in individual soup mugs, from a container at the table or from a soup bar. The increasing use of soups bars has resulted from the widespread public acceptance of salad bars in virtually all types of foodservice operations. Soup bars may offer two or more soups and, when appropriate, a variety of garnishes, such as bacon, croutons, cheeses, chives or other items that complement the flavor of soups.

Salads and salad dressings may be served in a variety of ways. A selection of dressings may be offered with the salad ingredients or served in individual containers accompanying the salad. The salads may be displayed in covered containers, on serving lines, or in attractive salad bowls. The salad and salad dressing sections of this book offer many suggestions for combinations and methods of service for salads, ranging from simple Hearts of Lettuce to more elaborate Chef's and specialty salads.

HOUSE DRESSING

	1 Quart	2 Quarts	1 Gallon	2 Gallons
Tarragon	1 Tbsp.	2 Tbsp.	¼ cup	½ cup
Vinegar, tarragon	2 Tbsp.	¼ cup	½ cup	1 cup
Mayonnaise	2 cups	1 qt.	2 qt.	1 gal.
Sour Cream	1¼ cups	2½ cups	1 qt. 1 cup	2 qt. 2 cups
Parsley, fresh, minced	½ cup	1 cup	2 cups	1 qt.
Capers, minced	⅓ cup	⅔ cup	1⅓ cups	2⅔ cups
Green Onion, minced	¼ cup	½ cup	1 cup	2 cups
Lemon Juice, fresh	2 Tbsp.	¼ cup	½ cup	1 cup
Anchovy Filet, minced	1	2	4	8
Garlic Clove, minced	1	2	4	8

1. Soak tarragon in tarragon vinegar for 15 minutes.
2. Combine all ingredients and blend well.
3. Refrigerate covered until ready to use.

COOKED SALAD DRESSINGS

COOKED SALAD DRESSING
(Small Amounts)

	1 Gallon	2 Gallons	3 Gallons	4 Gallons
Mustard, dry	½ oz.	1 oz.	1½ oz.	2 oz.
Salt	2 oz.	4 oz.	6 oz.	8 oz.
Flour, all-purpose	8 oz.	1 lb.	1 lb. 8 oz.	2 lb.
Sugar	1 lb. 5 oz.	2 lb. 10 oz.	3 lb. 15 oz.	5 lb. 4 oz.
Water	2 qt.	1 gal.	1 gal. 2 qt.	2 gal.
Vinegar, cider	1 qt.	2 qt.	3 qt.	1 gal.
Eggs, whole	10 *or* 2 cups	20 *or* 1 qt.	30 *or* 1 qt. 2 cups	40 *or* 2 qt.
Oil, salad	1½ cups	3 cups	1 qt. ½ cup	1 qt. 2 cups

1. Weigh dry ingredients. Put in steam kettle.
2. Add water to dry ingredients in steam kettle. Stir until smooth.
3. Cook until mixture thickens, stirring frequently with a wire whip. While mixture is cooking, measure the eggs, vinegar, and oil. After mixture thickens, cook 5 minutes longer.
4. Add vinegar and stir.
5. Beat eggs slightly. Add some of the hot mixture to eggs. Then return eggs to mixture in kettle and stir rapidly. Turn off heat and allow to stand in kettle 5 minutes.
6. Add oil. Stir until mixed.
7. Store in refrigerator until needed.

Note: At the completion of cooking, this salad dressing may be thin. It thickens in the refrigerator when thoroughly chilled.

COOKED SALAD DRESSING
(Large Amounts)

	8 Gallons	12 Gallons	16 Gallons	24 Gallons
Water	4 gal.	6 gal.	8 gal.	12 gal.
Mustard, dry	4 oz.	6 oz.	8 oz.	12 oz.
Salt	1 lb.	1 lb. 8 oz.	2 lb.	3 lb.
Flour, all-purpose	4 lb.	6 lb.	8 lb.	12 lb.
Sugar	10 lb. 8 oz.	15 lb. 12 oz.	21 lb.	31 lb. 8 oz.
Vinegar, cider	2 gal.	3 gal.	4 gal.	6 gal.
Eggs, whole	80 *or* 1 gal.	120 *or* 1 gal. 2 qt.	160 *or* 2 gal.	240 *or* 3 gal.
Oil, salad	3 qt.	1 gal. 2 cups	1 gal. 2 qt.	2 gal. 1 qt.

1. Heat water in steam kettle.
2. Combine all dry ingredients. Add gradually to water in kettle.
3. Cook until mixture thickens or begins to simmer. After mixture reaches a simmer, cook 5 minutes longer.
4. Add vinegar, stir until well-mixed, and return to a boil.
5. Beat eggs slightly. Add some of the hot mixture to the eggs.
6. Add egg mixture all at once to the hot mixture in kettle and combine rapidly. Turn off heat and allow mixture to stand in kettle 5 minutes.
7. Add oil. Stir until mixed.
8. Store covered in the refrigerator, in 1-gal. jars or in 5-gal. stock pots until needed.

Note: At the completion of cooking, this salad dressing may be thin. It thickens in the refrigerator when thoroughly chilled.

COMBINATION DRESSINGS

COMBINATION DRESSING

	1 Gal. 1 Qt. 2 Cups	2 Gal. 3 Qt.	5 Gal. 2 Qt.	11 Gallons
Mayonnaise	3 qt.	1 gal. 2 qt.	3 gal.	6 gal.
Salad Dressing, cooked	2 qt. 2 cups	1 gal. 1 qt.	2 gal. 2 qt.	5 gal.

1. While it is still warm, gradually pour cooked salad dressing into mayonnaise, using #2 speed of mixer. Beat until dressing is of a smooth consistency.
2. Combination dressing may also be made when both mayonnaise and cooked salad dressing are cold. Combine in mixer or mix small amounts with a wire whip.

Note: Combination Dressing is excellent served on fish salads, jellied vegetable salads and when used in coleslaws.

CHEESE DRESSING

	1 Quart	2 Quarts	3 Quarts	1 Gallon
Combination Dressing	1 qt.	2 qt.	3 qt.	1 gal.
Cheese, grated fine	6 oz.	12 oz.	1 lb. 2 oz.	1 lb. 8 oz.
Cream, light	¼ cup	½ cup	¾ cup	1 cup

1. Mix enough to combine thoroughly.

PIMIENTO CHEESE DRESSING

	1 Quart	2 Quarts	3 Quarts	1 Gallon
Combination Dressing	1 qt.	2 qt.	3 qt.	1 gal.
Cheese, grated fine	6 oz.	12 oz.	1 lb. 2 oz.	1 lb. 8 oz.
Pimiento, ⅜″ pieces	6 oz.	12 oz.	1 lb. 2 oz.	1 lb. 8 oz.
Cream, light	¼ cup	½ cup	¾ cup	1 cup

1. Mix enough to combine.

DEVILED SMITHFIELD HAM DRESSING

	1 Quart	2 Quarts	3 Quarts	1 Gallon
Combination Dressing	1 qt.	2 qt.	3 qt.	1 gal.
Deviled Smithfield Ham	4 oz.	8 oz.	12 oz.	1 lb.

1. Mix enough to thoroughly combine.

CREAM, FRENCH, AND SPECIAL DRESSINGS

CREAM DRESSING BASE

	1 Qt. 1 Cup	2 Qt. 2 Cups	1 Gal. 1 Qt.	2 Gal. 2 Qt.
Fruit Juices, canned, hot	3 cups	1 qt. 2 cups	3 qt.	1 gal. 2 qt.
Flour, all-purpose	2½ oz.	5 oz.	10 oz.	1 lb. 4 oz.
Sugar	2 oz.	4 oz.	8 oz.	1 lb.
Salt	1½ tsp.	1 Tbsp.	1 oz.	2 oz.
Mustard, dry	½ tsp.	1 tsp.	2 tsp.	1 Tbsp. 1 tsp.
Fruit Juices, canned, cold	1 cup	2 cups	1 qt.	2 qt.
Eggs, whole	4 or ¾ cup	8 or 1½ cups	16 or 3 cups	32 or 1 qt. 2 cups

1. Heat the first amount of fruit juices to boiling.
2. Sift flour, sugar, salt, and mustard.
3. Add cold fruit juices and eggs to sifted dry ingredients. Stir with a wire whip until no lumps remain.
4. Add cold juice mixture to hot juice all at once and cook until thickened, stirring constantly. After mixture has thickened, cook a few minutes longer in order to remove starch taste. Remove from heat and cool.
5. Refrigerate until ready to combine with whipped cream or whipped topping.

Note: Suggested Fruit Juices are peach, pear, apricot, or a mixture of these juices drained from cans. A combination of pineapple and pear juice (half of each kind) is particularly good, although pineapple juice alone is not satisfactory. Canned fruit juices must be light in color. Do not use dark-colored juices such as cherry.

Note: This base without whipped cream can be held a week. Do not add whipped cream until base is cold.

LEMON OR LIME CREAM DRESSING

	2 Quarts	1 Gallon	2 Gallons	4 Gallons
Cream, heavy	2 cups	1 qt.	2 qt.	1 gal.
Sugar	2 Tbsp.	1½ oz.	3 oz.	6 oz.
Lemon *or* Lime				
Rind, grated	¾ tsp.	1½ tsp.	1 Tbsp.	½ oz.

1. Whip heavy cream until stiff. Add sugar.
2. Combine cold, cream dressing base with corresponding amounts of whipped cream.
3. Add lemon rind, if lemon cream dressing is desired. Add lime rind for lime cream dressing.

Note: Do not add whipped cream until ready for service. Mix only amount needed for one day.

Note: Whip topping may be used in place of heavy cream. Do not add sugar because topping when whipped is sweet enough. Follow directions on the can for whip topping. Use the following *whipped* amounts:

Whip Topping	1 qt.	2 qt.	1 gal.	2 gal.

PINEAPPLE CREAM DRESSING BASE
(Golden Cream Dressing Base)

	1 Qt. 1 Cup	2 Qt. 2 Cups	1 Gal. 1 Qt.	2 Gal. 2 Qt.
Water, hot	3 cups	1 qt. 2 cups	3 qt.	1 gal. 2 qt.
Sugar	8 oz.	1 lb.	2 lb.	4 lb.
Flour, all-purpose	2½ oz.	5 oz.	10 oz.	1 lb. 4 oz.
Salt	1½ tsp.	1 Tbsp.	1 oz.	2 oz.
Paprika	¼ tsp.	½ tsp.	1 tsp.	2 tsp.
Mustard, dry	¼ tsp.	½ tsp.	1 tsp.	2 tsp.
Orange Juice	½ cup	1 cup	2 cups	1 qt.
Lemon Juice	½ cup	1 cup	2 cups	1 qt.
Pineapple Juice	½ cup	1 cup	2 cups	1 qt.
Eggs, whole	4 or ¾ cup	8 or 1½ cups	16 or 3 cups	32 or 1 qt. 2 cups

1. Heat water to boiling.
2. Sift sugar, flour, salt, paprika, and mustard.
3. Add cold fruit juice and eggs to sifted dry mixture. Stir with a wire whip until no lumps remain.
4. Add cold juice mixture to hot water all at once and cook until thickened, stirring constantly. After mixture has thickened, cook a few minutes longer in order to remove starch taste. Remove from heat and cool.
5. Refrigerate until used.

PINEAPPLE CREAM DRESSING
(Golden Fruit Salad Dressing)

	2 Quarts	1 Gallon	2 Gallons	4 Gallons
Cream, heavy, unwhipped	1 cup	2 cups	1 qt.	2 qt.

1. Whip heavy cream until stiff.
2. Combine the Pineapple Cream Dressing Base (see preceding formula) with corresponding amounts of whipped cream.

Note: Do not add whipped cream until ready for service. Mix only amount needed for one day.

GERALINE HARDWICK

Figure 9   Salad dressing is important for eye and taste appeal. Pear and Cranberry Salad served in a lettuce cup with a Golden Fruit Salad Dressing is an attractive individual salad that may be served as an a la carte item or as the introduction to a meal.

SESAME LIME DRESSING FOR TROPICAL
OR WESTERN FRUIT SALAD

	1 Quart	2 Quarts	1 Gallon
Egg Yolks	4	8	16
Salt	1 Tbsp.	1 oz.	2 oz.
Sugar	3½ oz.	7 oz.	14 oz.
Ginger, ground	1 tsp.	2 tsp.	1 Tbsp. 1 tsp.
Lime Juice	1 cup	2 cups	1 qt.
Oil, salad	3 cups	1 qt. 2 cups	3 qt.
Sesame Seed, toasted	2 Tbsp.	¼ cup	½ cup

1. Blend the egg yolk, salt, sugar, ginger, and lime juice in a blender or bowl of mixer.
2. Use low speed of blender or medium if using beater.
3. Gradually add oil while blending to make the dressing light and thick.
4. Stir in the toasted sesame seeds.
5. Chill for at least 1 hour.
6. Dressing may be stored in refrigerator indefinitely. This salad dressing looks like a soft mayonnaise but has a flavor of lime.

FRENCH DRESSINGS

RED FRENCH DRESSING

	2 Qt. 2 Cups	1 Gal. 1 Qt.	3 Gal. 3 Qt.	7 Gal. 2 Qt.
Cornstarch	1½ oz.	3 oz.	9 oz.	1 lb. 2 oz.
Water, cold	¾ cup	1½ cups	1 qt. ½ cup	2 qt. 1 cup
Water, boiling	¾ cup	1½ cups	1 qt. ½ cup	2 qt. 1 cup
Paprika, Spanish	1 oz.	2 oz.	6 oz.	12 oz.
Water, hot	¾ cup	1½ cups	1 qt. ½ cup	2 qt. 1 cup
Salt	2¼ oz.	4½ oz.	13½ oz.	1 lb. 11 oz.
Sugar	6 oz.	12 oz.	2 lb. 4 oz.	4 lb. 8 oz.
Vinegar, cider	1⅞ cups	3¾ cups	2 qt. 3¼ cups	1 gal. 1 qt. 2½ cups
Oil, salad	1 qt. 1½ cups	2 qt. 3 cups	2 gal. 1 cup	4 gal. 2 cups
Onion, grated	¾ tsp.	1½ tsp.	1 Tbsp. 1½ tsp.	3 Tbsp.

1. Weigh cornstarch, paprika, salt, and sugar.
2. Dissolve cornstarch in cold water. Dissolve paprika in hot water.
3. Add boiling water to cornstarch and cook until paste is transparent and thick, or for 3 to 5 minutes, stirring constantly with wire whip.
4. Add paprika which has been dissolved in hot water, and cook approximately 1 minute (this will neutralize the raw taste of the paprika).
5. To the hot paste add salt and sugar and mix well. Using a sieve, strain into mixer bowl while still hot.
6. Use wire balloon whip and beat the paste in mixer while gradually and alternately adding the vinegar and oil. Beat continuously at #3 speed.
7. While dressing is beating, grate onion. Add grated onion to dressing. Beat only until onion juice is well-mixed. Onion may also be finely chopped.
8. Store covered in refrigerator until served. Stir well before using.

Note: If dressing is to be served immediately, double the amount of grated onion.

Note: This starch base holds the seasonings and oil in suspension and will not separate if a good emulsion is formed when the dressing is made.

CHIVE DRESSING

	1 Quart	3 Quarts	1 Gallon	3 Gallons
Red French Dressing	1 qt.	3 qt.	1 gal.	3 gal.
Chives, chopped fine	¼ cup	¾ cup	1 cup	3 cups

1. Wash chives and drain.
2. Chop fine.
3. Add to French Dressing (see preceding formula) and mix to combine.
4. Allow to stand at least 1 hour before serving so the flavor of the chives will be absorbed into the dressing.
5. Store covered in the refrigerator.

HORSERADISH FRENCH DRESSING

	1 Quart	3 Quarts	1 Gallon	3 Gallons
Red French Dressing	1 qt.	3 qt.	1 gal.	3 gal.
Horseradish	½ cup	1½ cups	2 cups	1 qt. 2 cups

1. Combine the horseradish and French Dressing and mix well.
2. Store covered in the refrigerator.

OLIVE FRENCH DRESSING

	1 Quart	3 Quarts	1 Gallon	3 Gallons
Red French Dressing	1 qt.	3 qt.	1 gal.	3 gal.
Stuffed Olives	1 cup	3 cups	1 qt.	3 qt.

1. Slice stuffed olives in thin slices and combine with French Dressing.
2. Store covered in the refrigerator.
3. Mix well before serving.

WHITE FRENCH DRESSING

	2 Qt. 2 Cups	1 Gal. 1 Qt.	5 Gallons	10 Gallons
Cornstarch	1½ oz.	3 oz.	12 oz.	1 lb. 8 oz.
Water, cold	½ cup	1 cup	1 qt.	2 qt.
Water, boiling	1 cup	2 cups	2 qt.	1 gal.
Paprika	½ tsp.	1 tsp.	1 Tbsp. 1 tsp.	½ oz.
Water, hot	¾ cup	1½ cups	1 qt. 2 cups	3 qt.
Mustard, dry	2 tsp.	1 Tbsp. 1 tsp.	1¼ oz.	2½ oz.
Salt	2¼ oz.	4½ oz.	1 lb. 2 oz.	2 lb. 4 oz.
Sugar	8 oz.	1 lb.	4 lb.	8 lb.
Vinegar, cider	1⅞ cups	3¾ cups	3 qt. 3 cups	1 gal. 3 qt. 2 cups
Oil, salad	1 qt. 1½ cups	2 qt. 3 cups	2 gal. 3 qt.	5 gal. 2 qt.
Onion, grated	¾ tsp.	1½ tsp.	2 Tbsp.	¼ cup
Garlic Cloves, quartered	2	4	16	32

1. Weigh or measure cornstarch, paprika, mustard, salt, and sugar.
2. Dissolve cornstarch in cold water. Dissolve paprika in hot water.
3. Add boiling water to cornstarch and cook until paste is transparent and thick, or for 3 to 5 minutes, stirring constantly with a wire whip.
4. To cornstarch paste add paprika, which has been dissolved in hot water and cook approximately 1 minute (this will neutralize the raw taste of the paprika).
5. To the hot paste add dry mustard, salt, and sugar and stir well. Using a sieve, strain paste into mixer bowl while still hot.
6. Use a wire balloon whip and whip hot paste on #3 speed of mixer for 2 minutes. While paste is beating, measure vinegar and oil.
7. Gradually add the oil alternately with the vinegar, continuing to beat on #3 speed all the time. Stop beating the dressing as soon as the oil

and vinegar have been added. Do not overbeat dressing at this point or it will become too thick. Dressing should have a thickened consistency but should not look whipped or fluffy, and should not hold its shape. Following are the approximate times which should be allowed for the addition of the oil and vinegar:

2 Qt.	1 Gal.	5 Gal.	10 Gal.
2 Cups	1 Qt.		
2 minutes	4 minutes	15 minutes	30 minutes

8. Add grated onion. Add garlic, which has been tied in a cheesecloth bag, and hold covered overnight in refrigerator to allow flavors to blend. Remove garlic from dressing after 1 day so flavor does not become too strong.
9. Store covered in refrigerator until served. Stir well before using.

Note: Garlic may be omitted. Amount of grated onion may be doubled if a dressing that is not garlic-flavored is preferred. Tossed salads should not be marinated with this dressing. Add dressing to salad just before serving.

CLEAR FRENCH DRESSING

	2 Quarts	**1 Gallon**	**2 Gallons**	**4 Gallons**
Oil, salad	1 qt. 2 cups	3 qt.	1 gal. 2 qt.	3 gal.
Vinegar, cider	2 cups	1 qt.	2 qt.	1 gal.
Salt	1¼ oz.	2½ oz.	5 oz.	10 oz.
Sugar	1¼ oz.	2½ oz.	5 oz.	10 oz.
Paprika	1 Tbsp. 1 tsp.	2 Tbsp. 2 tsp.	1½ oz.	3 oz.
Mustard, dry	2 tsp.	1 Tbsp. 1 tsp.	2 Tbsp. 2 tsp.	1½ oz.
Pepper, black	¼ tsp.	½ tsp.	1 tsp.	2 tsp.
Garlic Cloves, split, optional	8	16	32	64

1. Combine all ingredients and mix. Chill.

Note: Wine vinegar may be substituted for cider vinegar. This dressing is particularly good served with fresh citrus sections and greens.

CLEAR ITALIAN DRESSING

	1 Qt. 1 Cup	2 Qt. 2 Cups	1 Gal. 1 Qt.	2 Gal. 2 Qt.
Oil, salad	1 qt.	2 qt.	1 gal.	2 gal.
Vinegar, cider	1 cup	2 cups	1 qt.	2 qt.
Salt	1 Tbsp. 1 tsp.	1¼ oz.	2½ oz.	5 oz.
Celery Salt	2 tsp.	1 Tbsp. 1 tsp.	2 Tbsp. 2 tsp.	2 oz.
Pepper, white	2 tsp.	1 Tbsp. 1 tsp.	2 Tbsp. 2 tsp.	1¼ oz.
Mustard, dry	1 tsp.	2 tsp.	1 Tbsp. 1 tsp.	2 Tbsp. 2 tsp.
Cayenne	1 tsp.	2 tsp.	1 Tbsp. 1 tsp.	2 Tbsp. 2 tsp.
Garlic Cloves, minced	4	8	16	32
Hot Pepper Sauce	8 drops	16 drops	⅛ tsp.	¼ tsp.

1. Combine all ingredients and mix.
2. Chill. Stir well before using on salad.

Note: Garlic may be reduced to half. Other seasonings such as oregano and basil may also be added.

FRUIT FRENCH DRESSINGS

FRUIT FRENCH DRESSING I
(Lime Fruit French Dressing)

	1 Qt. 3 Cups	3 Qt. 2 Cups	1 Gal. 3 Qt.	3 Gal. 2 Qt.
Cornstarch	1 oz.	2 oz.	4 oz.	8 oz.
Water, cold	½ cup	1 cup	2 cups	1 qt.
Water, boiling	½ cup	1 cup	2 cups	1 qt.
Paprika	2 Tbsp.	1 oz.	2 oz.	4 oz.
Water, hot	2 Tbsp.	¼ cup	½ cup	1 cup
Salt	1 oz.	2 oz.	4 oz.	8 oz.
Sugar	6 oz.	12 oz.	1 lb. 8 oz.	3 lb.
Fruit Juices, canned, light	¾ cup	1½ cups	3 cups	1 qt. 2 cups
Lime Juice, fresh	1 cup	2 cups	1 qt.	2 qt.
Oil, salad	3¾ cups	1 qt. 3½ cups	3 qt. 3 cups	1 gal. 3 qt. 2 cups

1. Weigh or measure cornstarch, paprika, salt, and sugar.
2. Dissolve cornstarch in cold water. Dissolve paprika in hot water.
3. Add boiling water to cornstarch and cook until paste is transparent and thick, or for 3 to 5 minutes, stirring constantly with wire whip.
4. Add paprika, which has been dissolved in hot water and cook approximately 1 minute (this will neutralize the raw taste of paprika).
5. To the hot paste add salt and sugar and mix well. Using a sieve, strain into mixer bowl while still hot.
6. Use wire balloon whip and whip on #3 speed, gradually adding the canned fruit juices alternately with the oil, continuing to beat on #3 speed all the while.
7. Squeeze limes and add lime juice alternately with oil.
8. Store covered in refrigerator until served. Stir well before serving with fruit salads.

Note: Any light-colored fruit juice from a can is satisfactory. Peach, pear, or apricot juice, or a mixture of these with pineapple juice, may be used.

FRUIT FRENCH DRESSING II
(Lemon Fruit French Dressing)

	1 Quart	2 Quarts	1 Gallon	2 Gallons
Mustard, dry	¾ tsp.	1½ tsp.	1 Tbsp.	½ oz.
Salt	2 tsp.	1 Tbsp. 1 tsp.	1¼ oz.	2½ oz.
Sugar	4 oz.	8 oz.	1 lb.	2 lb.
Lemon Juice	1 cup	2 cups	1 qt.	2 qt.
Oil, salad	2 cups	1 qt.	2 qt.	1 gal.
Orange *or* Pineapple Juice	¼ cup	½ cup	1 cup	2 cups

1. Combine and mix dry ingredients in bowl of mixer.
2. Add enough lemon juice to make a thin paste.
3. Using balloon whip at #2 speed, add oil slowly until mixture becomes very heavy.
4. Alternately add remaining oil and fruit juices.

Note: This dressing holds well for several days. It is advisable to make it in amounts of 1 gal. or more.

CELERY SEED FRUIT FRENCH DRESSING

1. Add the following amounts of celery seed to the preceding formula for Fruit French Dressing II:

Celery Seed	½ tsp.	1 tsp.	2 tsp.	1 Tbsp. 1 tsp.

MINT FRUIT DRESSING

	1 Qt. 1½ Cups	2 Qt. 3 Cups	1 Gal. 1 Qt. 2 Cups	2 Gal. 3 Qt.
Cornstarch	1 oz.	2 oz.	4 oz.	8 oz.
Water, cold	½ cup	1 cup	2 cups	1 qt.
Water, boiling	½ cup	1 cup	2 cups	1 qt.
Sugar	6 oz.	12 oz.	1 lb. 8 oz.	3 lb.
Salt	1 Tbsp.	1 oz.	2 oz.	4 oz.
Pineapple Juice	¾ cup	1½ cups	3 cups	1 qt. 2 cups
Lemon Juice	¾ cup	1½ cups	3 cups	1 qt. 2 cups
Oil, salad	3 cups	1 qt. 2 cups	3 qt.	1 gal. 2 qt.
Peppermint Extract	¼ tsp.	½ tsp.	1 tsp.	2 tsp.
Green Food Color				

1. Weigh or measure sugar, salt, and cornstarch.
2. Dissolve cornstarch in cold water. Stir with a wire whip.
3. Add boiling water and cook until mixture is thick and transparent.
4. Add sugar and salt. Blend. Strain while hot through a sieve into mixer bowl.
5. Use wire balloon whip and, while beating continuously on #3 speed, add the combined fruit juices slowly, alternating with the oil.
6. Add peppermint extract and mix thoroughly.
7. Add a very small amount of green food color to provide a delicate green tint.
8. Store covered overnight for flavors to blend.
9. Stir or beat well before pouring over fruit salads.

Note: A combination of pineapple and apricot juice, using half of each, is also very good.

ORANGE FRUIT DRESSING

	2 Qt. 3 Cups	1 Gal. 1 Qt. 2 Cups	2 Gal. 3 Qt.	5 Gal. 2 Qt.
Water, boiling	1 qt.	2 qt.	1 gal.	2 gal.
Cinnamon	½ tsp.	1 tsp.	2 tsp.	1 Tbsp. 1 tsp.
Salt	2 tsp.	1 Tbsp. 1 tsp.	1¼ oz.	2½ oz.
Sugar	1 lb. 12 oz.	3 lb. 8 oz.	7 lb.	14 lb.
Cornstarch	3 oz.	6 oz.	12 oz.	1 lb. 8 oz.
Butter *or* Margarine	8 oz.	1 lb.	2 lb.	4 lb.
Orange Rind, grated	1 oz.	2 oz.	4 oz.	8 oz.
Orange Juice	1 qt.	2 qt.	1 gal.	2 gal.
Lemon Juice	¼ cup	½ cup	1 cup	2 cups

1. Heat water to boiling.
2. Weigh or measure and mix cinnamon, salt, sugar, and cornstarch.
3. Add dry ingredients gradually to boiling water. Cook until thickened, stirring constantly with a wire whip.
4. Add butter or margarine, orange rind, and fruit juices. Stir and cool.
5. Store in refrigerator covered until ready for use.
6. Serve over fruit salads.

ORANGE BLOSSOM DRESSING

	1 Quart	2 Quarts	1 Gallon
Cornstarch	3 Tbsp.	6 Tbsp.	¾ cup
Water, cold	¼ cup	½ cup	1 cup
Water, boiling	½ cup	1 cup	2 cups
Paprika	¼ tsp.	½ tsp.	1 tsp.
Water, hot	¼ cup	½ cup	1 cup
Sugar	¼ cup	½ cup	1 cup
Salt	½ tsp.	1 tsp.	2 tsp.
Mustard, dry	½ tsp.	1 tsp.	2 tsp.
Oil, salad	1⅜ cup	2¾ cup	1 qt. 1½ cups
Vinegar, cider	½ cup	1 cup	2 cups
Onion Juice	¼ tsp.	½ tsp.	1 tsp.
Fine Herbs	⅛ tsp.	¼ tsp.	½ tsp.
Garlic Cloves	½	1	2
Orange Juice	¾ cup	1½ cups	3 cups
Orange Rind, grated	2 Tbsp.	¼ cup	½ cup

Note: Make day before use.

1. Dissolve cornstarch in cold water. Add boiling water.
2. Cook until thick, for 3 to 5 minutes. Stir constantly.
3. Dissolve paprika in hot water.
4. Add paprika to cornstarch mixture and cook 1 minute.
5. Add sugar, salt, and mustard to mixture and mix.
6. Strain through a sieve to eliminate lumps.
7. Whip hot mixture while gradually adding oil alternately with vinegar, beating on fast speed all the time.
8. Add fine herbs and garlic clove. Mix. Chill and remove garlic after 24 hours.
9. Combine chilled dressing, orange juice, and orange rind.
10. Stir until thoroughly mixed. Refrigerate 1 to 2 hours to allow flavors to blend.

MARINATING DRESSINGS

OIL-VINEGAR MARINATING DRESSING

	1 Quart	2 Quarts	1 Gallon	2 Gallons
Oil, salad	2 cups	1 qt.	2 qt.	1 gal.
Vinegar, cider	2 cups	1 qt.	2 qt.	1 gal.
Salt	1 Tbsp.	1 oz.	2 oz.	4 oz.

1. Combine all ingredients. Mix thoroughly.
2. Put 2 cups dressing on each 12 × 20 × 2 pan of chopped lettuce or on 1 gal. 2 qt. chopped lettuce (2 lb. 8 oz. EP).
3. Marinate just before serving.

Note: This dressing has a tendency to separate quickly. It must be mixed thoroughly each time it is put on each salad. A ladle is good for stirring.

GARLIC MARINATING DRESSING

	1 Qt. 1 Cup	2 Qt. 2 Cups	1 Gal. 1 Qt.	2 Gal. 2 Qt.
Oil, salad	1 qt.	2 qt.	1 gal.	2 gal.
Vinegar, cider	½ cup	1 cup	2 cups	1 qt.
Garlic Cloves, large	1½	3	6	12
Onion, medium	1½	3	6	12
Salt	2¼ tsp.	1 Tbsp. 1½ tsp.	1½ oz.	3 oz.
Oregano, ground	¾ tsp.	1½ tsp.	1 Tbsp.	2 Tbsp.

1. Run all ingredients in blender for 2 minutes.
2. Store covered in the refrigerator.

Note: After blending this dressing looks as if it has been cooked with a cornstarch base. It is opaque in appearance. If it settles out in storage, blend again before using.

Note: This marinating dressing is high in garlic flavor but is excellent on a marinated lettuce salad. Garlic may be reduced to half if less garlic flavor is preferred.

CALICO DRESSING

	3 Cups	1 Qt. 2 Cups	3 Quarts	1 Gal. 2 Qt.
Oil, salad	1 cup	2 cups	1 qt.	2 qt.
Vinegar, cider	1½ cups	3 cups	1 qt. 2 cups	3 qt.
Onion, whole, EP	4 oz.	8 oz.	1 lb.	2 lb.
Sugar	2 oz.	4 oz.	8 oz.	1 lb.
Salt	1 Tbsp.	1 oz.	2 oz.	4 oz.
Mustard, dry	2 tsp.	1 Tbsp. 1 tsp.	½ oz.	1 oz.
Pepper, white	1 tsp.	2 tsp.	1 Tbsp. 1 tsp.	¾ oz.

1. Combine all ingredients in a blender. Blend well.
2. Chill covered in the refrigerator.
3. This dressing may be added to Calico Coleslaw (see p. 214) about 15 minutes before serving.

CAESAR SALAD DRESSING

	1 Cup	2 Cups	1 Quart	2 Quarts
Eggs, whole	2	4	8	16
Oil, salad	⅓ cup	⅔ cup	1⅓ cups	2⅔ cups
Lemon Juice	3 Tbsp.	6 Tbsp.	¾ cup	1½ cups
Worcestershire Sauce	¼ tsp.	½ tsp.	1 tsp.	2 tsp.
Parmesan Cheese, grated	½ cup	1 cup	2 cups	4 cups
Mustard, prepared	1 Tbsp.	2 Tbsp.	¼ cup	½ cup
Garlic Cloves, finely chopped	1½	3	6	12
Pepper, black	few grains	⅛ tsp.	¼ tsp.	½ tsp.

1. Combine all ingredients for salad dressing.
2. Mix thoroughly until smooth with French whip, or for larger amounts, use balloon whip in mixer. Chill thoroughly until ready to serve.
3. Combine salad dressing with greens in the following amounts:

Romaine	3 qt.	1 gal. 2 qt.	3 gal.	6 gal.
Salad Dressing	1 cup	2 cups	1 qt.	2 qt.
Croutons	6 oz.	12 oz.	1 lb. 8 oz.	3 lb.

Note: Vinegar or wine vinegar may be substituted for the lemon juice or half of each may be used.

WHITE HOUSE DRESSING

	2 Quarts	1 Gallon	2 Gallons	4 Gallons
Vinegar, white	3 cups	1 qt. 2 cups	3 qt.	1 Gal. 2 qt.
Oil, salad	2 cups	1 qt.	2 qt.	1 gal.
Sugar	1 lb.	2 lb.	4 lb.	8 lb.
Mustard, prepared	¼ cup	½ cup	1 cup	2 cups
Salt	1 oz.	2 oz.	4 oz.	8 oz.
Worcestershire Sauce, optional	¼ cup	½ cup	1 cup	2 cups
Green Pepper, chopped ¼", EP	6 oz.	12 oz.	1 lb. 8 oz.	3 lb.
Onion, chopped ¼", EP	6 oz.	12 oz.	1 lb. 8 oz.	3 lb.
Pimiento, chopped ¼", optional	4 oz.	8 oz.	1 lb.	2 lb.

1. Combine vinegar and oil.
2. Add sugar, prepared mustard, and salt. Add Worcestershire sauce if desired. Mix until sugar and salt are dissolved.
3. Add chopped green pepper, onion, and pimientos.
4. Let dressing stand at least 3 hours or covered overnight in refrigerator to blend ingredients.

Note: This dressing is very colorful and will keep under refrigeration for several months, but it is best served immediately if the red and green are to show on salad. It is quite sweet and clear without the Worcestershire sauce. The Worcestershire gives it a dark appearance and an excellent flavor.

VINAIGRETTE

	1 Qt. 2 Cups	3 Quarts	1 Gal. 2 Qt.
Oil, salad	3¾ cups	1 qt. 3½ cups	3 qt. 3 cups
Vinegar	1¼ cups	2½ cups	1 qt. 1 cup
Green Onion, chopped, EP	2 oz.	4 oz.	8 oz.
Parsley, chopped	½ cup	1 cup	2 cups
Salt	1½ Tbsp.	3 Tbsp.	3 oz.
Pepper	1½ Tbsp.	3 Tbsp.	6 Tbsp.
Garlic Powder	1 Tbsp.	2 Tbsp.	¼ cup
Oregano	½ Tbsp.	1 Tbsp.	2 Tbsp.

1. Combine all ingredients. Whisk to blend.
2. Refrigerate covered.

CREAMY SALAD DRESSING

	1½ Cups	3 Cups	1 Qt. 2 Cups	3 Quarts
Egg Yolk	2 tsp.	1 Tbsp. 1 tsp.	2 Tbsp. 2 tsp.	¼ cup 1 Tbsp. 1 tsp.
Mustard, Dijon	1 Tbsp. 1 tsp.	2 Tbsp. 2 tsp.	¼ cup 1 Tbsp. 1 tsp.	½ cup 2 Tbsp. 2 tsp.
Tabasco Sauce	2 drops	4 drops	8 drops	16 drops
Garlic, finely chopped	1 tsp.	2 tsp.	1 Tbsp. 1 tsp.	2 Tbsp. 2 tsp.
Salt	¼ tsp.	½ tsp.	1 tsp.	2 tsp.
Pepper, black, freshly ground	¼ tsp.	½ tsp.	1 tsp.	2 tsp.
Vinegar	2 tsp.	1 Tbsp. 1 tsp.	2 Tbsp. 2 tsp.	¼ cup 1 Tbsp. 1 tsp.
Oil, salad	1 cup	2 cups	1 qt.	2 qt.
Lemon Juice, fresh	2 tsp.	1 Tbsp. 1 tsp.	2 Tbsp. 2 tsp.	¼ cup 1 Tbsp. 1 tsp.
Cream, heavy	2 tsp.	1 Tbsp. 1 tsp.	2 Tbsp. 2 tsp.	¼ cup 1 Tbsp. 1 tsp.

1. Combine egg yolk, mustard, Tabasco sauce, garlic, salt, pepper, and vinegar in bowl of mixer.
2. Using balloon wire whip, beat until well-blended.
3. Add oil gradually while beating.
4. Continue beating until thickened and well-blended.
5. Add fresh lemon juice and heavy cream and beat until well-blended.
6. Refrigerate covered.

Note: This dressing is similar to a thin mayonnaise. It is used for coating salad greens. The dressing will coat the following amount of salad greens:

Salad Greens	1 gal. 2 qt.	3 gal.	6 gal.	12 gal.

CHEESE DRESSINGS

COTTAGE CHEESE DRESSING
(French Type)

	1 Qt. 2 Cups	3 Quarts	1 Gal. 2 Qt.	3 Gallons
Cottage Cheese, creamed	2½ cups	1 qt. 1 cup	2 qt. 2 cups	1 gal. 1 qt.
Sugar	3½ oz.	7 oz.	14 oz.	1 lb. 12 oz.
Salt	2 tsp.	1 Tbsp. 1 tsp.	1¼ oz.	2½ oz.
Mustard, dry	1 Tbsp. 1 tsp.	2 Tbsp. 2 tsp.	1¼ oz.	2½ oz.
Paprika	2 tsp.	1 Tbsp. 1 tsp.	2 Tbsp. 2 tsp.	1¼ oz.
Oil, salad	1½ cups	3 cups	1 qt. 2 cups	3 qt.
Catsup	½ cup	1 cup	2 cups	1 qt.
Vinegar	⅔ cup	1⅓ cups	2⅔ cups	1 qt. 1⅓ cups
Water	2 Tbsp.	¼ cup	½ cup	1 cup
Worcestershire Sauce	1 Tbsp. 1 tsp.	2 Tbsp. 2 tsp.	¼ cup 1 Tbsp. 1 tsp.	½ cup 2 Tbsp. 2 tsp.
Garlic Cloves, mashed	2	4	8	16
Tabasco Sauce	dash	few drops	1/16 tsp.	⅛ tsp.

1. Beat cottage cheese in mixer until creamy.
2. Add sugar, salt, dry mustard, and paprika and blend into cottage cheese until well-mixed.
3. Add all remaining ingredients and blend well.
4. Serve on any tossed salad or hearts of lettuce just before being served.

Note: Do not make too large a quantity of this dressing in advance. Make no more than can be used within 1 day.

ROQUEFORT OR BLEU CHEESE DRESSING

2 Tbsp. per Portion	1 Quart 32 Portions	2 Quarts 64 Portions	1 Gallon 128 Portions	2 Gallons 256 Portions
Roquefort or Danish Bleu Cheese	12 oz.	1 lb. 8 oz.	3 lb.	6 lb.
Cream Cheese	12 oz.	1 lb. 8 oz.	3 lb.	6 lb.
Sugar	1½ tsp.	1 Tbsp.	2 Tbsp.	2 oz.
Paprika	¾ tsp.	1½ tsp.	1 Tbsp.	2 Tbsp.
Oil, salad	1⅓ cups	2⅔ cups	1 qt. 1⅓ cups	2 qt. 2⅔ cups
Vinegar, cider	3 Tbsp.	¼ cup 2 Tbsp.	¾ cup	1½ cups

1. Put Roquefort or Bleu Cheese, cream cheese, sugar, and paprika in bowl of mixer.
2. On #2 speed, and using flat beater, add oil and vinegar alternately and quickly. Mix only until oil and vinegar are incorporated. Do not over-mix.

Note: There should be large flecks of Roquefort or Bleu Cheese in this dressing.

ROQUEFORT SOUR CREAM DRESSING

2 Tbsp. per Portion	2 Quarts 64 Portions	1 Gallon 128 Portions	2 Gallons 256 Portions	3 Gallons 384 Portions
Roquefort or Bleu Cheese Dressing	1 qt.	2 qt.	1 gal.	1 gal. 2 qt.
Sour Cream	1 qt.	2 qt.	1 gal.	1 gal. 2 qt.

1. Follow the preceding formula for Roquefort or Bleu Cheese Dressing.
2. Combine dressing with sour cream and mix with a wire whip.

CHEDDAR CHEESE DRESSING

	1½ Cups	3 Cups	1 Qt. 2 Cups	3 Quarts
Eggs, whole	1	2	4	8
Brown Sugar, packed	1 tsp.	2 tsp.	1 Tbsp. 1 tsp.	2 Tbsp. 2 tsp.
Salt	¾ tsp.	1½ tsp.	1 Tbsp.	1 oz.
Mustard, dry	½ tsp.	1 tsp.	2 tsp.	1 Tbsp. 1 tsp.
Worcestershire Sauce	½ tsp.	1 tsp.	2 tsp.	1 Tbsp. 1 tsp.
Horseradish, prepared	½ tsp.	1 tsp.	2 tsp.	1 Tbsp. 1 tsp.
Oil, salad	1 cup	2 cups	1 qt.	2 qt.
Vinegar	2 Tbsp.	¼ cup	½ cup	1 cup
Lemon Juice, fresh	2 Tbsp.	¼ cup	½ cup	1 cup
Cheddar Cheese, grated	2 oz.	4 oz.	8 oz.	1 lb.
Green Onions, finely chopped	1½	3	6	12

1. Combine eggs, brown sugar, salt, mustard, and Worcestershire sauce in a bowl.
2. Beat with mixer 2 to 3 minutes. Blend in horseradish.
3. Very slowly pour in half of the oil, beating constantly.
4. Add vinegar and lemon juice alternately with the remaining oil and beat 2 to 3 minutes longer.
5. Transfer to blender and mix for 10 to 15 seconds, until creamy. Do not allow to become as thick as mayonnaise.
6. Add cheese and onions and blend well. Refrigerate until ready to use.

NOUVELLE CUISINE DRESSINGS

AVOCADO DRESSING

	2 Cups	**1 Quart**	**2 Quarts**	**1 Gallon**
Spinach Leaves, fresh	5	10	20	40
Onion, chopped, EP	¼ cup	½ cup	1 cup	2 cups
Avocado, pitted, peeled	½	1	2	4
Oil, salad	⅜ cup	¾ cup	1½ cups	3 cups
Vinegar, red wine	⅜ cup	¾ cup	1½ cups	3 cups
Water	⅜ cup	¾ cup	1½ cup	3 cups
Eggs, hard-cooked	2	4	8	16
Salt	1½ tsp.	1 Tbsp.	2 Tbsp.	2 oz.

1. Place all ingredients in a blender.
2. Blend until smooth.
3. Cover and refrigerate.
4. Serve on sliced tomatoes which have been placed on a bed of spinach.

FLUFFY MINT DRESSING

	1½ Cups	3 Cups	1 Qt. 2 Cups	3 Quarts
Cottage Cheese, creamed	1 cup	2 cups	1 qt.	2 qt.
Sour Cream *or* Yogurt, plain	⅓ cup	⅔ cup	1⅓ cups	2⅔ cups
Orange Juice	3 Tbsp.	6 Tbsp.	¾ cup	1½ cups
Honey	1 Tbsp.	2 Tbsp.	¼ cup	½ cup
Mint Flakes	½ tsp.	1 tsp.	2 tsp.	1 Tbsp. 1 tsp.

1. In a mixing bowl, beat the cottage cheese with a whip at medium speed until fairly smooth and fluffy, about 5 minutes.
2. Add remaining ingredients to the cottage cheese. Mix at low speed until well-blended, about 1 minute.
3. Store covered in refrigerator up to 48 hours. If dressing separates, beat with a whip at low speed, about 1 minute.
4. Serve with fruit salads or fruit appetizers.

Note: Prepare a day ahead in order to allow flavors to blend. This formula may be made in a blender. Combine all ingredients in the blender and blend until smooth.

HERB GARLIC DRESSING

	2 Cups	1 Quart	2 Quarts	1 Gallon
Cottage Cheese, creamed	1¼ cups	2½ cups	1 qt. 1 cup	2 qt. 2 cups
Sour Cream *or* Yogurt, plain	¼ cup	½ cup	1 cup	2 cups
Milk	¼ cup	½ cup	1 cup	2 cups
Lemon Juice	1 Tbsp.	2 Tbsp.	¼ cup	½ cup
Parsley Flakes	1 tsp.	2 tsp.	1 Tbsp. 1 tsp.	2 Tbsp. 2 tsp.
Garlic Powder	½ tsp.	1 tsp.	2 tsp.	1 Tbsp. 1 tsp.
Onion Powder	½ tsp.	1 tsp.	2 tsp.	1 Tbsp. 1 tsp.
Mustard, dry	½ tsp.	1 tsp.	2 tsp.	1 Tbsp. 1 tsp.
Basil Leaf	½ tsp.	1 tsp.	2 tsp.	1 Tbsp. 1 tsp.
Salt	¼ tsp.	½ tsp.	1 tsp.	2 tsp.

1. In a mixing bowl, beat cottage cheese with paddle at medium speed until fairly smooth, about 5 minutes.
2. Add remaining ingredients to the cottage cheese. Mix at low speed until well-blended, about 2 minutes.
3. Store covered in refrigerator up to 3 days. If dressing separates, blend with whisk.
4. Serve with tossed green salads or sliced tomatoes.

Note: Prepare a day ahead in order to allow flavors to blend. This formula may be made in a blender. Combine all ingredients in the blender and blend until smooth. The Herb Garlic Dressing may also be used as a dip for appetizers, accompanied by Melba rounds or fresh vegetables.

SALAD DRESSING NATURELLE

	12 Portions	24 Portions	48 Portions
Broth, chicken	1 cup	2 cups	1 qt.
Oil, olive	½ cup	1 cup	2 cups
Vinegar, white wine	½ cup	1 cup	2 cups
Lemon Juice	½ cup	1 cup	2 cups
Parsley Flakes	2 Tbsp.	¼ cup	½ cup
Chervil	½ tsp.	1 tsp.	2 tsp.
Salt	1 tsp.	2 tsp.	1 Tbsp. 1 tsp.
Black Pepper, ground	½ tsp.	1 tsp.	2 tsp.
Tarragon Leaves	¼ tsp.	½ tsp.	1 tsp.

1. Combine all ingredients.
2. Mix well to combine.
3. Stir just before using.

Salad service in quantity foodservice operations may be divided into three general categories: 1) the small salad served as an accompaniment to a meal or as a garnish for sandwiches; 2) the large a la carte salad which ordinarily serves as a meal in itself; and 3) the salad bar.

Small salads The wide variety of salads in the small salad category include 1) tossed salads; 2) both vegetable and fruited cole-slaws; 3) vegetable salads, such as the German Cucumber Salad; 4) fruit salads, such as the Waldorf Salad; and 5) gelatin salads, served either from molds or in squares. These small salads may be served in lettuce cups or on a plate with chicory or other greens. A light, small salad can provide a substantial lift to a meal, a crisp texture, and a contrast in color and flavor. Served simply, the small salad is an important part of meal service in most quantity operations.

A la carte salads The a la carte salad often includes a protein item in addition to vegetables and/or fruit. The protein ingredient may be any one of such foods as deviled, halved, or sliced hard-cooked eggs, cottage cheese or julienne cheese strips, cold cuts, cream cheese balls, turkey or chicken in various forms, and meat or fish. The large a la carte salad may be served on a bed of shredded lettuce or flat greens, or served in a large lettuce cup. A mixture of tossed salad greens may be used as a base and the protein item— such as julienne chicken, ham, beef, or a combination of all three items—placed on top of the greens in a bowl. This type of salad is often included on the menu as a "Chef's Salad" and is usually served with a choice of dressings.

Salad bars Salad bars have become an important part of the quantity foodservice industry in facilities ranging from family and fast food restaurants to colleges and universities. A recent survey in *Institutions/Volume Feeding Magazine* revealed that more than one-third of all restaurants and institutional foodservices include a salad bar. Other surveys indicate that 46 percent of potential restaurant customers rank the salad bar among their most important considerations when selecting a restaurant.

The salad bar provides an opportunity to respond to customer interest and to increase profits through effective merchandising, reduced labor costs, and the utilization of leftovers. There is virtually no limit to the items that can be included on a salad bar. Greens and other tossed salad ingredients, prepared salads such as chicken, tuna, macaroni, potato, slaws, and various bean salads, a variety of relishes and marinated vegetables, watermelon pickles, chili peppers, and others may be included. More expensive items such as avocado, crab, crisply fried bacon bits, and assorted cheeses may also be incorporated into salad bar service if they are treated as garnishes rather than primary ingredients.

The placement of the salad bar within the overall traffic and seating patterns of the restaurant and the arrangement of food on the bar are important in creating interest and promoting effective utilization. While the variety and mix of salads is important, the placement of foods for appearance and convenience is a key factor. An attractive arrangement of salad ingredients in the sequence of preparation—first the greens, then the other vegetables followed by the salad dressings and garnishes respectively—is not only logical, but adds to the convenience and appeal of the bar as well.

The selection of salad dressings available is also important to the success of a salad bar. The dressings may include a variety of the many excellent commercial products on the market, a selection of special dressings made on the premises, or a combination of these. One highly successful chain of restaurants featuring salad bars purchases commercial blue cheese dressing, adds chunks of blue cheese and a little garlic salt before service, and calls it their house dressing.

Two basic types of salad bar equipment are available. The first—a portable, four- to six-foot insulated, ice pan salad bar—uses ice to cool all ingredients and requires a drain that must be emptied frequently. These units are particularly well-suited to smaller restaurants and, because they are portable, to certain types of hotel, school, and other quantity operations. The second type of salad bar is a self-contained unit equipped with a compressor refrigeration unit to chill food, although ice may be used for decoration if the unit has a drain. Because it requires an electrical outlet and because of its size, weight, expanded display area, and other factors, this unit is usually a semistationary fixture. In many states a sneeze guard is required for salad bars and other "open" serving units. The guard is designed to protect food from contamination, to aid in maintaining freshness, and may serve as a decorative feature of the bar.

Proper maintenance, cleanliness, and stocking of the bar are vital to its success. Considerable care must be taken to ensure that all ingredients are fresh, that wilted greens are replaced, that proper temperatures are maintained for prepared salads in which bacterial growth is a hazard, and that the bar and containers are kept clean and fresh-looking at all times. The salad bar offers many advantages, but it also requires considerable attention to detail and careful planning.

Innovations in salad preparation Many innovations are taking place in the preparation of salads for quantity foodservice. While the majority of operations still prepare salads on the premises, others have found it more economical to buy prepared salads from a commercial source. Both small and large salads may be purchased ready for service in individual portions.

Central kitchen preparation of salads and other food items has become a major factor in many large cities where commercial, quantity operations process salads and make them available to smaller units. Some of the larger restaurant chain operations, with many satellite units, build their own vegetable or salad preparation facility in a large central commissary where they manufacture salads for distribution to their various outlets. As an example, large quantities of cabbage for coleslaw may be cleaned and shredded at a central location, packed in polyethylene bags, and sent to the point of service. In many instances, dressing is prepared and packed in pure pak or other containers and sent with the basic ingredients. The foodservice employee need only mix so many bags of cabbage with so many containers of dressing.

Salad formulas of the future, such as coleslaw, may be written: 5 Poly Bags + 1 Pure Pak Dressing = 100 Portions Coleslaw. While some of the formulas in this section can be expanded for use in central kitchen facilities, the majority have been developed for use in individual kitchens.

TOSSED SALADS

The tossed salad, a perennial favorite, is a simple combination of various crisp greens. Although Iceberg lettuce usually predominates in tossed salads, various other types of lettuce such as Bibb, romaine, or escarole may be mixed with the Iceberg to provide contrasts in flavor, color, and texture. A few leaves of dark green spinach give contrast in color; sliced radishes, cucumbers, and sprigs of watercress may be mixed with the greens or placed on top as a garnish; and cubes or wedges of tomato may be added just before serving.

Several types of lettuce are available, with variations in texture, color, and flavor, and all are acceptable for use in tossed salads. The *Bibb* (or *Limestone*) and *Boston* (or *Butterhead*) lettuces are small, soft, loose-leaf varieties with light green outer leaves and light yellow inner leaves. *Romaine* or *Cos* lettuce is a dark green, cylindrical head with stiff leaves and a comparatively rough texture. *Escarole* is a broad, slightly curled, well-branched head with light center leaves and is somewhat bitter in taste. *Iceberg* lettuce, also known as *Crisphead*, is the most familiar and most widely-used salad green in foodservices. The medium green outer leaves become pale green toward the core and the head is compact and tightly folded. Iceberg is also the most readily available year-round due to the new storage techniques and staggered growing seasons.

In addition to the standard varieties, *Lamb's Tongue* or *Field Lettuce*—which grows in small clumps with small, tongue-shaped leaves on delicate stems—and *Leaf Lettuce*—with loose-curled leaves branching from a stalk and ranging from a maroon to a dark or light green—may be used. Special attention must be paid to leaf lettuce, which loses moisture twice as fast as head lettuce. There are two types of *Endive:* a branched head of curly leaves sometimes called *Chicory,* and the *Belgian* or *French* varieties, characterized by a cylindrical small head and blond leaves. Both types are somewhat bitter and should not be used as the primary ingredient in a salad for this reason.

Because these several types of lettuce will vary in price, the individual operator must decide on the type to be used. The salad

UNITED FRESH FRUIT AND VEGETABLE ASSOCIATION

Figure 10   There is an almost endless number of coleslaw serving variations. Even a simple slaw becomes a treat for the eye and taste when it is properly prepared and served with a touch of imagination. Fruit, pepper rings, olives, tomatoes, and many other vegetables are excellent additions to many basic slaws.

menu of one famous restaurant chain features tossed Bibb lettuce leaves as a standard, while other operators prefer the crispness of romaine or Iceberg.

CARE OF GREENS

Successful salad preparation begins with the purchase of quality greens and a system for keeping greens fresh, crisp, and cold with maximum yield and minimum loss of nutrients. Only fresh, young greens should be purchased. Those that are overmature, wilted, shriveled, discolored, or that show signs of decay should be avoided. Because greens deteriorate from day to day even under refrigeration, it is important that they be ordered only in proper amounts. Careful planning and inventory control can be used to determine the amount of greens needed for any meal or on any given day.

Salad greens should be prepared as soon as possible after they have been purchased. They should never be allowed to stand for any length of time at room temperatures because they will wilt and deteriorate rapidly after they have been washed and prepared for use.

STORAGE OF LETTUCE

Lettuce purchased from a supplier may be fresh from the field, or it may have been held in commercial storage if there is a surplus on the market. Iceberg lettuce can be expected to keep in storage for two to three weeks at steady, low temperatures. Lettuce freezes at 31.7°F and should be stored as close as possible to that temperature. The optimal temperature is 32°F to 35°F, but storage under 40°F is adequate to ensure freshness, flavor, and a long shelf life. A high relative humidity of 85 to 95 percent should be maintained during storage.

SAFE TEMPERATURES FOR LETTUCE

IF LETTUCE READS

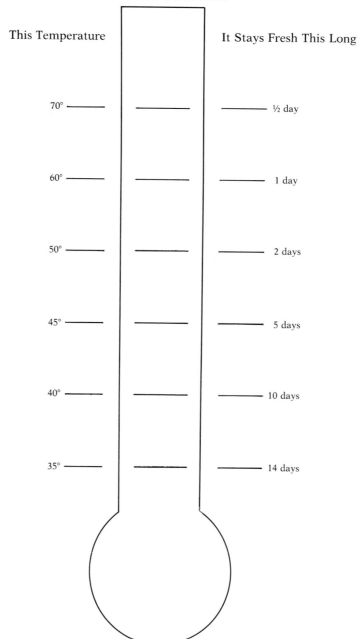

This Temperature

It Stays Fresh This Long

70° — — ½ day

60° — — 1 day

50° — — 2 days

45° — — 5 days

40° — — 10 days

35° — — 14 days

Store lettuce at 40°F or under for best balance of freshness and flavor.

It is important to allow for proper air circulation and to avoid tight "packing" of lettuce with other foods during storage. Lettuce should be stored away from ethylene-producing fruits such as apples, bananas, and pears because ethylene hastens decay in vegetables—particularly lettuce and other leafy greens.

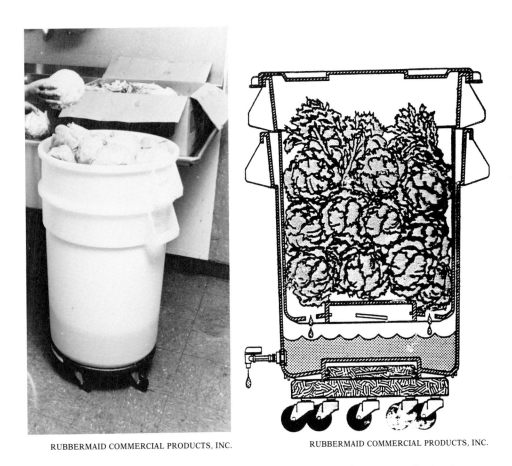

RUBBERMAID COMMERCIAL PRODUCTS, INC.   RUBBERMAID COMMERCIAL PRODUCTS, INC.

Figure 12A and 12B   Proper storage is important to the service of crisp lettuce. It is possible to crisp and store lettuce in a single container shown here. The plastic container with a drain spigot will not rust or transfer food odors and it simplifies the storage of lettuce.

PRECUT, PACKAGED LETTUCE AND SALAD MIX

Precut lettuce was developed especially for the quantity food-service industry as a labor-saving innovation, and there has been a steady increase in its use. It is available in most areas in either five- or ten-pound clear poly bags which should be refrigerated at 34°F. Precut lettuce may be purchased shredded, chopped, or combined with other vegetables in a salad mix that is ready for use in tossed salads or at the salad bar.

PREPARATION OF LETTUCE

Lettuce is often served lacking in the crispness necessary for an appetizing and appealing salad. Because crispness is of such importance, the following steps for preparing lettuce are recommended:

1. The head should be carefully washed and the outer leaves removed. If the outer leaves are in good condition, they may be used in tossed salads, sandwiches, soups, or in wilted lettuce salads.
2. Lettuce heads may be cored by whacking them, core-side down, on a counter or board to force the core up. The core may be cut out with a sharp-pointed, stainless steel knife.
3. The head should be held under the cold water faucet and water allowed to run briskly into the cavity. The weight of the water, together with a gentle movement of the fingers, will separate the leaves slightly without tearing or damaging them. If a large amount of lettuce is to be prepared, the cores should be removed and the lettuce should stand, cavity down, in cold water in the sink for ten to twenty minutes.
4. The lettuce should be allowed to drain for at least five minutes. Gentle shaking of the drained heads will remove most of the excess water.
5. The heads should be arranged, cavity down, in a container with a false bottom. The container should be tightly covered. The false bottom or rack prevents the lettuce from coming in contact with any excess water.

6. The containers should be placed in the refrigerator as soon as possible. Lettuce should be refrigerated at 32°F to 40°F and allowed to chill for twenty-four hours before serving. If lettuce is properly covered and air excluded, it will not turn brown in the refrigerator during the chilling and crisping process.

7. After washing and draining have been completed, the leaves may be separated, placed in a covered container, and refrigerated. Whether the heads are separated before or after refrigeration, it is important that they be stored at the proper temperature and the leaves kept from contact with any excess water.

PROCESSING IN QUANTITY

Large quantities of Iceberg lettuce may be power-shredded in a power cutter. A greens machine is also available for quick drying of lettuce and other greens. Lettuce crispers and salad dispensers are additional pieces of equipment available to aid in the preparation of salad greens.

PREPARATION OF "CUT" GREENS

The following procedures are recommended for the preparation of cut greens:

1. Remove the tough and discolored outer parts from the greens. (This procedure should be followed for the entire amount to be prepared before continuing to the next step.)

2. Double sinks should be filled two-thirds full with cold water. For crinkly leafed greens, such as Bibb lettuce or spinach, which can be very sandy, use lukewarm water. The warmer water temperature causes the leaves to flatten slightly and makes it easier to remove the sand. Whenever possible, it is preferable to tear greens rather than to cut them. Use a cutting board to cut greens to the desired size, and place them into the cold water immediately.

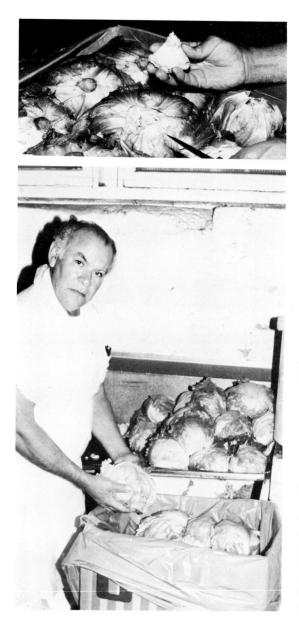

Figure 13A-B-C-D   Production procedures for large quantities of lettuce are shown here. (a) Core heads of lettuce with a stainless steel knife and submerge in lukewarm water for a few minutes to restore moisture; (b) After thorough draining, place in tightly closed containers for refrigeration; (c) Next, process in a power cutter filled with ice water; (d) Last, thoroughly drain again before assembling the salad.

3. Cut or tear the required amounts of greens in the proportion to be used in the salad (one part chicory, one part celery cabbage, one part romaine, and one part Iceberg, for example). All greens should be cut or torn into half-inch or one-inch pieces with the exception of the celery cabbage, which should be cut quite fine.

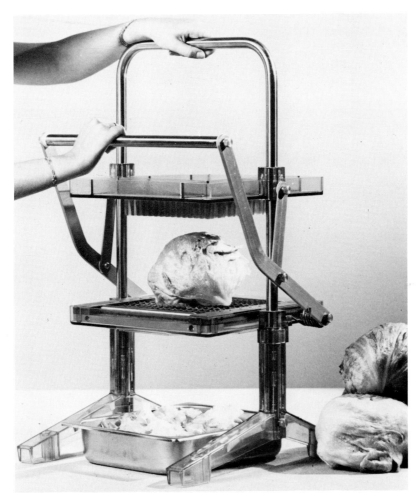

SILVER KING, STEVENS LEE COMPANY

Figure 14   A lettuce cutter is one of the many pieces of special equipment available to aid in salad preparation and in the production of comparatively small quantities of salads.

4. Without crowding the sink, cut as many greens as possible into the first water. There should be enough room in the sink for the greens to float freely for proper washing. It is better to do repeat batches of greens than to overcrowd those in the sink.

SILVER KING, STEVENS LEE COMPANY

Figure 15   Several models of refrigerated salad dispensers are available for use in quantity foodservices. These dispensers provide readily available, crisped greens for use in salads.

5. Using a mesh basket or perforated deep pans, transfer the greens from the first sink to the second sink of clear, cold water and repeat the washing process.

6. Drain and rinse the first sink. Fill it two-thirds full with cold water, transfer the greens to it, and wash them once more. Then drain the water from the sink and allow the greens to stand until excess water has drained.

7. Remove the cut greens and transfer them to mesh refrigerator baskets lined with clean cloths. These cloths absorb excess moisture and, when used to cover the basket, exclude air from the greens.

8. Store the cut greens in the refrigerator at 32°F to 40°F for several hours or overnight to chill and crisp. The greens may also be refrigerated in any tightly covered or air-proof container, such as polyethylene bags.

9. When preparing greens in great quantities by continuous processing, it may be necessary to use an automatic vegetable washer, tumble dry, and then store in polyethylene bags.

The success of tossed salads depends largely on the freshness and crispness of the greens and vegetables used in preparation. If these suggestions are carefully followed, the end result should be salads that are attractive and appealing in taste and texture.

TOMATO PREPARATION METHODS

Tomatoes are included in the majority of tossed salads; proper preparation and chilling are important to ensure their firmness. The simplest method of peeling tomatoes is to place them in a wire basket or colander and dip them into boiling water until the skins begin to loosen. When a gentle push causes the skin to move away from the flesh, the tomatoes should be plunged into cold water to cool. The skins and cores can then be removed. Tomatoes should be placed on trays and stored in the refrigerator until needed. This procedure should be completed well in advance of serving time so that the tomatoes will be well-chilled and firm when added to the salad.

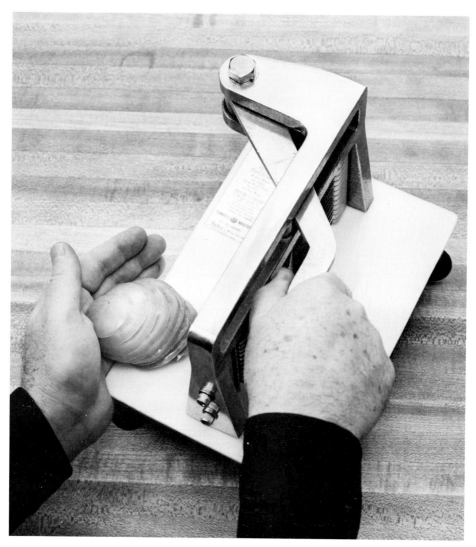

Figure 16   The quick and efficient hand-operated tomato slicer saves time in salad preparation and provides uniform tomato slices.

FARMER'S TOSSED SALAD

½ Cup Portion 12 × 20 × 2 Pan	1 Gal. 2 Qt. 48 Portions 1 Pan	3 Gallons 96 Portions 2 Pans	6 Gallons 192 Portions 4 Pans	12 Gallons 384 Portions 8 Pans
Lettuce, Iceberg, EP	2 lb.	4 lb.	8 lb.	16 lb.
Spinach, EP	2 oz.	4 oz.	8 oz.	1 lb.
Carrots, cubed ¼", EP	8 oz.	1 lb.	2 lb.	4 lb.
Celery, sliced ¼", EP	1 lb.	2 lb.	4 lb.	8 lb.
Radishes, sliced, EP, optional	4 oz.	8 oz.	1 lb.	2 lb.

1. Remove cores and any dark brown outside leaves from Iceberg lettuce.
2. Remove stems from spinach, leaving only the green leaves.
3. Wash lettuce and spinach. Drain thoroughly.
4. Cut greens into bite-size pieces and combine in specified amounts.
5. Cube carrots and slice celery on slicing machine.
6. Slice radishes if used.
7. Add carrots and celery to lettuce and spinach. Toss together.
8. Sprinkle 4 oz. radishes on top of each pan, if radishes are used.

Note: It requires approximately 2 heads lettuce AP to yield 2 lb. EP. Weights of lettuce vary.

Note: A half-cup of mixed vegetables may also be put into a salad bowl and sprinkled with sliced radishes for garnish.

TOSSED GARDEN GREEN SALAD

½ Cup Portion 12 × 20 × 2 Pan	1 Gal. 2 Qt. 48 Portions 1 Pan	3 Gallons 96 Portions 2 Pans	6 Gallons 192 Portions 4 Pans	12 Gallons 384 Portions 8 Pans
Lettuce, Iceberg, EP	1 lb. 8 oz.	3 lb.	6 lb.	12 lb.
Romaine, EP	8 oz.	1 lb.	2 lb.	4 lb.
Spinach, EP	2 oz.	4 oz.	8 oz.	1 lb.
Tomatoes, AP, blanched, peeled	3 lb. *or* 9 medium	6 lb. *or* 18 medium	12 lb. *or* 36 medium	24 lb. *or* 72 medium
Onions, red, sliced ⅛", EP	2	4	8	16

1. Remove cores from Iceberg lettuce and romaine. Remove any dark or brown outer leaves.
2. Remove stems from spinach.
3. Wash all greens. Drain greens thoroughly.
4. Cut greens into bite-size pieces and combine in specified amounts. Be sure that the combination of light and dark green leaves is equal and attractive. This is very important with this salad.
5. Store in pans, colanders, or poly bags in refrigerator until serving time.
6. Blanche and peel tomatoes. Store in refrigerator until serving time. Cut tomatoes in cubes and slice red onions very thin.
7. Put ½ cup salad greens in a salad bowl.
8. Serve 4 to 6 tomato cubes per salad on top and at edges, and 2 to 3 sliced onion rings on center top of salad.

Note: It requires approximately 2 heads of lettuce AP to yield 1 lb. 8 oz. to 2 lb. EP. Weights of lettuce vary.

EASY CAESAR SALAD

1 Cup Portion	6 Portions	12 Portions	24 Portions	48 Portions
Romaine, chopped ½″ to 1″, EP	3 bunches *or* 3 qt.	6 bunches *or* 1 gal. 2 qt.	12 bunches *or* 3 gal.	24 bunches *or* 6 gal.
Bread for ¼″ Croutons	6 slices	12 slices	24 slices	48 slices
Butter	4 oz.	8 oz.	1 lb.	2 lb.

1. Cut or tear romaine into ½″ to 1″ (or bite-size) pieces.
2. Wash thoroughly and crisp in refrigerator for several hours or overnight. If still wet when ready to combine with dressing, it may be necessary to pat dry with paper towels. It is important that no water cling to leaves and the greens be well-chilled and crisp.
3. Cut bread slices into croutons. Drizzle butter over croutons and toast in a slow oven until crisp, or about 1 hour.
4. Combine greens, croutons, and Caesar Dressing at the time of service (the formula for Caesar Dressing can be found on page 172).

Note: Lettuce may be substituted for half of the romaine if desired.

Note: If croutons are already buttered and on hand, the weight amounts are as follows:

Buttered Croutons	6 oz.	12 oz.	1 lb. 8 oz.	3 lb.

Note: This salad is particularly well suited to service at a table. The dressing, croutons and greens should be mixed at the table just before serving. Do not allow to stand. Three quarts of greens will serve a generous portion for 6 to 8 people.

GARDEN SPINACH SALAD

½ Cup Portion 12 × 20 × 2 Pan	1 Gal. 2 Qt. 48 Portions 1 Pan	3 Gallons 96 Portions 2 Pans	6 Gallons 192 Portions 4 Pans	12 Gallons 384 Portions 8 Pans
Lettuce, Iceberg, EP	1 lb. 8 oz.	3 lb.	6 lb.	12 lb.
Spinach, EP	8 oz.	1 lb.	2 lb.	4 lb.
Radishes, sliced ⅛″, EP	1 lb.	2 lb.	4 lb.	8 lb.
Celery, sliced ⅛″, EP	1 lb.	2 lb.	4 lb.	8 lb.

1. Remove cores from Iceberg lettuce and any dark or brown outside leaves.
2. Remove stems from spinach, leaving only the green leaves.
3. Wash lettuce and spinach. Drain thoroughly.
4. Cut greens into bite-size pieces and combine in specified amounts.
5. Slice stem ends from radishes and remove leaves from celery.
6. Slice radishes and celery on machine. Add to spinach and lettuce.
7. Store in pans, colander, or poly bags in refrigerator until serving time.

Note: It requires approximately 2 heads of lettuce AP to yield 1 lb. 8 oz. to 2 lb. EP. Weights of lettuce vary.

RED CABBAGE TOSSED SALAD

½ Cup Portion 12 × 20 × 2 Pan	1 Gal. 2 Qt. 48 Portions 1 Pan	3 Gallons 96 Portions 2 Pans	6 Gallons 192 Portions 4 Pans	12 Gallons 384 Portions 8 Pans
Red Cabbage, shredded, EP	8 oz.	1 lb.	2 lb.	4 lb.
Celery, sliced ⅛″, EP	8 oz.	1 lb.	2 lb.	4 lb.
Lettuce, chopped 1″, EP	2 lb.	4 lb.	8 lb.	16 lb.

1. Combine and toss all ingredients.
2. Use a clear marinating dressing—2 cups per pan for 1 gal. 2 qt.

MEXICAN TOSSED SALAD

½ Cup Portion 12 × 20 × 2 Pan	1 Gal. 2 Qt. 48 Portions 1 Pan	3 Gallons 96 Portions 2 Pans	6 Gallons 192 Portions 4 Pans	12 Gallons 384 Portions 8 Pans
Cabbage, shredded, EP	1 lb.	2 lb.	4 lb.	8 lb.
Romaine, or Escarole, EP	1 head or 8 oz.	2 heads or 1 lb.	4 heads or 2 lb.	8 heads or 4 lb.
Lettuce, Iceberg, chopped 1", EP	1 med. head or 1 lb.	2 med. heads or 2 lb.	4 med. heads or 4 lb.	8 med. heads or 8 lb.
Scallions, chopped ¼", EP	1 bunch or ½ oz.	2 bunches or 1 oz.	4 bunches or 2 oz.	8 bunches or 4 oz.
Green Peppers, chopped ¼", EP, optional	8 oz.	1 lb.	2 lb.	4 lb.
Pimiento, chopped ¼", optional	2 oz.	4 oz.	8 oz.	1 lb.

1. Shred cabbage. Wash, drain, and refrigerate to crisp.
2. Chop or tear romaine or escarole and lettuce into bite-size pieces (about ½" to 1").
3. Clean and chop the scallions. Clean and dice the green peppers. Dice pimiento if used.
4. Combine ingredients as for tossed salad.
5. Use 2 cups White House Dressing per pan or per 1 gal. 2 qt. mixture (the formula for White House Dressing can be found on p. 173).

COLESLAW

Coleslaws are usually divided into two basic categories: 1) vegetable slaws and 2) fruited slaws. Within these two categories are further subdivisions including the creamy slaws which use mayonnaise, sour cream, or combination dressing base, and the marinated slaws which use a marinating (oil and vinegar) dressing or a transparent type of fruit dressing. Creamy-style coleslaw is more than twice as popular as the vinaigrette-style slaws.

All vegetable slaws consist of combinations of vegetables such as carrots, green pepper, or parsley with cabbage as the major ingredient. Fruited slaws use a high percentage of fruit, such as apples, pineapple, or grapes, in addition to cabbage. Many other ingredients, such as raisins or peanuts, may be used in both vegetable and fruited slaws.

On the overall salad menu, coleslaws are second only to tossed salads in popularity and rank first in terms of quantity of preparation, simply because they are considerably less expensive than other salads to prepare and there is comparatively little waste.

It should be noted that yields may vary somewhat when testing coleslaws in small amounts of fifty portions and when actually preparing 1,000 portions. The slaw packs down in the larger amount because of the sheer weight of the shredded cabbage; therefore, the number of portions may be reduced. In addition, cabbage yields vary greatly depending on the established preparation procedures and, to some extent, on the person doing the cutting or shredding. Some employees prefer to remove all outside green leaves from the cabbage, resulting in waste as high as 25 to 30 percent. If most of the outer green leaves are shredded, the waste may be reduced to as low as 10 to 15 percent. The green leaves should be used as much as possible because they are high in nutritive value and make a more colorful coleslaw. In winter months, when cabbage may be totally white, green pepper, chopped parsley, and pimiento are necessary to provide the color contrast so important to a good slaw.

Figure 17 The shredded cabbage that forms the base for slaws may be combined with other vegetables and fruit, and served with various dressings to provide variety on a quantity foodservice menu.

205

CABBAGE PREPARATION

Cabbage for slaws may be shredded or minced. Cabbage for use in the majority of slaws is shredded, and minced for use in a relish. A minced cabbage may be prepared by running it through the vegetable slicer plate twice, or it may be minced more quickly in a cutter mixer, if such equipment is available. The peppers, dressing, and other ingredients may also be added with the green cabbage leaves. While this process represents a considerable savings of time, the running time of the cutter mixer must be carefully controlled. The conventional vegetable slicer plate is not satisfactory for continuous processing or shredding of cabbage. If substantial quantities are needed, high speed vegetable cutters or slaw shredders should be used.

HOBART MANUFACTURING COMPANY

Figure 18a   This counter-top machine with a speed drive and shredding plate makes it easy to shred small quantities of vegetables or cheese for salads.

Figure 18b and 18c   Counter-top (b) or floor model (c) shredding equipment is available for cutting or shredding cabbage, lettuce, and other salad ingredients. This type of equipment is designed for use in medium or large operations.

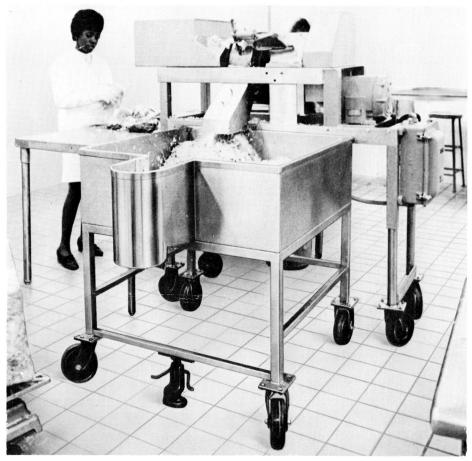

Figure 18d   Special floor model equipment is available for shredding or slicing large quantities of lettuce or cabbage for salads.

Cabbage is often very sandy, and the washing of large amounts can present several problems. It may be necessary to wash and drain the cabbage several times, shredding it into large vegetable bins beforehand if desired. In extremely large quantities, it may be more expedient to core and wash the heads and drain the vegetable bins thoroughly before shredding.

Cabbage wilts considerably when washed in water unless it is thoroughly drained. Adequate draining also prevents the problems that may result when water clings to the cabbage and dilutes the salad dressing. After thorough draining, the cabbage should be crisped in the refrigerator or packed in polyethylene bags for ease in handling on the premises or for shipping. If cabbage is to be stored, it should be treated with an antioxidant to prevent wilting.

To crisp shredded or chopped cabbage, it should be covered and left in the refrigerator until thoroughly chilled. In small quantities, it may be placed in ice water and put in the refrigerator to chill and crisp. When the latter method is used, the cabbage must be thoroughly drained before preparation of the slaw.

Some operations mix large amounts of slaw in a cold steam kettle. In others, where service takes place over a period of hours, coleslaw is mixed in small batches of fifty to 100 portions to keep the serving line supplied with fresh slaw. In this case, mixing can be accomplished easily in a 48-quart bowl on a dolly. Some slaws, such as the Creamy Coleslaw, improve when permitted to stand long enough for the flavors to blend. Others, such as the Combination Slaw, should be mixed just before serving to ensure a flavor and texture of quality. Specific directions for marinating or holding have been included in the individual formulas.

In small quantities, slaw may be served from the mixing container or may be placed in $12 \times 20 \times 2$ pans for portioning at the point of service. The yield per pan has been included in most formulas, although the gallon or portion yield will usually be of the greatest use.

VARIATIONS IN COLESLAW

The considerable amounts of juice that often remain from pickles or relishes can be substituted for vinegar in vegetable coleslaw formulas. Usually it will be necessary to decrease the amount of sugar used if such a substitution is made. Other possible variations include the use of Savoy cabbage, Celery (Chinese) cabbage, or red cabbage. Still other variations are possible in the dressings served on slaws (several appropriate dressings may be found in the Salad Dressing section).

CREAMY COLESLAW

½ Cup Portion 12 × 20 × 2 Pan	1 Gal. 2 Qt. 48 Portions 1 Pan	3 Gallons 96 Portions 2 Pans	6 Gallons 192 Portions 4 Pans	12 Gallons 384 Portions 8 Pans
Cabbage, shredded, EP	6 lb.	12 lb.	24 lb.	48 lb.
Green Pepper, chopped fine, EP	8 oz.	1 lb.	2 lb.	4 lb.
Onion, chopped fine, EP	2 oz.	4 oz.	8 oz.	1 lb.
Parsley, chopped fine, EP	½ oz.	1 oz.	2 oz.	4 oz.
Pimiento, cubed ¼", optional	4 oz.	8 oz.	1 lb.	2 lb.
Mayonnaise	1 qt.	2 qt.	1 gal.	2 gal.
Vinegar, cider	1 cup	2 cups	1 qt.	2 qt.
Sugar	6 oz.	12 oz.	1 lb. 8 oz.	3 lb.
Salt	2 tsp.	1 Tbsp. 1 tsp.	1¼ oz.	2½ oz.
Pepper	½ tsp.	1 tsp.	2 tsp.	1 Tbsp. 1 tsp.

Note: One medium head of cabbage yields 3 lb. EP shredded cabbage. One very large head of cabbage yields 5 lb. EP.

1. Shred cabbage using vegetable slicer plate of machine.
2. Wash cabbage, drain, and refrigerate to crisp.
3. Add chopped green pepper, onion, parsley, and pimiento to cabbage and mix.
4. Combine mayonnaise, vinegar, and seasonings. Stir until smooth and well-mixed.
5. Add dressing to vegetables. Combine thoroughly to mix.
6. Refrigerate 1 hour before serving. Toss occasionally while in refrigerator. It's important that the cabbage marinate in dressing and be mixed occasionally while marinating.

CREAMY CABBAGE AND PEPPER SLAW

1. Follow the preceding formula for Creamy Coleslaw, increasing the green pepper in the following amounts:

Green Pepper, chopped fine, EP	1 lb.	2 lb.	4 lb.	8 lb.

CREAMY CABBAGE AND CARROT SLAW
(Confetti Coleslaw)

½ Cup Portion 12 × 20 × 2 Pan	1 Gal. 2 Qt. 48 Portions 1 Pan	3 Gallons 96 Portions 2 Pans	6 Gallons 192 Portions 4 Pans	12 Gallons 384 Portions 8 Pans
Cabbage, shredded, EP	4 lb.	8 lb.	16 lb.	32 lb.
Carrots, shredded, EP	2 lb.	4 lb.	8 lb.	16 lb.
Green Pepper, chopped fine, EP	8 oz.	1 lb.	2 lb.	4 lb.
Onion, chopped fine, EP	2 oz.	4 oz.	8 oz.	1 lb.
Parsley, chopped fine, EP	½ oz.	1 oz.	2 oz.	4 oz.
Mayonnaise	1 qt.	2 qt.	1 gal.	2 gal.
Vinegar, cider	1 cup	2 cups	1 qt.	2 qt.
Sugar	6 oz.	12 oz.	1 lb. 8 oz.	3 lb.
Salt	2 tsp.	1 Tbsp. 1 tsp.	1¼ oz.	2½ oz.
Pepper	½ tsp.	1 tsp.	2 tsp.	1 Tbsp. 1 tsp.

1. Shred cabbage using vegetable slicer plate of machine.
2. Wash cabbage, drain, and refrigerate to crisp.
3. Add shredded carrots, chopped green pepper, onion, and parsley to cabbage and mix.
4. Combine mayonnaise, vinegar, and seasonings. Stir until smooth and well-mixed.
5. Add dressing to vegetables. Combine thoroughly to mix.
6. Refrigerate 1 hour before serving. Toss occasionally while in refrigerator. It is important that the cabbage marinate in dressing and be mixed occasionally while marinating.

CREAMY CABBAGE AND CUCUMBER SLAW

1. Follow the preceding formula for Creamy Cabbage and Carrot Slaw, substituting cucumber for the carrots in the following amounts:

Cucumbers, cubed ¼″, EP	2 lb.	4 lb.	8 lb.	16 lb.

CREAMY CABBAGE, CARROT, AND RAISIN SLAW

1. Using the formula for Creamy Cabbage and Carrot Slaw, add the following amounts of raisins:

Raisins	1 lb.	2 lb.	4 lb.	8 lb.

CREAMY CABBAGE, CARROT, AND PEANUT SLAW
(Southern Slaw)

1. Using the formula for Creamy Cabbage and Carrot Slaw, add the following amounts of peanuts:

Peanuts	1 lb.	2 lb.	4 lb.	8 lb.

COMBINATION COLESLAW

½ Cup Portion 12 × 20 × 2 Pan	1 Gal. 2 Qt. 48 Portions 1 Pan	3 Gallons 96 Portions 2 Pans	6 Gallons 192 Portions 4 Pans	12 Gallons 384 Portions 8 Pans
Cabbage, shredded, EP	9 lb.	18 lb.	36 lb.	72 lb.
Pimiento, chopped ¼″, optional	4 oz.	8 oz.	1 lb.	2 lb.
Combination Dressing	1 qt. 2 cups	3 qt.	1 gal. 2 qt.	3 gal.

1. Shred cabbage. Chop pimiento if used. Combine. (Pimiento need not be used if cabbage is very green; however, it is a colorful addition.)
2. Add Combination Dressing (see p. 154) to cabbage and pimiento. Toss together lightly.
3. Put 1 gal. 2 qt. in each 12 × 20 × 2 pan for 48 ½-cup portions per pan.

Note: This slaw should be mixed just before serving. If mixed 2 hours ahead of time, it develops an off-flavor. Mix just before serving and in small relays or amounts if possible.

YANKEE COLESLAW
(Coleslaw with Sour Cream Dressing)

½ Cup Portion 12 × 20 × 2 Pan	1 Gal. 2 Qt. 48 Portions 1 Pan	3 Gallons 96 Portions 2 Pans	6 Gallons 192 Portions 4 Pans	12 Gallons 384 Portions 8 Pans
Cabbage, shredded, EP	6 lb.	12 lb.	24 lb.	48 lb.
Sugar	6 oz.	12 oz.	1 lb. 8 oz.	3 lb.
Salt	1 oz.	2 oz.	4 oz.	8 oz.
Pepper, white	½ tsp.	1 tsp.	2 tsp.	1 Tbsp. 1 tsp.
Vinegar	½ cup	1 cup	2 cups	1 qt.
Sour Cream	1½ cups	3 cups	1 qt. 2 cups	3 qt.

1. Shred cabbage finely.
2. Combine sugar, salt, pepper, and vinegar. Mix until sugar is dissolved.
3. Add seasoned vinegar to sour cream, mixing lightly to thoroughly blend.
4. Add dressing to cabbage shortly before serving. Mix lightly.

CALICO COLESLAW

½ Cup Portion 12 × 20 × 2 Pan	3 Gallons 96 Portions 2 Pans	6 Gallons 192 Portions 4 Pans	12 Gallons 384 Portions 8 Pans	24 Gallons 768 Portions 16 Pans
Cabbage, shredded, EP	8 lb.	16 lb.	32 lb.	64 lb.
Corn, whole kernel, drained	1 #10 can	2 #10 cans	4 #10 cans	1 case 2 #10 cans
Onion, chopped fine, EP	1 lb. 4 oz.	2 lb. 8 oz.	5 lb.	10 lb.
Green Pepper, chopped fine, EP	8 oz.	1 lb.	2 lb.	4 lb.
Pimiento, chopped ¼″	1 lb.	2 lb.	4 lb.	8 lb.
Calico Dressing	3 cups	1 qt. 2 cups	3 qt.	1 gal. 2 qt.

1. Shred cabbage finely, using vegetable slicer plate of machine.
2. Wash, drain, and refrigerate to crisp.
3. Drain whole kernel corn.
4. Combine all vegetables and stir to mix.
5. Add Calico Dressing (see p. 172) and toss to mix.

VEGETABLE COLESLAW

½ Cup Portion 12 × 20 × 2 Pan	1 Gal. 2 Qt. 48 Portions 1 Pan	3 Gallons 96 Portions 2 Pans	6 Gallons 192 Portions 4 Pans	12 Gallons 384 Portions 8 Pans
Peas, frozen, cooked	2 lb. 8 oz.	5 lb.	10 lb.	20 lb.
Sugar	1½ oz.	3 oz.	6 oz.	12 oz.

Cabbage,
  shredded *or*
  minced, EP
	2 lb.	4 lb.	8 lb.	16 lb.

Carrots, cubed ¼″, EP	1 lb.	2 lb.	4 lb.	8 lb.
Celery, cubed ¼″, EP	1 lb.	2 lb.	4 lb.	8 lb.
White French Dressing	3 cups	1 qt. 2 cups	3 qt.	1 gal. 2 qt.

Tomatoes, AP cut
  in cubes,
  optional
	4 lb.	8 lb.	16 lb.	32 lb.

1. Add sugar to water. Cook frozen peas in water. Drain peas and chill in refrigerator.
2. Shred or mince cabbage. Cube carrots and celery.
3. Wash vegetables and allow to drain. Put in refrigerator to crisp.
4. Combine cold peas, cabbage, carrots, and celery.
5. Toss together lightly with White French Dressing (see p. 163).
6. Serve in vegetable dishes. Top each ½-cup serving with 1 Tbsp. fresh tomato cubes if desired.

Note: Tomatoes may be tossed in with other vegetables and dressing if preferred. This will increase the specified yields. Tomatoes should be firm and tossed just before serving.

MEXICAN CABBAGE RELISH

½ Cup Portion 12 × 20 × 2 Pan	1 Gal. 2 Qt. 48 Portions 1 Pan	3 Gallons 96 Portions 2 Pans	6 Gallons 192 Portions 4 Pans	12 Gallons 384 Portions 8 Pans
Cabbage, minced, EP	5 lb.	10 lb.	20 lb.	40 lb.
Green Pepper, chopped ¼", EP	8 oz.	1 lb.	2 lb.	4 lb.
Celery, chopped ¼", EP	8 oz.	1 lb.	2 lb.	4 lb.
Pimiento, chopped ¼"	4 oz.	8 oz.	1 lb.	2 lb.
Onion, chopped fine, EP	¾ oz.	1½ oz.	3 oz.	6 oz.
Parsley, chopped fine, EP	½ oz.	1 oz.	2 oz.	4 oz.
Vinegar, cider	3 cups	1 qt. 2 cups	3 qt.	1 gal. 2 qt.
Sugar	1 lb. 8 oz.	3 lb.	6 lb.	12 lb.
Salt	1 Tbsp.	1 oz.	2 oz.	4 oz.
Pepper	¼ tsp.	½ tsp.	1 tsp.	2 tsp.

1. Prepare all vegetables as directed.
2. Wash and drain all vegetables except pimiento. Combine all vegetables.
3. Combine vinegar, sugar, salt, and pepper.
4. Add vinegar dressing to mixed vegetables. Toss to combine again. Refrigerate.

Note: Vegetables may be pre-prepared and washed a day ahead.

MEXICAN COLESLAW

½ Cup Portion 12 × 20 × 2 Pan	1 Gal. 2 Qt. 48 Portions 1 Pan	3 Gallons 96 Portions 2 Pans	6 Gallons 192 Portions 4 Pans	12 Gallons 384 Portions 8 Pans
Cabbage, shredded, EP	4 lb.	8 lb.	16 lb.	32 lb.
Celery, cubed ¼", EP	1 lb. 8 oz.	3 lb.	6 lb.	12 lb.
Green Pepper, chopped ¼", EP	4 oz.	8 oz.	1 lb.	2 lb.
Pimiento, chopped ¼"	4 oz.	8 oz.	1 lb.	2 lb.
Vinegar	1⅓ cups	2⅔ cups	1 qt. 1⅓ cups	2 qt. 2⅔ cups
Water	⅓ cup	⅔ cup	1⅓ cups	2⅔ cups
Oil	⅓ cup	⅔ cup	1⅓ cups	2⅔ cups
Sugar	8 oz.	1 lb.	2 lb.	4 lb.
Salt	1 oz.	2 oz.	4 oz.	8 oz.

1. Shred cabbage finely, using vegetable slicer plate of machine.
2. Wash, drain, and refrigerate to crisp.
3. Combine vinegar, water, oil, sugar, and salt. Mix until sugar and salt are dissolved.
4. Add all vegetables to dressing or vice versa.
5. Toss to combine. Refrigerate.

CABBAGE AND PARSLEY COLESLAW
(Marinated Coleslaw)

½ Cup Portion 12 × 20 × 2 Pan	1 Gal. 2 Qt. 48 Portions 1 Pan	3 Gallons 96 Portions 2 Pans	6 Gallons 192 Portions 4 Pans	12 Gallons 384 Portions 8 Pans
Cabbage, shredded, EP	6 lb. 4 oz.	12 lb. 8 oz.	25 lb.	50 lb.
Parsley, chopped fine, EP	2 oz. to 4 oz.	4 oz. to 8 oz.	8 oz. to 1 lb.	1 lb. to 2 lb.
Onion, chopped fine, EP	4 oz.	8 oz.	1 lb.	2 lb.
Oil, salad	½ cup 2 Tbsp.	1¼ cup	2½ cups	1 qt. 1 cup
Vinegar, cider	⅞ cup	1¾ cup	3½ cups	1 qt. 3 cups
Sugar	7 oz.	14 oz.	1 lb. 12 oz.	3 lb. 8 oz.
Salt	2 Tbsp. or 1 oz.	2 oz.	4 oz.	8 oz.

1. Shred cabbage finely using vegetable slicer plate of machine.
2. Wash cabbage, drain and refrigerate to crisp.
3. Add chopped parsley and onion to shredded cabbage. Use larger amounts of parsley only if cabbage is white. If cabbage is green, use smaller amounts of parsley. Mix lightly to distribute uniformly.
4. Combine oil, vinegar, sugar, and salt, mixing until sugar and salt are dissolved.
5. Mix dressing thoroughly before adding to salad ingredients.
6. Add dressing shortly before serving to prevent excessive wilting of vegetables.

RED CABBAGE TOSS

½ Cup Portion 12 × 20 × 2 Pan	1 Gal. 2 Qt. 48 Portions 1 Pan	3 Gallons 96 Portions 2 Pans	6 Gallons 192 Portions 4 Pans	12 Gallons 384 Portions 8 Pans
Red Cabbage, shredded, EP	2 lb. 8 oz.	5 lb.	10 lb.	20 lb.
Cauliflower, sliced thin, EP	1 lb. 12 oz.	3 lb. 8 oz.	7 lb.	14 lb.
Celery, sliced thin, EP	1 lb.	2 lb.	4 lb.	8 lb.
Onion, chopped fine, EP	6 oz.	12 oz.	1 lb. 8 oz.	3 lb.
Sugar	4 oz.	8 oz.	1 lb.	2 lb.
Salt	1 Tbsp. 1 tsp.	1¼ oz.	2½ oz.	5 oz.

Vinegar	1⅓ cups	2⅔ cups	1 qt.
			   1⅓ cups
				2 qt.
				   2⅔ cups

Oil, salad	¾ cup	1½ cups	3 cups	1 qt.

1. Shred cabbage finely, using vegetable slicer plate of machine.
2. Wash cabbage, drain, and refrigerate to crisp.
3. Combine cabbage, cauliflowerets, celery, and onion.
4. Combine ingredients for dressing. Stir until sugar is dissolved.
5. Add dressing to vegetables, mixing lightly.
6. Chill for 1 hour.
7. Garnish with cauliflower flowerets and/or green pepper rings.

CABBAGE, PINEAPPLE, AND RAISIN SALAD

½ Cup Portion 12 × 20 × 2 Pan	1 Gal. 2 Qt. 48 Portions 1 Pan	3 Gallons 96 Portions 2 Pans	6 Gallons 192 Portions 4 Pans	12 Gallons 384 Portions 8 Pans
Cabbage, shredded, EP	4 lb.	8 lb.	16 lb.	32 lb.
Pineapple Tidbits, drained	1 #10 can	2 #10 cans	4 #10 cans	1 case 2 #10 cans
Raisins	1 lb.	2 lb.	4 lb.	8 lb.
Mayonnaise	1 qt.	2 qt.	1 gal.	2 gal.
Pineapple Syrup, drained from fruit	1 cup	2 cups	1 qt.	2 qt.
Sugar	4 oz.	8 oz.	1 lb.	2 lb.

Note: One #10 can of pineapple tidbits yields 2 qts. (well-packed) when drained. Crushed pineapple, which is less expensive, may be substituted for pineapple tidbits.

1. Shred cabbage finely, using vegetable slicer plate of machine.
2. Wash cabbage, drain, and refrigerate to crisp.
3. Add well-drained pineapple tidbits and raisins to drained cabbage.
4. Combine mayonnaise, pineapple syrup, and sugar. Stir to mix thoroughly.
5. Add the mayonnaise dressing to the cabbage, pineapple, and raisin mixture. Combine thoroughly to mix.
6. Put 1 gal. 2 qt. mixture (well-packed) into each 12 × 20 × 2 pan.
7. Chill thoroughly in refrigerator before serving.
8. It is important that some of the dressing be portioned into pans or into serving dishes along with cabbage.

Note: If cabbage is white throughout the head, as in midwinter, add chopped parsley for additional color. This salad is most attractive if green cabbage is used.

GERALINE HARDWICK

Figure 19   The Cabbage, Pineapple, and Raisin Salad is a popular variation of the basic Coleslaw formula. The pineapple and raisins provide an interesting contrast in color and texture. The dressing is made with a combination of pineapple juice, sugar, and mayonnaise.

CABBAGE, PINEAPPLE, AND PEANUT BUTTER SLAW

1. Use the preceding formula for Cabbage, Pineapple and Raisin Salad. Omit raisins if desired. Peanuts may be substituted for raisins if desired.
2. Soften the peanut butter by adding the pineapple juice to it in the mixer. Use a flat beater. Add the following amounts of peanut butter to the dressing:

| Peanut Butter | 2 oz. | 4 oz. | 8 oz. | 1 lb. |

CABBAGE, PINEAPPLE, AND GRAPE SALAD

½ Cup Portion 12 × 20 × 2 Pan	1 Gal. 2 Qt. 48 Portions 1 Pan	3 Gallons 96 Portions 2 Pans	6 Gallons 192 Portions 4 Pans	12 Gallons 384 Portions 8 Pans
Cabbage, shredded, EP	6 lb.	12 lb.	24 lb.	48 lb.
Pineapple Tidbits, drained	½ #10 can	1 #10 can	2 #10 cans	4 #10 cans
Grapes, Red, Tokay or Emperor Malaga	2 lb.	4 lb.	8 lb.	16 lb.
Mayonnaise	2 cups	1 qt.	2 qt.	1 gal.
Cooked Salad Dressing	2 cups	1 qt.	2 qt.	1 gal.

1. Shred cabbage finely, using vegetable slicer plate of machine.
2. Wash cabbage, drain, and refrigerate to crisp.
3. Halve and seed the grapes. Add grapes and well-drained pineapple to cabbage.
4. Combine mayonnaise and Cooked Salad Dressing (see pp. 141–152).
5. Add dressing to cabbage, pineapple, and grapes.
6. Serve ½ cup in a vegetable dish or in a small lettuce cup. Garnish with 4 or 5 grape halves.

Note: Green grapes, whole or halved, may be substituted for red grapes.

Note: If Cooked Salad Dressing is not on hand, the following may be substituted for the combination of mayonnaise and dressing:

Mayonnaise	1 qt.	2 qt.	1 gal.	2 gal.
Pineapple Syrup	1 cup	2 cups	1 qt.	2 qt.
Sugar	4 oz.	8 oz.	1 lb.	2 lb.

CABBAGE AND APPLE SALAD

½ Cup Portion 12 × 20 × 2 Pan	1 Gal. 2 Qt. 48 Portions 1 Pan	3 Gallons 96 Portions 2 Pans	6 Gallons 192 Portions 4 Pans	12 Gallons 384 Portions 8 Pans
Cabbage, shredded, EP	6 lb.	12 lb.	24 lb.	48 lb.
Red Apples, cubed ½", EP	2 lb. 8 oz.	5 lb.	10 lb.	20 lb.
Raisins, optional	1 lb.	2 lb.	4 lb.	8 lb.
Mayonnaise	1 qt.	2 qt.	1 gal.	2 gal.
Pineapple Syrup	1 cup	2 cups	1 qt.	2 qt.
Sugar	4 oz.	8 oz.	1 lb.	2 lb.

1. Shred cabbage finely, using vegetable slicer plate of machine.
2. Wash cabbage, drain, and refrigerate to crisp.
3. Cube apples, leaving red peel on for color.
4. Add apples and raisins to cabbage. Combine thoroughly.
5. Combine mayonnaise, pineapple syrup, and sugar.
6. Add the mayonnaise dressing to the cabbage, apples, and raisins. Combine thoroughly to mix.
7. Serve ½ cup in a vegetable dish or in a small lettuce cup. Garnish with raisins or apple cubes if desired.

FRUITED COLESLAW

½ Cup Portion 12 × 20 × 2 Pan	1 Gal. 2 Qt. 48 Portions 1 Pan	3 Gallons 96 Portions 2 Pans	6 Gallons 192 Portions 4 Pans	12 Gallons 384 Portions 8 Pans
Cabbage, shredded, EP	2 lb. 8 oz.	5 lb.	10 lb.	20 lb.
Red Apples, cubed ½", EP	2 lb. 8 oz.	5 lb.	10 lb.	20 lb.
Carrots, grated, EP	1 lb. 8 oz.	3 lb.	6 lb.	12 lb.
Raisins	1 lb.	2 lb.	4 lb.	8 lb.
Fruit French Dressing II	1 qt.	2 qt.	1 gal.	2 gal.

1. Shred cabbage finely, using vegetable slicer plate of machine.
2. Wash cabbage, drain, and refrigerate to crisp.
3. Shred carrots by running through grater plate.
4. Cube apples, leaving red peel on for color.
5. Combine cabbage, carrots, apples, and raisins.
6. Add Fruit French Dressing II (see p. 167) and mix to lightly combine.
7. Refrigerate and stir well before serving.

PINEAPPLE VEGETABLE SLAW

½ Cup Portion 12 × 20 × 2 Pan	1 Gal. 2 Qt. 48 Portions 1 Pan	3 Gallons 96 Portions 2 Pans	6 Gallons 192 Portions 4 Pans	12 Gallons 384 Portions 8 Pans
Cabbage, shredded, EP	1 lb. 8 oz.	3 lb.	6 lb.	12 lb.
Carrots, grated, EP	1 lb. 8 oz.	3 lb.	6 lb.	12 lb.
Celery, sliced ¼", EP	1 lb.	2 lb.	4 lb.	8 lb.

Pineapple
   Tidbits,
   drained
	1 #10 can	2 #10 cans	4 #10 cans	1 case 2
				   #10 cans

Fruit French Dressing II	3 cups	1 qt. 2 cups	3 qt.	1 gal. 2 qt.

1. Shred cabbage finely, using vegetable slicer plate of machine.
2. Wash cabbage, drain, and refrigerate to crisp.
3. Add well-drained pineapple tidbits to cabbage, carrots, and celery.
4. Add the Fruit French Dressing II (see p. 167) to the pineapple and vegetable mixture. Combine thoroughly to mix.
5. Put 1 gal. 2 qt. mixture (well-packed) into each 12 × 20 × 2 pan.
6. Chill thoroughly in refrigerator before serving.

SMALL VEGETABLE SALADS

While small tossed salads and coleslaws are the most widely-served of the small vegetable salads, lettuce salads, marinated vegetable salads, and vegetable relishes are frequently served in quantity foodservice operations.

SHELLEY MANUFACTURING COMPANY

Figure 19a   This vegetable drier will dry up to one case of lettuce every sixty seconds. The inner liner is removable so that greens may be washed, dried, and chilled in the same polyethylene container.

LETTUCE SALADS

The familiar Heart of Lettuce Salad is served frequently in institutional operations. When preparing Heart of Lettuce, the large outer leaves of the head may be removed, crisped in the refrigerator, and used as a base for service. The inner head should be cut into wedges, crisped, and thoroughly chilled. Although Iceberg lettuce is usually preferred for this type of salad, a whole head of Bibb lettuce with a garnish of cherry tomatoes is an excellent substitute. The center heart of romaine, with the outside leaves removed for use in tossed or Caesar salads, is an interesting variation. French and Roquefort dressings are those most frequently served on lettuce salads, although Russian and Thousand Island dressings may be offered.

In lieu of the Heart of Lettuce Salad, lettuce may be shredded or cubed in chunks and served in a salad bowl or on a salad plate. Wedges of tomato make an effective garnish. A deep green sprig of watercress provides an excellent contrast to the light green of the lettuce and the red of the tomatoes.

Heart of Lettuce servings are often weighed for portion control and to ensure that guests receive the same-size portion each time. Portion weights will depend on the type of service and cost factors.

MARINATED VEGETABLES

The familiar marinated vegetable salads have a tart taste because they are usually covered with an oil and vinegar dressing. The basic oil and vinegar mixture may include additional flavoring ingredients of onion, parsley, mustard, paprika, sugar, salt, and other seeds, spices, and herbs. When onions are used for added flavor they may be sliced, grated, or chopped. Beans of all kinds, beets, tomatoes, and cucumbers are among the vegetables that lend themselves particularly well to marinating. The salads may be served in vegetable dishes or paper souffle cups with a serving of dressing. These salads are particularly effective when served as part of a menu featuring a bland item that requires added contrast in flavor and texture. Care should be taken not to include too many marinated items in one menu.

In addition to the popular oil and vinegar dressing, vegetables may be marinated with a French-type dressing. For example, canned, diced beets are excellent when marinated with a Fruit French Dressing. If leftover vegetables are pleasing in taste and appearance, they can be combined, marinated with a French dressing, and served either as appetizers or small salads.

VEGETABLE RELISHES

Vegetable relish items, such as carrot and celery sticks, play an important part in some foodservice operations—particularly in school foodservices in which specific nutritional requirements must be met. Other operations serve vegetable relishes as a part of a luncheon plate, and nearly all operations use vegetable relishes on occasion as a garnish for sandwiches in place of, or in addition to, pickles. Among the more popular types of vegetables used for relish service are carrot sticks, celery sticks, cauliflower flowerets, cherry tomatoes or tomato wedges, cucumber slices or cucumber fingers, radishes, olives, and green pepper strips or rings.

HEARTS OF LETTUCE SALAD

3 oz. Portions	48 Portions	96 Portions	192 Portions	384 Portions
Lettuce, Iceberg, light heads	12 heads *or* ½ crate	24 heads *or* 1 crate	2 crates	4 crates

4 oz. Portions	48 Portions	96 Portions	192 Portions	384 Portions
Lettuce, Iceberg, heavy heads	8 heads	16 heads	32 heads *or* 1⅓ crates	64 heads *or* 2⅔ crates

1. Core lettuce and remove dark, bruised, or thick outer leaves. Some outer leaves may be saved for use as underliner for lettuce hearts.
2. Wash lettuce and drain. Lettuce heads may be put in perforated pans which are set in solid pans. In this way, water will drain from the lettuce heads.
3. When lettuce heads have drained, cut each head into 4 portions if the lettuce heads are light in weight. This will yield an approximate 3-oz. lettuce heart. If heads are heavy, cut them into 6 portions. This will yield an approximate 4-oz. lettuce heart.
4. Lettuce hearts may be returned to the same perforated pan for further draining, approximately 24 portions per 4″ pan. Use outer leaves to cover hearts and store in refrigerator to crisp until serving time.
5. When ready to serve, make a lettuce cup of outer leaves and place lettuce heart on the cup. Serve on a flat salad plate.
6. Serve with 2 Tbsp. Thousand Island, Russian, Roquefort (Domestic Blue Cheese), or Red French Dressing.

Note: All ingredient calculations are based on 24 heads per crate, which is one of the most common packs of lettuce.

MARINATED LETTUCE SALAD

½ Cup Portion 12 × 20 × 2 Pan	3 Gallons 96 Portions 2 Pans	6 Gallons 192 Portions 4 Pans	12 Gallons 384 Portions 8 Pans	24 Gallons 768 Portions 16 Pans
Lettuce, AP, *or*	6 heads *or* ¼ crate	12 heads *or* ½ crate	24 heads *or* 1 crate	48 heads *or* 2 crates
Lettuce, trimmed, EP	3 gal. *or* 5 lb.	6 gal. *or* 10 lb.	12 gal. *or* 20 lb.	24 gal. *or* 40 lb.

1. Approximately 3 medium heads, AP, should be used per 12 × 20 × 2 pan. When trimmed and cut this yields 1 gal. 2 qt. per 12 × 20 × 2 pan *or* 2 lb. 8 oz. per 12 × 20 × 2 pan.
2. Cut or tear lettuce into bite-size pieces.
3. Put 1 gal. 2 qt. in each 12 × 20 × 2 pan.
4. A ½-cup portion may also be put in a salad bowl. Garnish with tomato wedges and watercress.
5. Serve with Oil-Vinegar Dressing or with Garlic Marinating Dressing (see p. 171).

MARINATED GARDEN TOMATOES

½ Cup Portion	48 Portions	96 Portions	192 Portions	384 Portions
Tomatoes, AP	10 lb.	20 lb.	40 lb.	80 lb.
Onion, sliced, ⅛", EP	1 lb.	2 lb.	4 lb.	8 lb.
Parsley, chopped, EP	2 oz.	4 oz.	8 oz.	1 lb.
Oil, salad	1 qt.	2 qt.	1 gal.	2 gal.
Vinegar, cider	2 cups	1 qt.	2 qt.	1 gal.
Sugar	1 oz.	2 oz.	4 oz.	8 oz.
Salt	1 oz.	2 oz.	4 oz.	8 oz.
Pepper, white	2 tsp.	1 Tbsp. 1 tsp.	¾ oz.	1½ oz.

Note: Tomatoes should be firm for this formula.

1. Blanch tomatoes in very hot water. Peel and core. Slice tomatoes into ¼" slices. Place sliced tomatoes in a flat pan no more than 2 slices deep. Tomatoes also may be cubed ½" to 1" if preferred.
2. Layer onion slices on top of and between sliced tomatoes. If tomatoes are cubed instead of sliced, the onion may be chopped and sprinkled on top of tomatoes.
3. Chill tomatoes in refrigerator while preparing dressing.
4. Combine chopped parsley, oil, vinegar, sugar, salt, and pepper.
5. Pour dressing evenly over pan of tomatoes and allow to marinate in refrigerator at least 15 minutes to blend flavors.
6. Serve ½ cup in a vegetable dish with some of the dressing on each serving of tomatoes.

GERMAN CUCUMBERS

½ Cup Portion	48 Portions	96 Portions	192 Portions	384 Portions
Cucumbers, sliced ⅛″, AP	10 lb.	20 lb.	40 lb.	80 lb.
Water	1 gal.	2 gal.	4 gal.	8 gal.
Salt	2 oz.	4 oz.	8 oz.	1 lb.
Onion, coarsely grated or chopped, EP	6 oz.	12 oz.	1 lb. 8 oz.	3 lb.
Parsley, chopped, EP	¼ oz.	½ oz.	1 oz.	2 oz.
Water	3 cups	1 qt. 2 cups	3 qt.	1 gal. 2 qt.
Vinegar, cider	3 cups	1 qt. 2 cups	3 qt.	1 gal. 2 qt.
Sugar	1 lb.	2 lb.	4 lb.	8 lb.
Salt	2 oz.	4 oz.	8 oz.	1 lb.

1. Soak sliced cucumbers in brine made by combining first amounts of water and salt. Soak for 30 minutes.
2. Combine onion, parsley, second amount of water, vinegar, sugar, and second amount of salt.
3. Drain cucumbers from brine and add vinegar dressing to sliced cucumbers.
4. Refrigerate for 1 hour before serving to allow flavors to blend.

COLD SPICED BEETS

½ Cup Portion 12 × 20 × 4 Pan	48 Portions 1 Pan	96 Portions 2 Pans	192 Portions 4 Pans	384 Portions 8 Pans
Beets, diced or sliced, drained	2 #10 cans	4 #10 cans	1 case 2 cans	2 cases 4 cans
Onion, sliced ⅛″, EP	8 oz.	1 lb.	2 lb.	4 lb.
Beet Juice, drained from beets	1 qt.	2 qt.	1 gal.	2 gal.
Vinegar, cider	1 qt.	2 qt.	1 gal.	2 gal.
Sugar	1 lb.	2 lb.	4 lb.	8 lb.
Salt	1 oz.	2 oz.	4 oz.	8 oz.
Cinnamon, ground	¼ oz.	½ oz.	1 oz.	2 oz.
Allspice, ground	¼ oz.	½ oz.	1 oz.	2 oz.
Cloves, whole	¼ oz.	½ oz.	1 oz.	2 oz.

1. Drain beets. There is approximately 1 qt. of beet juice in each #10 can. Reserve specified amount of juice. Put 2 #10 cans of drained beets in each pan.
2. Add 8 oz. onions to beets in each pan. Combine.
3. Combine beet juice, vinegar, sugar, salt, and spices. Bring to a boil. Simmer for 15 minutes. The sauce will become somewhat syrupy. Remove from heat and allow to stand for 1 hour.
4. Strain beet juice mixture and add 2 qt. to drained beets and onions in pan.
5. Cover beets and allow them to chill overnight in liquid before serving.

PICKLED BEETS

Heaping ½ Cup Portion	48 Portions	96 Portions	192 Portions	384 Portions
Beets, sliced or diced, drained	2 #10 cans	4 #10 cans	1 case 2 cans	2 cases 4 cans
Beet Juice	2 qt.	1 gal.	2 gal.	4 gal.
Vinegar	1 qt. 1 cup	2 qt. 2 cups	1 gal. 1 qt.	2 gal. 2 qt.
Sugar	2 lb.	4 lb.	8 lb.	16 lb.
Salt	1½ tsp.	1 Tbsp.	1 oz.	2 oz.
Cinnamon, ground	1 tsp.	2 tsp.	1 Tbsp. 1 tsp.	2 Tbsp. 2 tsp.
Allspice, ground	1½ tsp.	1 Tbsp.	2 Tbsp.	1 oz.
Cloves, whole	2 tsp.	1 Tbsp. 1 tsp.	2 Tbsp. 2 tsp.	¼ cup 1 Tbsp.

1. Drain beets, reserving beet juice as specified in formula.
2. Combine beet juice, vinegar, sugar, salt, and spices. (Cloves may be tied in a cheesecloth bag.)
3. Bring syrup to a boil, reduce heat, and simmer for 15 minutes.
4. Strain syrup to remove cloves, or remove bag if cloves have been tied in a bag.
5. Pour hot syrup over beets.
6. Allow to stand in refrigerator overnight before using.

Note: Chopped onions are often added to pickled beets for color. Use the following amounts:

Onion, chopped ¼", EP				
	2 oz.	4 oz.	8 oz.	1 lb.

MARINATED BEET SALAD

½ Cup Portion 12 × 20 × 2 Pan	48 Portions 1 Pan	96 Portions 2 Pans	192 Portions 4 Pans	384 Portions 8 Pans
Beets, diced, drained	2 #10 cans	4 #10 cans	1 case 2 cans	2 cases 4 cans
Fruit French Dressing II	1 qt.	2 qt.	1 gal.	2 gal.

1. Drain beets and marinate in Fruit French Dressing II overnight in refrigerator (see p. 167).
2. Stir well before serving.

MARINATED GREEN BEANS
(Mild Flavor)

½ Cup Portion 12 × 20 × 2 Pan	1 Gal. 3 Qt. 48 Portions 1 Pan	3 Gal. 2 Qt. 96 Portions 2 Pans	7 Gallons 192 Portions 4 Pans	14 Gallons 384 Portions 8 Pans
Green Beans, canned, cut, and undrained	2 #10 cans	4 #10 cans	1 case 2 cans	2 cases 4 cans
Onion, finely chopped, EP	12 oz.	1 lb. 8 oz.	3 lb.	6 lb.
Vinegar	2 cups	1 qt.	2 qt.	1 gal.
Salt	1 Tbsp.	1 oz.	2 oz.	4 oz.

1. Combine all ingredients.
2. Refrigerate at least 2 hours.

Note: These beans may also be covered and refrigerated overnight.

Figure 20   Pickled Green Beans in one-quarter or one-half cup portions add variation to salad menus and may also be served as a vegetable accompaniment to any meal. The combination of green and wax beans in equal amounts provides a contrast in color and increases the eye-appeal of the serving.

PICKLED GREEN BEANS
(Strong Flavor)

½ Cup Portion 12 × 20 × 2 Pan	1 Gal. 3 Qt. 48 Portions 1 Pan	3 Gal. 2 Qt. 96 Portions 2 Pans	7 Gallons 192 Portions 4 Pans	14 Gallons 384 Portions 8 Pans
Green Beans, canned, cut, and drained	2 #10 cans	4 #10 cans	1 case 2 cans	2 cases 4 cans
Onion, sliced	8 oz.	1 lb.	2 lb.	4 lb. 1 gal.
Oil, salad	3 cups	1 qt. 2 cups	3 qt.	2 qt.
Vinegar, cider	1 qt. 2 cups	3 qt.	1 gal. 2 qt.	3 gal.
Sugar, brown	1 lb.	2 lb.	4 lb.	8 lb.
Salt	1 Tbsp. 1 tsp.	1¼ oz.	2½ oz.	5 oz.
Pepper, white	½ tsp.	1 tsp.	2 tsp.	1 Tbsp. 1 tsp.

1. Drain beans.
2. Add thinly sliced onions to green beans.
3. Combine oil, vinegar, sugar, salt, and pepper.
4. Add dressing to beans and onions. Combine lightly so that beans will remain whole.
5. Marinate several hours. Stir occasionally.
6. Serve as a vegetable or small salad.

Note: Green and waxed beans combined in equal amounts make an attractive combination.

GREEN AND WAX BEANS VINAIGRETTE

½ Cup Portion 12 × 20 × 2 Pan	1 Gal. 2 Qt. 48 Portions 1 Pan	3 Gallons 96 Portions 2 Pans	6 Gallons 192 Portions 4 Pans	12 Gallons 384 Portions 8 Pans
Beans, green and wax, cut and drained	2 #10 cans	4 #10 cans	1 case 2 cans	2 cases 4 cans
Chives, chopped, EP	¼ oz.	½ oz.	1 oz.	2 oz.
Parsley, chopped, EP	¼ oz.	½ oz.	1 oz.	2 oz.
Oil, salad	3 cups	1 qt. 2 cups	3 qt.	1 gal. 2 qt.
Vinegar, cider	1½ cups	3 cups	1 qt. 2 cups	3 qt.
Salt	1 Tbsp.	1 oz.	2 oz.	4 oz.
Paprika	1 Tbsp.	2 Tbsp.	1 oz.	2 oz.
Mustard, dry	1 Tbsp.	2 Tbsp.	1 oz.	2 oz.

1. Combine 1 can of green beans and 1 can of wax beans in a colander and drain. Put beans into a 12 × 20 × 2 pan.
2. Repeat process until all beans are used.
3. Combine all remaining ingredients for dressing and stir thoroughly.
4. Put 1 qt. dressing over beans in each pan.
5. Refrigerate for 1 hour.

Note: If parsley is not available, use double amount of chives. Scallion tops may be substituted for chives.

Note: Green and Wax Beans Vinaigrette may also be served hot or cold as a vegetable accompaniment.

TWO-BEAN SALAD
(Salad Makai)

½ Cup Portion 12 × 20 × 2 Pan	1 Gal. 2 Qt. 48 Portions 1 Pan	3 Gallons 96 Portions 2 Pans	6 Gallons 192 Portions 4 Pans	12 Gallons 384 Portions 8 Pans
Kidney Beans, drained	2 qt. *or* 3 lb.	1 gal. *or* 6 lb.	2 gal. *or* 12 lb.	4 gal. *or* 24 lb.
Lima Beans, frozen, cooked, drained	2 qt. *or* 3 lb.	1 gal. *or* 6 lb.	2 gal. *or* 12 lb.	4 gal. *or* 24 lb.
Celery, chopped ¼″, EP	1 lb. 12 oz.	3 lb. 8 oz.	7 lb.	14 lb.
Green Pepper, chopped ¼″, EP	8 oz.	1 lb.	2 lb.	4 lb.
Onion, sliced ⅛″, EP	6 oz.	12 oz.	1 lb. 8 oz.	3 lb.
Pimiento, chopped	1 cup	2 cups	1 qt.	2 qt.
Sugar	3½ oz.	7 oz.	14 oz.	1 lb. 12 oz.
Clear French Dressing *or* Clear Italian Dressing	3 cups	1 qt. 2 cups	3 qt.	1 gal. 2 qt.

1. Combine ingredients and toss well. (The formulas for Clear French Dressing and Clear Italian Dressing may be found on pp. 164 and 165.)
2. Allow to stand for at least 1 hour before serving.

Note: This salad may be served in a large bowl for buffets. Line a large wooden bowl with lettuce and fill with bean salad.

THREE-BEAN SALAD
(Southern Bean Salad)

Heaping ½ Cup Portion 12 × 20 × 2 Pan	2 Gal. 1 Qt. 48 Portions 1 Pan	4 Gal. 2 Qt. 96 Portions 2 Pans	9 Gallons 192 Portions 4 Pans	18 Gallons 384 Portions 8 Pans
Green Beans, cut and drained	1 #10 can	2 #10 cans	4 #10 cans	1 case 2 cans
Wax Beans, cut and drained	1 #10 can	2 #10 cans	4 #10 cans	1 case 2 cans
Red Kidney Beans, cooked, drained, and chilled	3 qt. *or* 1 #10 can	1 gal. 2 qt. *or* 2 #10 cans	3 gal. *or* 4 #10 cans	6 gal. *or* 1 case 2 cans
Onion, chopped fine, EP	12 oz.	1 lb. 8 oz.	3 lb.	6 lb.
Green Pepper, chopped fine, EP	12 oz.	1 lb. 8 oz.	3 lb.	6 lb.
Vinegar	3 cups	1 qt. 2 cups	3 qt.	1 gal. 2 qt.
Oil, salad	1½ cups	3 cups	1 qt. 2 cups	3 qt.
Sugar	1 lb. 8 oz.	3 lb.	6 lb.	12 lb.
Salt	1 oz.	2 oz.	4 oz.	8 oz.
Pepper	1 tsp.	2 tsp.	1 Tbsp. 1 tsp.	2 Tbsp. 2 tsp.

1. Combine beans, onions, and green pepper.
2. Combine vinegar, oil, sugar, salt, and pepper.
3. Add dressing to beans. Combine and allow to pickle in dressing for 1 hour. All beans may be chilled a day ahead.

Note: This salad is very sweet. Sugar may be decreased. Salad may also be marinated with Clear French Dressing or Clear Italian Dressing (see pp. 164 and 165).

FOUR-BEAN SALAD

1. Follow the preceding formula for Three-Bean Salad, using half kidney beans and half navy beans.
2. The Two-Bean Salad on p. 238 may be turned into a Four-Bean Salad by decreasing the kidney beans and limas to half and substituting green and wax beans for the other half.

CARROT, CELERY, AND RAISIN SALAD

½ Cup Portion 12 × 20 × 2 Pan	3 Quarts 24 Portions ½ Pan	1 Gal. 2 Qt. 48 Portions 1 Pan	3 Gallons 96 Portions 2 Pans	6 Gallons 192 Portions 4 Pans
Carrots, shredded, EP	2 lb.	4 lb.	8 lb.	16 lb.
Celery, cubed ½", EP	1 lb.	2 lb.	4 lb.	8 lb.
Raisins, seedless	8 oz.	1 lb.	2 lb.	4 lb.

Golden Cream
  Dressing base
	1½ cups	3 cups	1 qt. 2
			  cups
				3 qt.

Cream, heavy, unwhipped	1 cup	2 cups	1 qt.	2 qt.

1. Shred carrots and cube celery.
2. Combine shredded carrots, celery, and raisins.
3. Whip heavy cream until stiff.
4. Combine Golden Cream Dressing Base with whipped cream (see p. 158).
5. Add dressing to carrot mixture and combine thoroughly.
6. Put 1 gal. 2 qt. in each 12 × 20 × 2 pan.

Note: Whip Topping may be used in place of heavy cream in the following amounts:

Topping, whipped	2 cups	1 qt.	2 qt.	1 gal.

SMALL FRUIT SALADS

Small fruit salads may be served as accompaniments to a luncheon or dinner. They include the Waldorf Salad and its many variations, any pleasing combination of fresh and canned fruits, and a third grouping—such as Pear-Cranberry Salad—in which one fruit dominates and the other serves as a garnish.

WALDORF AND ITS VARIATIONS

Although Waldorf Salad is frequently made with mayonnaise, it often lacks flavor and texture. The Waldorfs in this section have been combined with an easily prepared cream dressing utilizing the canned fruit juices often discarded in quantity operations. The cream dressing base holds well for several days in the refrigerator and may therefore be made in quantities greater than those needed for one day or for one specific formula. When thoroughly chilled, the cream dressing base should be combined with whipped cream and added to cubed apples, celery, and/or other ingredients.

The heavy cream is expensive and adds to the cost of producing a Waldorf salad superior in flavor. There are several nondairy whip toppings on the market that can be substituted for whipped cream. Heavy cream doubles in volume when whipped, and whip topping trebles or quadruples in volume when mixed with a liquid and whipped. It is important that the manufacturer's directions be followed when substituting a whip topping for whipped cream. In addition to being a less expensive product and producing a greater volume, the nondairy whip topping has the added advantages of greater stability after whipping, longer refrigerated storage life, less tendency to sour, and fewer calories per serving.

SMALL COMBINATION FRUIT SALADS

It often happens in quantity foodservices that many "odds and ends" of fruit are leftover from partially used cans, from sectioned fresh fruit or melon, or from servings of fruit compote. These leftovers can be combined to form appealing small fruit salads. They may be combined with cream dressing or mixed and served in a lettuce cup with a tablespoon of cream dressing on top. Because the combination fruit salad is simply a conglomeration of fruits, it requires no specific formula for preparation. It is recommended, however, that one or more fresh and one or more canned or frozen fruits be included in a combination fruit salad.

WALDORF SALAD

½ Cup Portion 12 × 20 × 2 Pans	3 Quarts 24 Portions ½ Pan	1 Gal. 2 Qt. 48 Portions 1 Pan	3 Gallons 96 Portions 2 Pans	6 Gallons 192 Portions 4 Pans
Apples, cubed ½″, EP	2 lb. 8 oz.	5 lb.	10 lb.	20 lb.
Celery, cubed ¼″, EP	12 oz.	1 lb. 8 oz.	3 lb.	6 lb.
Walnuts or Pecans, optional	4 oz.	8 oz.	1 lb.	2 lb.
Cream Dressing Base	1½ cups	3 cups	1 qt. 2 cups	3 qt.
Cream, heavy	1 cup	2 cups	1 qt.	2 qt.
Sugar	1 Tbsp.	2 Tbsp.	1½ oz.	3 oz.
Lemon Rind, grated, optional	¼ tsp.	½ tsp.	1 tsp.	2 tsp.

1. Cube apples, leaving red peel on for color.
2. Combine apples and cubed celery. Add nuts, if used.
3. Whip cream until stiff. Add sugar. Add lemon rind, if used.
4. Combine Cream Dressing Base with whipped cream (see page 156).
5. Add dressing to apple mixture and combine thoroughly.
6. Put 1 gal. 2 qt. in each 12 × 20 × 2 pan.

Note: Whip Topping may be used in place of heavy cream. Use the following amounts and eliminate sugar:

Whip Topping, whipped	2 cups	1 qt.	2 qt.	1 gal.

Figure 21   Waldorf Salad may be served in a lettuce cup and garnished with any number of items ranging from chopped nuts to dates. The bright red peel should be left on the apples to provide a sharp color contrast.

WALDORF RAISIN OR WALDORF DATE SALAD

	24 Portions	48 Portions	96 Portions	192 Portions
Raisins *or*	4 oz.	8 oz.	1 lb.	2 lb.
Dates	4 oz.	8 oz.	1 lb.	2 lb.

1. Follow the preceding formula for Waldorf Salad, adding either raisins or dates. They may be used in addition to the nuts, or they may be substituted for them.

APPLE, CARROT, AND RAISIN SALAD

½ Cup Portion 12 × 20 × 2 Pan	3 Quarts 24 Portions ½ Pan	1 Gal. 2 Qt. 48 Portions 1 Pan	3 Gallons 96 Portions 2 Pans	6 Gallons 192 Portions 4 Pans
Apples, cubed ½", EP	2 lb. 8 oz.	5 lb.	10 lb.	20 lb.
Carrots, shredded, EP	8 oz.	1 lb.	2 lb.	4 lb.
Celery, cubed ¼", EP	4 oz.	8 oz.	1 lb.	2 lb.
Raisins	4 oz.	8 oz.	1 lb.	2 lb.
Cream Dressing Base	1½ cups	3 cups	1 qt. 2 cups	3 qt.
Cream, heavy	1 cup	2 cups	1 qt.	2 qt.
Sugar	1 Tbsp.	2 Tbsp.	1½ oz.	3 oz.
Lemon Rind, grated	¼ tsp.	½ tsp.	1 tsp.	2 tsp.

1. Cube apples, leaving red peel on for color.
2. Combine apples, shredded carrots, cubed celery, and raisins.
3. Whip heavy cream until stiff. Add sugar and lemon rind.
4. Combine Cream Dressing Base with whipped cream (see p. 156).
5. Add dressing to apple mixture and combine thoroughly.
6. Put 1 gal. 2 qt. in each 12 × 20 × 2 pan.

Note: Whip Topping may be used in place of heavy cream. Use the following amounts and eliminate sugar:

Whip Topping, whipped	2 cups	1 qt.	2 qt.	1 gal.

PINEAPPLE OR PEAR WALDORF SALAD

	24 Portions	48 Portions	96 Portions	192 Portions
Pineapple, tidbits				
or	8 oz.	1 lb.	2 lb.	4 lb.
Pears, diced	8 oz.	1 lb.	2 lb.	4 lb.

1. Follow the preceding formula for Apple, Carrot, and Raisin Salad, omitting raisins if desired, and substituting pineapple or pears for carrots.

PEANUT BUTTER WALDORF SALAD

½ Cup Portion 12 × 20 × 2 Pan	1 Gal. 2 Qt. 48 Portions 1 Pan	3 Gallons 96 Portions 2 Pans	6 Gallons 192 Portions 4 Pans	12 Gallons 384 Portions 8 Pans
Dressing Base	3 cups	1 qt. 2 cups	3 qt.	1 gal. 2 qt.
Lemon Juice	½ cup	1 cup	2 cups	1 qt.
Pineapple Juice	½ cup	1 cup	2 cups	1 qt.
Orange Juice	½ cup	1 cup	2 cups	1 qt.
Sugar	7 oz.	14 oz.	1 lb. 12 oz.	3 lb. 8 oz.
Eggs, whole	4	8	16	32
Peanut Butter	**2 oz.**	**4 oz.**	**8 oz.**	**1 lb.**
Salad				
Apples, cubed ½", EP	5 lb.	10 lb.	20 lb.	40 lb.
Celery, cubed ¼", EP	1 lb.	2 lb.	4 lb.	8 lb.
Heavy Cream	1 cup	2 cups	1 qt.	2 qt.

1. Heat juices over hot water or in steam kettle.
2. Combine eggs and sugar. Add some of the hot juices to the egg and sugar mixture. Stir to combine.
3. Add all of the egg, sugar, and juice mixture at once to the remaining hot juices.
4. Stir constantly until thickened or until mixture coats the spoon.
5. Add peanut butter and stir until peanut butter is dissolved. A few

flecks of peanut butter left in the mixture are not objectionable. Chill
thoroughly.

6. Cube apples and celery.
7. Whip heavy cream and add to peanut butter dressing base.
8. Add dressing to cubed apples and celery.
9. Combine thoroughly.
10. Serve ½ cup in a lettuce cup and sprinkle shredded coconut on top,
    if desired.

PINEAPPLE-PEANUT BUTTER WALDORF SALAD

1. Follow the preceding formula for Peanut Butter Waldorf Salad, adding
   the following amounts of pineapple and marshmallows to the apples
   and celery:

	1 Gal. 3 Qt. 56 Portions	3 Gal. 2 Qt. 112 Portions	7 Gallons 224 Portions	14 Gallons 448 Portions
Pineapple Tidbits, well- drained	½ #10 can	1 #10 can	2 #10 cans	4 #10 cans
Marshmallows, miniature	8 oz.	1 lb.	2 lb.	4 lb.

PEACH, PEAR, OR PINEAPPLE CRANBERRY SALAD

½ Cup Portion 12 × 20 × 2 Pan	48 Portions 2 Pans	96 Portions 4 Pans	192 Portions 8 Pans	384 Portions 16 Pans
Peach Halves, 25- 30 count *or*	2 #10 cans	4 #10 cans	1 case 2 cans	2 cases 4 cans
Bartlett Pear Halves, 40-50 count, *or*	*or* 1 #10 can	*or* 2 #10 cans	*or* 4 #10 cans	*or* 1 case 2 cans
Pineapple Slices, 52 count	*or* 1 #10 can	*or* 2 #10 cans	*or* 4 #10 cans	*or* 1 case 2 cans
Cranberries, fresh, finely chopped	8 oz.	1 lb.	2 lb.	4 lb.
Sugar	8 oz.	1 lb.	2 lb.	4 lb.
Cottage Cheese, optional	3 lb.	6 lb.	12 lb.	24 lb.
Lettuce, 1-lb. heads	2	4	8	16

1. Drain peach halves, Bartlett pear halves, or pineapple slices.
2. Chop cranberries in the food cutter.
3. Add sugar immediately to chopped cranberries. Combine thoroughly. Store in refrigerator for 1 hour. Adding sugar to cranberries immediately aids in retaining the red color.
4. Set up salad with small lettuce cup. Place peach, pear, or pineapple slice on lettuce cup. Place a #50 scoop of cottage cheese on center of peach or pear half or pineapple slice. (Cottage cheese is optional.) Put 1 tsp. cranberries to side of cottage cheese, or place in center of fruit if cottage cheese is not used.
5. Serve with 1 Tbsp. Cream Dressing or Golden Cream Dressing (see pp. 156–158).

Note: This salad is especially festive at Christmas. Pears may be tinted a light green for this occasion. A sprig of watercress is perfect with this salad when a lettuce cup is used. Curly chicory may also be used in place of lettuce cups.

PINEAPPLE, BANANA, AND PRUNE SALAD

½ Cup Portion 12 × 20 × 2 Pan	48 Portions 2 Pans	96 Portions 4 Pans	192 Portions 8 Pans	384 Portions 16 Pans
Pineapple Slices, 52 count	1 #10 can	2 #10 cans	4 #10 cans	1 case 2 cans
Bananas	2½ lb.	5 lb.	10 lb.	20 lb.
Prunes, dried, cooked	1 lb.	2 lb.	4 lb.	8 lb.
Lettuce, 1-lb. heads	2	4	8	16

1. Drain pineapple slices. Save juice for coating bananas.
2. Set up salad with small lettuce cup. Put 24 small lettuce cups in each 12 × 20 × 2 pan (if salads are to be transported). Put 1 slice of pineapple on each lettuce cup. Put 1 pitted prune in center of pineapple. Cut bananas into ½" slices. Dip into pineapple juice for coating. Put 3 or 4 banana slices on pineapple.
3. Serve with Orange Fruit Dressing or Red French Dressing (see pp. 169 and 161).

Note: Do not slice bananas far ahead of service. They will become soggy if allowed to stand in pineapple juice. Put banana slices on salad just before sending out or setting up for service.

PEACH AND BANANA SALAD

½ Cup Portion 12 × 20 × 2 Pan	48 Portions 2 Pans	96 Portions 4 Pans	192 Portions 8 Pans	384 Portions 16 Pans
Peach Halves, 25-30 count	2 #10 cans	4 #10 cans	1 case 2 cans	2 cases 4 cans
Pineapple Chunks, optional	1 #10 can	2 #10 cans	4 #10 cans	1 case 2 cans
Bananas	1 dozen	2 dozen	4 dozen	8 dozen
Peanut Butter	1 cup	2 cups	1 qt.	2 qt.
Lettuce *or* Escarole, 1-lb. heads	3	6	12	24

1. Drain peach halves and pineapple chunks.
2. Slice bananas lengthwise. Cover ½ banana with peanut butter and top with other half. Bananas may need to be coated with peach or pineapple juice in order to prevent browning.
3. Set up salad with lettuce or escarole cup. Place peach on cup with center facing up. Fill center with bananas sliced ½″ thick. Place 2 pineapple chunks, if desired, to the side of sliced banana chunk.
4. Serve each portion with 2 Tbsp. Orange Fruit Dressing (see p. 169).

GELATIN SALADS

Gelatin salads may be made using either unflavored or flavored gelatin, although the flavored gelatins are preferred in institutional foodservice. The two methods most frequently used for preparing gelatin salads are: 1) to heat half the water to boiling, add the gelatin, mix well, and add the remainder of the water cold; and 2) to heat approximately one fourth of the liquid to boiling, add gelatin, mix thoroughly, and add the remainder of water in the form of ice. The object of both methods is to solidify the product quickly. While the second method is the quickest, ice machines that produce cubes or crushed ice must be available for quantity production. A gallon measure, or five- or ten-gallon stock pots for larger amounts, should be filled with ice. Water must be added to cover, providing the specified amount of liquid. Because large amounts of ice are not always available in an institution, most formulas in this section have been established with the first method. The Golden Glow Salad has been established using both methods so that the two procedures can be compared.

The directions in Golden Glow I state that the gelatin mixture should be poured and allowed to chill until syrupy before the fruits and vegetable are added. This method is simple when only a few pans are made, but becomes quite laborious when large quantities are prepared. In Golden Glow II, the fruit and vegetable are added to the dissolved gelatin mixture in the kettle before it is panned. This one-kettle, ice method is faster than adding fruits or vegetables to panned gelatin. The availability of ice, the type of equipment used, and the quantity prepared will determine the best method to be used in preparing gelatin salads or gelatin desserts.

Lemon and/or lime crystals or concentrates are ingredients that save substantial amounts of time and storage space. The crystals need only be dissolved in water, and concentrates need only be diluted. Golden Glow II has been established using lemon crystals; however, if fresh lemon juice is preferred, it may be substituted in the amount indicated for "water for crystals."

The directions for the Golden Glow Salad state that the mixture should be placed in pans. This method provides a square cut portion, but many operations prefer to serve a molded salad. The Golden

GERALINE HARDWICK

Figure 22   The simple uses of light colored gelatins (such as lemon) or dark colored (such as strawberry) along with variations in serving can provide interest to the gelatin salad menu.

Glow and other salads may be molded as well as panned, although dipping gelatin salads into molds and then unmolding is more time-consuming than putting the salad into pans and cutting it in squares.

ASPICS

There are two familiar types of aspics, the one using tomato juice as a base being the most well-known. The second type contains a broth base and is commonly known as a clear aspic. Both types use unflavored gelatin as a stabilizing agent.

The basic tomato aspic forms an important part of a quantity menu for special events and/or buffets. A basic formula has been included in this section, along with suggestions for variations. Although the flavor does not appeal to everyone, a tomato aspic is low in calories and high in Vitamin C. A deviled egg set in a tomato aspic provides an excellent low calorie, high food value luncheon item.

STANDARD RATIOS AND PURCHASE UNITS

One tablespoon of unflavored gelatin will set two cups of liquid—even an acidic liquid such as tomato juice. There are four tablespoons of unflavored gelatin to an ounce. One ounce of unflavored gelatin will set two quarts of liquid; two ounces will set one gallon. A higher ratio may be needed for items prepared in ring molds because these products must be very stiff in order to prevent breaking when removing from the mold.

A one-pound, eight-ounce box of flavored gelatin will set one gallon of liquid or thirty-two portions per $12 \times 20 \times 2$ pan (cut 8×4). In a gelatin salad, fruit and/or vegetables are added. In most instances an acidic juice (such as pineapple or lemon juice) is included to enhance flavor. The ratio per $12 \times 20 \times 2$ pan then becomes one pound of flavored gelatin, two quarts and two cups of liquid (no more than two cups of the liquid as an acid juice), and two quarts of fruit and/or vegetable per pan.

Flavored gelatin may be purchased in containers of many sizes.

Two of the more familiar sizes are the one-pound, eight-ounce box and the number ten can. It is also available in fifty-pound drums for large operations. Although it would be more convenient to specify a number of boxes or cans, the *weight* of the gelatin has been listed to avoid confusion resulting from variations in purchase units.

Several factors are important in the successful preparation of flavored gelatin salads. The quality of the dry gelatin mixture is undoubtedly the most important. Both flavor and gelling capability (bloom count in the range of 200) are important for all gelatin salads but particularly if the gelatin is to carry fruit and/or vegetables. *Bloom* is the term used to measure the ability of a gelatin to form a gel or to describe its gel strength. The higher the bloom, the greater the ability to gel. There are many inexpensive gelatins on the market with a low bloom strength and an objectionable flavor. Because many of these inexpensive products do not have satisfactory gelling qualities, it pays to spend a little more to buy a flavored gelatin of high quality. If a gelatin of high bloom count is not purchased, it may be necessary to either delete gelatin salads during very hot seasons or to greatly increase the ratio of gelatin. In addition, some flavored gelatins may lose their bloom strength if stored for long periods of time at high temperatures. In this case, the tiny gelatin granules will form large clumps. If a cook (who has been using a standard formula day after day) suddenly finds 1,000 portions of a 200 bloom count gelatin unset (or if it looks set and becomes watery upon portioning), the storage and temperature factors may be the reason. If gelatin does not gel, it is either of low bloom count, too old, or stored at either high temperatures or under excessively humid conditions.

The second most important factor in the successful preparation of flavored gelatin salads is the use of boiling water to dissolve the gelatin. While some authorities maintain that gelatin will dissolve properly at 185°F (or even at 140°F to 165°F), it is recommended that boiling water be used as a part of the liquid content. If the water is not boiling when the dry gelatin is added, the mixture should be stirred and brought to a boil. If a temperature lower than boiling is used, the gelatin may appear to be completely dissolved but may have a granular texture when it sets.

Fresh or frozen fresh pineapple should never be used in preparing a gelatin salad. Even the juice of fresh pineapple should not be used because the fresh fruit and juice contain an enzyme called bromelin that digests the gelatin. It is a disheartening experience to add leftover fruit that includes fresh pineapple to a gelatin salad, refrigerate it overnight, and then find an unset mixture in the morning.

Gelatin salads made with flavored gelatin may be served with any cream dressing. Aspics are best served with a mayonnaise or combination dressing. The dressing should complement the salad, but never overpower it.

GOLDEN GLOW I
(Orange, Carrot, and Pineapple Salad)

Cut 8 × 4 12 × 20 × 2 Pan	32 Portions 1 Pan	64 Portions 2 Pans	128 Portions 4 Pans	256 Portions 8 Pans
Water, boiling	1 qt.	2 qt.	1 gal.	2 gal.
Gelatin, orange *or* lemon	1 lb.	2 lb.	4 lb.	8 lb.
Water, cold	1 qt.	2 qt.	1 gal.	2 gal.
Lemon Juice	½ cup	1 cup	2 cups	1 qt.
Salt	¼ tsp.	½ tsp.	1 tsp.	2 tsp.
Pineapple Juice	1½ cups	3 cups	1 qt. 2 cups	3 qt.
Pineapple, crushed and drained	½ #10 can *or* 1 qt.	1 #10 can *or* 2 qt.	2 #10 cans *or* 1 gal.	4 #10 cans *or* 2 gal.
Carrots, AP	1 lb.	2 lb.	4 lb.	8 lb.
or	*or*	*or*	*or*	*or*
Carrots, shredded, EP	12 oz.	1 lb. 8 oz.	3 lb.	6 lb.

1. Add gelatin to boiling water. Stir to dissolve completely.
2. Add cold water, lemon juice, pineapple juice, and salt. Stir to mix.
3. Put 2 qt. 2 cups gelatin mixture into each 12 × 20 × 2 pan. Allow to chill until syrupy.
4. Add 1 qt. crushed pineapple and 1 qt. (12 oz. EP) shredded carrots to each 12 × 20 × 2 pan. Stir to mix in each pan.
5. Chill in refrigerator overnight until set.
6. Cut each pan 8 × 4 for 32 portions per pan.

Note: If drained pineapple juice is short, add water to arrive at the required amount.

Figure 23   This Golden Glow Salad and other gelatin salads may be prepared by heating half of the water to a boil, adding gelatin, and then adding the remainder of water, cold or by the "ice method", in which a quarter of the water required is heated to boiling, the gelatin is added, and then the remainder of water added in the form of ice.

GOLDEN GLOW II
(Orange, Carrot, and Pineapple Salad—Ice Method)

Cut 8 × 4 12 × 20 × 2 Pan	64 Portions 2 Pans	128 Portions 4 Pans	256 Portions 8 Pans	384 Portions 12 Pans
Pineapple, crushed and drained	1 #10 can	2 #10 cans	4 #10 cans	1 case
Water, boiling	1 qt.	2 qt.	1 gal.	1 gal. 2 qt.
Gelatin, orange	2 lb.	4 lb.	8 lb.	12 lb.
Ice and Water	3 qt.	1 gal. 2 qt.	3 gal.	4 gal. 2 qt.
Lemon Crystals	½ oz.	1 oz.	2 oz.	3 oz.
Water, for crystals	1 cup	2 cups	1 qt.	1 qt. 2 cups
Pineapple Juice	3 cups	1 qt. 2 cups	3 qt.	1 gal. 2 cups
Salt	½ tsp.	1 tsp.	2 tsp.	1 Tbsp.
Carrots, AP	2 lb.	4 lb.	8 lb.	12 lb.
or	*or*	*or*	*or*	*or*
Carrots, shredded, EP	1 lb. 8 oz.	3 lb.	6 lb.	9 lb.

1. Drain crushed pineapple. Chill in refrigerator if possible. Save juice.
2. Add gelatin to boiling water in steam kettle. Stir to dissolve completely, then turn off steam.
3. Add ice and water. Be sure to fill gallon of ice cubes with water.
4. Combine lemon crystals with water for crystals.
5. Add lemon juice, pineapple juice, and salt. Stir to mix.
6. Add crushed, drained pineapple, and shredded carrots to kettle. Stir to mix thoroughly.
7. Put a heaping 1-gal. of mixture into each 12 × 20 × 2 pan.
8. Chill in refrigerator to set, preferably overnight.
9. Cut pans 8 × 4 for 32 portions per pan.

Note: If drained pineapple juice is short, add water to arrive at required amount of pineapple juice listed above.

CRUNCHY BLACKBERRY ISLE SALAD

Cut 8 × 4 12 × 20 × 2 Pan	32 Portions 1 Pan	64 Portions 2 Pans	128 Portions 4 Pans	256 Portions 8 Pans
Water, boiling	1 qt.	2 qt.	1 gal.	2 gal.
Gelatin, blackberry	1 lb.	2 lb.	4 lb.	8 lb.
Water, cold	1 qt. 2 cups	3 qt.	1 gal. 2 qt.	3 gal.
Lemon Juice, optional	¼ cup	½ cup	1 cup	2 cups
Salt	½ tsp.	1 tsp.	2 tsp.	1 Tbsp. 1 tsp.

Pineapple,
   crushed,
   drained
	1 qt.
	   2 cups
		3 qt.	1 gal. 2 qt.	3 gal.

Celery, chopped
   ¼″, EP
	2 cups *or*
	   8 oz.
		1 qt. *or*
		   1 lb.
			2 qt. *or*
			   2 lb.
				1 gal. *or*
				   4 lb.

Pecans, chopped,
   optional
	1 cup *or*
	   4 oz.
		2 cups *or*
		   8 oz.
			1 qt. *or*
			   1 lb.
				2 qt. *or*
				   2 lb.

1. Add blackberry gelatin to boiling water. Stir to dissolve completely.
2. Add cold water, lemon juice, and salt. Stir to mix.
3. Put 2 qt. 2 cups gelatin mixture in each 12 × 20 × 2 pan. Allow to become syrupy.
4. Add 1 qt. 2 cups crushed pineapple and 2 cups chopped celery to each pan. Stir to distribute evenly.
5. Add nuts if used.
6. Chill in refrigerator overnight.

GRAPE ISLE SALAD

Follow the preceding formula for Crunchy Blackberry Isle Salad, substituting grape gelatin for blackberry gelatin.

BLACKBERRY PINEAPPLE SLAW

Eliminate the specified amount of pineapple, celery and nuts in the Crunchy Blackberry Isle Salad formula and add the following:

Pineapple, crushed and drained	1 qt. *or* ½ #10 can	2 qt. *or* 1 #10 can	1 gal. *or* 2 #10 cans	2 gal. *or* 4 #10 cans
Cabbage, chopped or shredded, EP	1 qt. *or* 12 oz.	2 qt. *or* 1 lb. 8 oz.	1 gal. *or* 3 lb.	2 gal. *or* 6 lb.

1. Put 1 qt. crushed pineapple and 1 qt. chopped or shredded cabbage in each pan.

JELLIED LIME, PINEAPPLE, AND CELERY SALAD

Cut 8 × 4 12 × 20 × 2 Pan	32 Portions 1 Pan	64 Portions 2 Pans	128 Portions 4 Pans	256 Portions 8 Pans
Water, boiling	1 qt.	2 qt.	1 gal.	2 gal.
Gelatin, lime	1 lb.	2 lb.	4 lb.	8 lb.
Water, cold	1 qt.	2 qt.	1 gal.	2 gal.
Pineapple Juice	2 cups	1 qt.	2 qt.	1 gal.
Pineapple, crushed or tidbits, drained	½ #10 can *or* 1 qt.	1 #10 can *or* 2 qt.	2 #10 cans *or* 1 gal.	4 #10 cans *or* 2 gal.
Celery, finely sliced, EP	1 qt. *or* 1 lb.	2 qt. *or* 2 lb.	1 gal. *or* 4 lb.	2 gal. *or* 8 lb.
Cheese, optional	8 oz.	1 lb.	2 lb.	4 lb.

1. Add gelatin to boiling water. Stir to dissolve completely.
2. Add cold water and pineapple juice. Stir to mix.
3. Put 2 qt. 2 cups gelatin mixture into each 12 × 20 × 2 pan. Allow to chill until syrupy.
4. Put 1 qt. pineapple (crushed or tidbits) and 1 qt. (or 1 lb. EP) sliced celery into each 12 × 20 × 2 pan. Stir to mix in each pan.
5. Chill in refrigerator overnight until set.
6. Cut each pan 8 × 4 for 32 portions per pan.

Figure 24   This Jellied Lime, Pineapple, and Celery Salad is a colorful addition
to the salad menu.

JELLIED PEACH SLAW

Cut 8 × 4 12 × 20 × 2 Pan	32 Portions 1 Pan	64 Portions 2 Pans	128 Portions 4 Pans	256 Portions 8 Pans
Water, boiling	1 qt.	2 qt.	1 gal.	2 gal.
Gelatin, cherry	1 lb.	2 lb.	4 lb.	8 lb.
Water, cold	1 qt. 1 cup	2 qt. 2 cups	1 gal. 1 qt.	2 gal. 2 qt.
Lemon Juice	1 cup	2 cups	1 qt.	2 qt.
Peaches, diced and drained	1 qt. *or* ½ #10 can	2 qt. *or* 1 #10 can	1 gal. *or* 2 #10 cans	2 gal. *or* 4 #10 cans
Cabbage, shredded fine, EP	1 qt. *or* 12 oz.	2 qt. *or* 1 lb. 8 oz.	1 gal. *or* 3 lb.	2 gal. *or* 6 lb.

1. Add gelatin to boiling water. Stir to dissolve completely.
2. Add cold water and lemon juice. Stir to mix.
3. Put 2 qt. 2 cups gelatin mixture into each 12 × 20 × 2 pan. Chill until syrupy.
4. Add 1 qt. diced peaches and 1 qt. shredded (or chopped) cabbage to each pan. Stir until well-mixed.
5. Chill in refrigerator overnight.

JELLIED PINEAPPLE SLAW

1. The preceding Jellied Peach Slaw is excellent with pineapple substituted for peaches in the following amounts:

Pineapple Tidbits, crushed and drained	1 qt. *or* ½ #10 can	2 qt. *or* 1 #10 can	1 gal. *or* 2 #10 cans	2 gal. *or* 4 #10 cans

Note: This salad is particularly attractive for Christmas. It has a beautiful combination of the red gelatin color and the white flecks of chopped cabbage throughout.

JELLIED PINEAPPLE-CRANBERRY SLAW

Cut 8 × 4 12 × 20 × 2 Pan	32 Portions 1 Pan	64 Portions 2 Pans	128 Portions 4 Pans	256 Portions 8 Pans
Cooked **Cranberries**				
Water, boiling	¾ cup	1½ cups	3 cups	1 qt. 2 cups
Sugar	8 oz.	1 lb.	2 lb.	4 lb.
Cranberries, raw	8 oz.	1 lb.	2 lb.	4 lb.
Gelatin Salad				
Water, boiling	1 qt.	2 qt.	1 gal.	2 gal.
Gelatin, cherry	1 lb.	2 lb.	4 lb.	8 lb.
Water, cold	1 qt. 1 cup	2 qt. 2 cups	1 gal. 1 qt.	2 gal. 2 qt.
Lemon Juice	1 cup	2 cups	1 qt.	2 qt.
Cranberries, cooked	2 cups	1 qt.	2 qt.	1 gal.
Pineapple, tidbits or crushed, drained	2 cups	1 qt. *or* ½ #10 can	2 qt. *or* 1 #10 can	1 gal. *or* 2 #10 cans
Cabbage, shredded fine or chopped, EP	1 qt. *or* 12 oz.	2 qt. *or* 1 lb. 8 oz.	1 gal. *or* 3 lb.	2 gal. *or* 6 lb.

1. Cook the cranberries a day ahead and chill in the refrigerator overnight.
2. To prepare gelatin salad, add gelatin to boiling water. Stir to dissolve completely.
3. Add cold water and lemon juice. Stir to mix.
4. Add cooked cranberries.
5. Put 3 qt. mixture into 12 × 20 × 2 pan. Chill until syrupy.
6. Add 2 cups pineapple (crushed or tidbits) and 1 qt. cabbage (shredded or chopped) to each pan. Stir until well-mixed.
7. Chill in refrigerator overnight.

JELLIED LEMON OR LIME WALDORF SALAD

4-oz. Molds 12 × 20 × 2 Pan	32 Portions 1 Pan	64 Portions 2 Pans	128 Portions 4 Pans	256 Portions 8 Pans
Water, boiling	1 qt.	2 qt.	1 gal.	2 gal.
Gelatin, lemon *or* lime	1 lb.	2 lb.	4 lb.	8 lb.
Water, cold	1 qt. 3½ cups	3 qt. 3 cups	1 gal. 3 qt.	3 gal. 3 qt.
Lemon Juice	½ cup	1 cup	2 cups	1 qt.
Salt	1 tsp.	2 tsp.	1 Tbsp. 1 tsp.	1¼ oz.

Walnuts *or*
  Pecans,
  chopped ¼",
  optional
	2 oz.	4 oz.	8 oz.	1 lb.

Celery, cubed ¼", EP	8 oz. *or* 2 cups	1 lb. *or* 1 qt.	2 lb. *or* 2 qt.	4 lb. *or* 1 gal.

Red Apples, AP,
  unpeeled,
  cubed ¼", EP
	1 lb. 12 oz.
	or 1 qt.
	2 cups
		3 lb. 8 oz.
		or 3 qt.
			7 lb. *or*
			1 gal.
			2 qt.
				14 lb. *or*
				3 gal.

1. Add gelatin to boiling water. Stir until completely dissolved.
2. Add cold water, lemon juice, and salt. Stir to mix.
3. Chill gelatin mixture in pans in refrigerator (3 qt. per pan) until slightly thickened or syrupy.
4. Add nuts, celery, and apples to slightly thickened gelatin mixture, Put in pans or 4-oz. fluted molds.
5. Chill in refrigerator overnight until set.

Note: This salad is more attractive in individual molds than in pans. If 12 × 20 × 2 pans are used, put the following into each pan when slightly thickened: 2 oz. nuts, 2 cups celery, 1 qt. 2 cups apples, and 3 qt. gelatin mixture. Chill overnight in refrigerator until set. Cut pans 8 × 4.

Note: This salad also may be made with any red gelatin such as strawberry or raspberry. Omit lemon juice with red colors and increase amounts of cold water to the following:

Water, cold	2 qt.	1 gal.	2 gal.	4 gal.

JELLIED CRANBERRY WALDORF

Cut 8 × 4 12 × 20 × 2 Pan	96 Portions 3 Pans	192 Portions 6 Pans	384 Portions 12 Pans	768 Portions 24 Pans
Water, boiling	3 qt.	1 gal. 2 qt.	3 gal.	6 gal.
Gelatin, strawberry	3 lb.	6 lb.	12 lb.	24 lb.
Sugar	4 lb.	8 lb.	16 lb.	32 lb.
Water, cold	3 qt.	1 gal. 2 qt.	3 gal.	6 gal.
Cranberries, raw	4 lb.	8 lb.	16 lb.	32 lb.
Oranges	6	12	24	48
Celery, chopped ¼″, EP	2 lb.	4 lb.	8 lb.	16 lb.

Apples, raw,
    unpeeled, diced
    ¼″, EP
	2 lb.	4 lb.	8 lb.	16 lb.

1. Add gelatin and sugar to boiling water. Stir to dissolve completely.
2. Add cold water.
3. Grind cranberries with oranges. Add to gelatin mixture.
4. Add chopped celery and apples.
5. Put approximately 1 gal. mixture in each 12 × 20 × 2 pan.
6. Chill overnight in refrigerator until firm.

Figure 25   Jellied Waldorf Salads served in crisp lettuce cups are popular and inexpensive items in virtually every quantity foodservice operation. These colorful salads have been set in individual molds, turned onto the lettuce cup, and garnished with parsley and apple slices.

JELLIED AUTUMN GINGER ALE WALDORF

4-oz. Molds *or* 4-oz. Souffle Cups 12 × 20 × 2 Pan	32 Portions 1 Pan	64 Portions 2 Pans	128 Portions 4 Pans	256 Portions 8 Pans
Water, boiling	1 qt.	2 qt.	1 gal.	2 gal.
Gelatin, lemon	1 lb. 4 oz.	2 lb. 8 oz.	5 lb.	10 lb.
Pineapple Syrup *or* Juice, cold	1 qt.	2 qt.	1 gal.	2 gal.
Ginger Ale, dry	1 qt.	2 qt.	1 gal.	2 gal.
Black Walnuts *or* Pecans, chopped ¼″	4 oz.	8 oz.	1 lb.	2 lb.
Pineapple Tidbits, Diced Pears, *or* Peaches, drained	2 cups	1 qt.	2 qt.	1 gal.
Red Apples, AP, unpeeled cubed ½″, EP	1 lb. 12 oz. *or* 1 qt. 2 cups	3 lb. 8 oz. *or* 3 qt.	7 lb. *or* 1 gal. 2 qt.	15 lb. *or* 3 gal.

1. Add gelatin to boiling water. Stir until dissolved completely.
2. Add cold pineapple juice and cool over crushed ice.
3. When this mixture begins to thicken, add the ginger ale.
4. Add pineapple tidbits, pears, or peaches, along with nuts and apples, to slightly thickened gelatin mixture.
5. Put in fluted 4-oz. molds or put 1 gal. in each 12 × 20 × 2 pan.
6. Chill in refrigerator overnight until set.

Note: White seedless grapes may be substituted for pineapple tidbits, diced pears, or peaches.

CIDER WALDORF SALAD MOLDS

4-oz. Molds 12 × 20 × 2 Pan	32 Portions 1 Pan	64 Portions 2 Pans	128 Portions 4 Pans	256 Portions 8 Pans
Apple Cider, hot	1 qt.	2 qt.	1 gal.	2 gal.
Gelatin, lemon *or*				
apple	1 lb. 8 oz.	3 lb.	6 lb.	12 lb.
Apple Cider, cold	2 qt.	1 gal.	2 gal.	4 gal.
Lemon Juice	½ cup	1 cup	2 cups	1 qt.
Salt	1 tsp.	2 tsp.	1 Tbsp. 1 tsp.	1¼ oz.
Carrots, grated, EP	6 oz.	12 oz.	1 lb. 8 oz.	3 lb.
Celery, chopped ¼″, EP	8 oz.	1 lb.	2 lb.	4 lb.
Red Apples, unpeeled and cubed ¼″, AP	1 lb. *or* 1 qt.	2 lb. *or* 2 qt.	4 lb. *or* 1 gal.	8 lb. *or* 2 gal.

1. Add gelatin to boiling cider. Stir to dissolve completely.
2. Add cold cider, lemon juice, and salt. Stir to mix.
3. Chill gelatin mixture in refrigerator.
4. When syrupy, add grated carrots, chopped celery, and apples. Mix to combine.
5. Put into pans or fluted 4-oz. molds and refrigerate overnight.

Note: Apple juice may be used in place of cider, but cider gives the salad its tangy flavor.

CRANBERRY JEWEL SALAD

Cut 8 × 4 12 × 20 × 2 Pan	64 Portions 2 Pans	128 Portions 4 Pans	256 Portions 8 Pans	512 Portions 16 Pans
Water, boiling	1 qt. 2 cups	3 qt.	1 gal. 2 qt.	3 gal.
Gelatin, raspberry	1 lb. 8 oz.	3 lb.	6 lb.	12 lb.
Water, cold	1 qt.	2 qt.	1 gal.	2 gal.
Oranges, whole	6	12	24	48
Cranberry Sauce, whole *or* jellied	1 #10 can	2 #10 cans	4 #10 cans	1 case 2 #10 cans

1. Add raspberry gelatin to boiling water. Stir until dissolved completely.
2. Add cold water and stir to mix. Chill in refrigerator until mixture becomes slightly thickened or syrupy.
3. Wash and remove blemishes from oranges. Cut into quarters and remove seeds.
4. Put quarters through food chopper or put in blender.
5. Add ground orange mixture to canned, whole cranberry sauce. (If jellied cranberry sauce is used, beat with wire or balloon whip until smooth and then add oranges.)
6. Fold cranberry and orange mixture into slightly thickened raspberry gelatin.
7. Put 3 qt. 2 cups into each 12 × 20 × 2 pan.
8. Serve in squares as a salad on lettuce or chicory, or serve as a relish. If served as a relish, the salad may be molded in paper souffle cups.

CRANBERRY-ORANGE STAR SALAD

4-oz. Star Molds	32 Portions	64 Portions	128 Portions	256 Portions
Cranberries, fresh	2 lb.	4 lb.	8 lb.	16 lb.
Oranges, fresh, medium *or* large	4	8	16	32
Sugar	2 lb. 8 oz.	5 lb.	10 lb.	20 lb.
Water, boiling	1 qt. 2 cups	3 qt.	1 gal. 2 qt.	3 gal.
Gelatin, lemon flavored	1 lb.	2 lb.	4 lb.	8 lb.

1. Grind cranberries and oranges together in the food cutter until pieces are very small. No large chunks of orange or cranberry should be visible.
2. Add sugar to cranberry and orange mixture. Mix thoroughly. Allow to stand 1 to 2 hours if possible.
3. Dissolve lemon gelatin in boiling water. Allow to cool while cranberry, orange, and sugar mixture is standing.
4. At end of 1 or 2 hours, combine gelatin with cranberries.
5. Dip into 4-oz. star molds.
6. Refrigerate overnight.

Note: This is excellent as a relish in a 2-oz. souffle cup. Portions would be double the number listed.

CHERRY-CRANBERRY MIST

4-oz. Souffle Cup	48 Portions	96 Portions	192 Portions	384 Portions
Water, boiling	1 qt.	2 qt.	1 gal.	2 gal.
Gelatin, cherry	12 oz.	1 lb. 8 oz.	3 lb.	6 lb.
Sugar	1 lb. 5 oz.	2 lb. 10 oz.	5 lb. 4 oz.	10 lb. 8 oz.
Lemon Juice	¼ cup	½ cup	1 cup	2 cups
Pineapple Juice	1 qt.	2 qt.	1 gal.	2 gal.
Celery, chopped ⅛″, EP	1 lb. *or* 1 qt.	2 lb. *or* 2 qt.	4 lb. *or* 1 gal.	8 lb. *or* 2 gal.
Cranberries, raw, chopped *or* ground	1 lb. *or* 1 qt.	2 lb. *or* 2 qt.	4 lb. *or* 1 gal.	8 lb. *or* 2 gal.
Oranges, ground fine	4 *or* 3 cups	8 *or* 1 qt. 2 cups	16 *or* 3 qt.	32 *or* 1 gal. 2 qt.
Pineapple, crushed and drained	1 qt. *or* ½ #10 can	2 qt. *or* 1 #10 can	1 gal. *or* 2 #10 cans	2 gal. *or* 4 #10 cans
Pecans, chopped, optional	8 oz.	1 lb.	2 lb.	4 lb.

1. Add gelatin and sugar to boiling water. Stir to dissolve completely.
2. Add lemon juice and pineapple juice. Stir to mix.
3. While gelatin mixture is cooling, chop celery. Grind cranberries and oranges separately or chop finely in food cutter.
4. Combine celery, cranberries, oranges, and crushed pineapple. Mix to combine evenly.
5. Using #16 scoop, portion fruit into 4-oz. souffle cups.
6. Divide gelatin liquid into half and reserve second half.
7. Pour first half of liquid gelatin mixture over fruit in souffle cups. Pour only enough liquid over fruit to barely cover.
8. Put souffle cups in refrigerator until solid. This requires a long time, preferably overnight. Refrigerate remaining liquid overnight. It will set but may be melted.
9. Melt liquid, cool, and then pour remaining liquid on solid, congealed fruit. In this manner, a top of beautiful red-colored gelatin shows, and the fruit is in the bottom of the souffle.

Note: This is a soft congealed salad, and cannot be unmolded. The salad is not attractive if all of the gelatin mixture is poured on at the beginning. If the souffle cup is filled with the gelatin to the top, the fruit rises. The Cherry Cranberry Mist is excellent served with turkey salad or in place of cranberry sauce or relish, along with hot sliced turkey over dressing.

MOLDED PEACH AND STUFFED PRUNE SALAD

Cut 8 × 4 12 × 20 × 2 Pan	32 Portions 1 Pan	64 Portions 2 Pans	128 Portions 4 Pans	256 Portions 8 Pans
Water, boiling	1 qt.	2 qt.	1 gal.	2 gal.
Gelatin, lemon *or*				
red-colored	12 oz.	1 lb. 8 oz.	3 lb.	6 lb.
Water, cold	1 qt. 2 cups	3 qt.	1 gal. 2 qt.	3 gal.
Peach Halves, 30-				
35 count, drained	1 #10 can	2 #10 cans	4 #10 cans	1 case 2 cans
Prunes, cooked				
and pitted	2 cups	1 qt.	2 qt.	1 gal.
Cream Cheese	1 lb.	2 lb.	4 lb.	8 lb.
Milk	¼ cup	½ cup	1 cup	2 cups

1. Add gelatin to boiling water. Stir to dissolve completely.
2. Add cold water.
3. Put drained peach halves in pans 8 × 4. Pear halves may be used instead of peach halves. Place cut side up.
4. Put 2 qt. 2 cups dissolved gelatin mixture over peaches in each pan. Peaches should just be barely covered.
5. Combine cream cheese with milk. Using flat paddle, soften cheese until it will pass through a pastry tube.
6. Fill prunes with cream cheese.
7. When gelatin is almost set, top the center of each peach with a stuffed prune. Chill overnight.

Note: The preparation process may be hastened by placing souffle cups (step 8) in the freezer for quick setting. As soon as souffle cups have gelled, they may be taken from the freezer, the remaining liquid poured on the fruit gelatin, and then refrigerated until set.

GERALINE HARDWICK

Figure 26   Pitted prunes filled with cream cheese are set in pear halves and/or pineapple slices in lemon gelatin to form this unusual salad that may be served in a lettuce cup or on a bed of romaine.

SANTA CLARA PRUNE SALAD

Cut 8 × 4 12 × 20 × 2 Pan	32 Portions 1 Pan	64 Portions 2 Pans	128 Portions 4 Pans	256 Portions 8 Pans
Water, boiling	2 qt.	1 gal.	2 gal.	4 gal.
Gelatin, raspberry	1 lb. 8 oz.	3 lb.	6 lb.	12 lb.
Sugar	4 oz.	8 oz.	1 lb.	2 lb.
Water, cold	2 qt.	1 gal.	2 gal.	4 gal.
Prunes, cooked and pitted, chopped ½″	1 lb. 8 oz.	3 lb.	6 lb.	12 lb.
Pineapple, crushed and drained	1 lb. 8 oz.	3 lb.	6 lb.	12 lb.
Walnuts or Pecans, broken, optional	4 oz.	8 oz.	1 lb.	2 lb.

1. Add gelatin and sugar to boiling water. Stir to dissolve completely.
2. Add cold water. Stir to mix and pour into pans. Chill.
3. When gelatin mixture begins to thicken, add 3 cups prunes and 3 cups pineapple to each pan.
4. Sprinkle 4 oz. nuts on top of each pan.
5. Chill overnight.

Note: This salad stands quite high in the pans.

SELF-LAYERED SALAD
(Jellied Grapefruit and Pear Salad)

Cut 8 × 4 12 × 20 × 2 Pan	32 Portions 1 Pan	64 Portions 2 Pans	128 Portions 4 Pans	256 Portions 8 Pans
Water, boiling	1 qt.	2 qt.	1 gal.	2 gal.
Gelatin, cherry	1 lb.	2 lb.	4 lb.	8 lb.
Water, cold	1 qt.	2 qt.	1 gal.	2 gal.
Lemon Juice	½ cup	1 cup	2 cups	1 qt.
Pineapple Juice	1½ cups	3 cups	1 qt. 2 cups	3 qt.
Salt	¼ tsp.	½ tsp.	1 tsp.	2 tsp.
Pears, diced, drained	1 qt. *or* ½ #10 can	2 qt. *or* 1 #10 can	1 gal. *or* 2 #10 cans	2 gal. *or* 4 #10 cans
Grapefruit Sections	1 qt.	2 qt.	1 gal.	2 gal.

1. Dissolve gelatin in boiling water. Stir until dissolved completely.
2. Add cold water, lemon juice, pineapple juice, and salt. Stir to mix.
3. In each 12 × 20 × 2 pan, put 1 qt. drained diced pears. Pour 2 qt. 2 cups gelatin mixture into each pan.
4. Float 1 qt. grapefruit sections on each pan. Chill in refrigerator overnight.

Note: Pears sink to bottom and grapefruit floats, creating a layer of gelatin in between when cut. Drained, sliced peaches and sliced bananas may be substituted for the pears and grapefruit in equal amounts.

MOLDED RED FRUIT SALAD

Cut 8 × 4 12 × 20 × 2 Pan	32 Portions 1 Pan	64 Portions 2 Pans	128 Portions 4 Pans	256 Portions 8 Pans
Water, boiling	1 qt.	2 qt.	1 gal.	2 gal.
Gelatin, red, flavored	1 lb.	2 lb.	4 lb.	8 lb.
Water, cold	1 qt. 2 cups	3 qt.	1 gal. 2 qt.	3 gal.
Salt	1 tsp.	2 tsp.	1 Tbsp. 1 tsp.	1¼ oz.
Fruit, well- drained	2 qt.	1 gal.	2 gal.	4 gal.

1. Add gelatin to boiling water. Stir until dissolved completely.
2. Add cold water and salt. Stir to mix.
3. Put 2 qt. 2 cups gelatin mixture into each 12 × 20 × 2 pan.
4. Chill until syrupy.
5. Add 2 qt. drained fruit to each pan and stir to distribute uniformly.
   Any combination of fruit, or fruit cocktail may be used.

RED GELATIN FRUIT SALAD
(Fruit Cocktail Salad)

Cut 8 × 4 12 × 20 × 2 Pan	32 Portions 1 Pan	64 Portions 2 Pans	128 Portions 4 Pans	256 Portions 8 Pans
Water, boiling	1 qt.	2 qt.	1 gal.	2 gal.

Red Gelatin,
  strawberry *or*
  raspberry
	1 lb.	2 lb.	4 lb.	8 lb.

Water, cold	2 qt.	1 gal.	2 gal.	4 gal.

Apricots, sliced
  and drained
	1 qt. *or* ½
	  #10 can
		2 qt. *or* 1
		  #10 can
			1 gal. *or* 2
			  #10 cans
				2 gal. *or* 4
				  #10 cans

Pears, diced and
  drained
	1 qt. *or* ½
	  #10 can
		2 qt. *or* 1
		  #10 can
			1 gal. *or* 2
			  #10 cans
				2 gal. *or* 4
				  #10 cans

1. Add gelatin to boiling water. Stir until completely dissolved.
2. Add cold water and put 3 qt. of gelatin mixture into each pan. Chill until syrupy.
3. Add 1 qt. of each drained fruit to each pan. Mix to combine.
4. Chill overnight in refrigerator.

Note: This salad is also attractive if pitted Bing cherries (drained) and diced pears (drained) are used. Use 1 qt. of each fruit per 12×20×2 pan. Fruit cocktail may also be used, 2 qt. (drained) per pan.

JELLIED PEAR, PINEAPPLE, AND ORANGE SALAD

Cut 8 × 4 12 × 20 × 2 Pan	32 Portions 1 Pan	64 Portions 2 Pans	128 Portions 4 Pans	256 Portions 8 Pans
Water, boiling	1 qt.	2 qt.	1 gal.	2 gal.
Gelatin, orange	1 lb.	2 lb.	4 lb.	8 lb.
Water, cold	1 qt.	2 qt.	1 gal.	2 gal.
Lemon Juice	½ cup	1 cup	2 cups	1 qt.
Pineapple Juice	1½ cups	3 cups	1 qt. 2 cups	3 qt.
Salt	¼ tsp.	½ tsp.	1 tsp.	2 tsp.
Pears, diced and drained	1 qt. *or* ½ #10 can	2 qt. *or* 1 #10 can	1 gal. *or* 2 #10 cans	2 gal. *or* 4 #10 cans
Pineapple, crushed and drained	1 qt. *or* ½ #10 can	2 qt. *or* 1 #10 can	1 gal. *or* 2 #10 cans	2 gal. *or* 4 #10 cans

1. Dissolve gelatin in boiling water.
2. Add cold water, lemon juice, and pineapple juice. Stir to mix.
3. When mixture is partially set, add drained diced pears and drained crushed pineapple.
4. Put heaping 1 gal. in each 12 × 20 × 2 pan or put 4 oz. (½ cup) in a fluted mold.
5. Chill in refrigerator overnight.

BRANDIED BLACK BING CHERRY MOLD

4-oz. Molds	32 Molds	64 Molds	128 Molds	256 Molds
Water, boiling	1 qt. 1 cup	2 qt. 2 cups	1 gal. 1 qt.	2 gal. 2 qt.
Gelatin, black raspberry, grape, cherry, *or* lemon	1 lb. 4 oz.	2 lb. 8 oz.	5 lb.	10 lb.
Black Bing Cherry Juice	1 qt. 1 cup	2 qt. 2 cups	1 gal. 1 qt.	2 gal. 2 qt.
Salt	1 tsp.	2 tsp.	1 Tbsp. 1 tsp.	1¼ oz.
Brandy	¼ cup	½ cup	1 cup	2 cups
Lemon Juice	¼ cup	½ cup	1 cup	2 cups
Black Bing Cherries, pitted and drained	1 #10 can *or* 2 qt. 2 cups	2 #10 cans *or* 1 gal. 1 qt.	4 #10 cans *or* 2 gal. 2 qt.	8 #10 cans *or* 5 gal.

1. Add gelatin to boiling water. Stir to dissolve thoroughly.
2. Add cherry juice, salt, brandy, lemon juice, and cherries. Since the amount of cherries and juice in a #10 can varies from time to time, add enough water to juice to bring to specified amount.
3. Chill until slightly thickened.
4. Put in 4-oz. molds and chill in refrigerator overnight.
5. Serve with a sweetened sour cream dressing, cream dressing, or as a dessert with sweetened whipped cream.

JELLIED GRAPE AND GRAPEFRUIT MOLD

4-oz. Mold 9 × 13 Pan	30 Portions 2 Pans	60 Portions 4 Pans	120 Portions 8 Pans	240 Portions 16 Pans
Grape Juice, unsweetened, boiling	1 qt. 2 cups *or* 1 46-oz. can	3 qt. *or* 2 46-oz. cans	1 gal. 2 qt. *or* 4 46-oz. cans	3 gal. *or* 8 46-oz. cans
Gelatin, grape, lemon, or blackberry	1 lb. 6 oz.	2 lb. 12 oz.	5 lb. 8 oz.	11 lb.
Pineapple Juice, unsweetened, cold	1 qt. 2 cups *or* 1 46-oz. can	3 qt. *or* 2 46-oz. cans	1 gal. 2 qt. *or* 4 46-oz. cans	3 gal. *or* 8 46-oz. cans
Salt	1 tsp.	2 tsp.	1 Tbsp. 1 tsp.	2 Tbsp. 2 tsp.
Grapefruit Sections, fresh *or* canned, drained	1 qt.	2 qt.	1 gal.	2 gal.

1. Dissolve gelatin in boiling grape juice. Stir with French whip until dissolved completely.
2. Add cold pineapple juice and salt.
3. Chill gelatin mixture over crushed ice or in pans in the refrigerator. When cool, add grapefruit sections.
4. Chill in refrigerator overnight until set. Cut 9×13 pans 5×3. If 12×20×2 pans are used, they should be cut 8×4 and the yield will vary.

Note: Grape and pineapple juice and gelatin mixture may be chilled until partially set, grapefruit sections stirred in, and mixture then put in 4-oz. fluted molds.

Note: If grapefruit sections are put in pans, be sure mixture is cold. Grapefruit sections will float. Grapefruit sections may be omitted. Chill juice mixture in flat pans overnight until set and serve as a dessert with sliced bananas and 1 tsp. whipped cream on top of each square.

SPICY ROSY APPLESAUCE MOLD
(Crimson Salad)

Cut 8 × 4 12 × 20 × 2 Pan	1 Gallon 32 Portions 1 Pan	2 Gallons 64 Portions 2 Pans	4 Gallons 128 Portions 4 Pans	8 Gallons 256 Portions 8 Pans
Water, boiling	1 qt.	2 qt.	1 gal.	2 gal.
Gelatin, lemon *or* apple	1 lb.	2 lb.	4 lb.	8 lb.
Cinnamon Imperial Candies	8 oz.	1 lb.	2 lb.	4 lb.
Applesauce, canned	1 #10 can	2 #10 cans	4 #10 cans	1 case 2 cans
Vinegar	¼ cup	½ cup	1 cup	2 cups

1. Add gelatin and cinnamon imperials to boiling water. Stir to dissolve completely.
2. Add applesauce and vinegar. Stir to blend.
3. Put a heaping 1 gal. of mixture in each 12 × 20 × 2 pan.
4. Chill in refrigerator overnight.

Note: A real beauty with roast pork, baked ham, or turkey.

JELLIED APPLESAUCE

Follow the preceding formula for Spicy Rosy Applesauce Mold, omitting the cinnamon imperials. The Jellied Applesauce may also be used as a dessert.

RED CHERRY RING MOLD

4-oz. Molds	24 Molds	48 Molds	72 Molds	96 Molds
Red Cherries, RSP, drained	½ #10 can	1 #10 can	1½ #10 cans	2 #10 cans
Gelatin, unflavored	1¼ oz.	2½ oz.	3¾ oz.	5 oz.
Water, cold	½ cup	1 cup	1½ cups	2 cups
Cherry Juice and Water, hot	2½ cups	1 qt. 1 cup	1 qt. 3½ cups	2 qt. 2 cups
Sugar	12 oz.	1 lb. 8 oz.	2 lb. 4 oz.	3 lb.
Salt	½ tsp.	1 tsp.	1½ tsp.	2 tsp.
Red Food Color	½ tsp.	1 tsp.	1½ tsp.	2 tsp.
Orange Juice	1 cup	2 cups	3 cups	1 qt.
Cottage Cheese	2 lb.	4 lb.	6 lb.	8 lb.

1. Hydrate (soften) gelatin in cold water.
2. Heat cherry juice and water to a boil.
3. Add softened gelatin to hot cherry juice and stir until gelatin has dissolved.
4. Add salt, red food color, and orange juice.
5. Arrange drained cherries in each ring mold.
6. Fill each mold to the top with gelatin mixture.
7. Chill overnight in the refrigerator until firm.
8. Unmold and serve with a #50 scoop of cottage cheese in center of ring mold.
9. Serve with 1 Tbsp. of Sour Cream Dressing (see following formula).
10. Garnish with chicory or watercress.

SOUR CREAM DRESSING

Sour Cream	2 cups	1 qt.	1 qt. 2 cups	2 qt.
Sugar, confectioner's	2 Tbsp.	1 oz.	1½ oz.	2 oz.

1. Combine sour cream and confectioner's sugar. Stir to mix.

RED RASPBERRY RING MOLD

4-oz. Mold	**24 Molds**	**48 Molds**	**72 Molds**	**96 Molds**
Raspberries, frozen, defrosted, and drained	1 qt.	2 qt.	3 qt.	1 gal.
Gelatin, unflavored	1 oz.	2 oz.	3 oz.	4 oz.
Water, cold	1 cup	2 cups	3 cups	1 qt.
Raspberry Juice, hot	1 qt.	2 qt.	3 qt.	1 gal.
Sugar	8 oz.	1 lb.	1 lb. 8 oz.	2 lb.
Red Color	½ tsp.	1 tsp.	1½ tsp.	2 tsp.

1. Defrost raspberries in refrigerator overnight.
2. Drain raspberries and save juice.
3. Soften gelatin in cold water.
4. Heat raspberry juice. Add sugar and heat to boiling.
5. Add softened gelatin and stir until gelatin has dissolved. Add red color.
6. Place 4 to 6 raspberries in each ring mold.
7. Pour gelatin mixture over raspberries.
8. Refrigerate overnight.
9. Unmold and serve with cottage cheese and Sour Cream Dressing (see preceding formula), or serve with ½ cup turkey salad in center of ring mold. Set up flat on plates and surround with chicory. This mold is very difficult to set up in lettuce cups.

PINEAPPLE COTTAGE CHEESE RING MOLD

4-oz. Molds	15 Molds	30 Molds	60 Molds	90 Molds
Pineapple Juice, hot	1½ cups	3 cups	1 qt. 2 cups	2 qt. 1 cup
Gelatin, unflavored	2 Tbsp.	1 oz.	2 oz.	3 oz.
Pineapple Juice, cold	½ cup	1 cup	2 cups	3 cups
Crushed Pineapple and Juice	1 cup	2 cups	1 qt.	1 qt. 2 cups
Cottage Cheese	1 lb. 8 oz.	3 lb.	6 lb.	9 lb.

1. Heat pineapple juice to boiling.
2. Hydrate (soften) gelatin in cold pineapple juice in a large bowl.
3. Add hot pineapple juice to softened gelatin and stir until gelatin has been dissolved.
4. Add crushed pineapple and juice and cottage cheese. Mix all ingredients together. Break up any large chunks of cottage cheese.
5. Put in ring molds. Chill in refrigerator overnight until set.
6. Unmold and serve with ½ cup fruit in center of mold.

Note: Set up on flat plates and surround with chicory. This mold is stiff enough to be set up in a lettuce cup.

LEMON-CHEESE MOLD

½ Cup Portions	24 Portions	48 Portions	96 Portions	192 Portions
Water, hot	1 cup	2 cups	1 qt.	2 qt.
Gelatin, lemon	6 oz.	12 oz.	1 lb. 8 oz.	3 lb.
Cream Cheese	1 lb.	2 lb.	4 lb.	8 lb.
Cottage Cheese	2 lb.	4 lb.	8 lb.	16 lb.
Cream, heavy	2 cups	1 qt.	2 qt.	1 gal.

1. Dissolve gelatin in boiling water. Allow to cool.
2. Blend cream cheese and cottage cheese in bowl of mixer for 5 to 10 minutes, or until smooth. Use flat beater for creaming.
3. Whip heavy cream until stiff. Fold whipped cream into cheese mixture.

4. Add cooled gelatin mixture and blend until smooth.
5. Put ½ cup mixture into individual pyrex custard cups.
6. Refrigerate overnight.
7. Unmold and serve cheese mold surrounded with fruit. This salad may be served in a large lettuce cup if a bed of shredded lettuce is used in center before placing mold on top.
8. This salad is particularly attractive if surrounded with fresh pineapple and whole strawberries.
9. Serve with a Lime Fruit French Dressing (see p. 166).

JELLIED LEMON-BANANA SALAD

Cut 8 × 4 12 × 20 × 2 Pan	1 Gal. 2 Qt. 32 Portions 1 Pan	3 Gallons 64 Portions 2 Pans	6 Gallons 128 Portions 4 Pans	12 Gallons 256 Portions 8 Pans
Water, boiling	2 qt.	1 gal.	2 gal.	4 gal.
Gelatin, lemon	1 lb. 8 oz.	3 lb.	6 lb.	12 lb.
Water, cold	2 qt.	1 gal.	2 gal.	4 gal.
Mayonnaise	2 cups	1 qt.	2 qt.	1 gal.
Bananas, sliced, EP	1 qt. 2 cups *or* 2 lb.	3 qt. *or* 4 lb.	1 gal. 2 qt. *or* 8 lb.	3 gal. *or* 16 lb.

1. Add gelatin to boiling water. Stir to dissolve completely.
2. Add cold water and mayonnaise. Mix to combine.
3. Refrigerate until thickened.
4. Put mixture in bowl of beater, add bananas, and whip on high speed in mixer for 5 minutes (begin on second speed to avoid splashing).
5. Put 1 gal. 2 qt. in each 12 × 20 × 2 pan.

Note: The following amounts of crushed pineapple (drained) may be added along with bananas:

Pineapple, crushed, drained	2 cups	1 qt.	2 qt.	1 gal.

BAN-ORAN-GEL

Cut 8 × 4 12 × 20 × 2 Pan	3 Quarts 32 Portions 1 Pan	1 Gal. 2 Qt. 64 Portions 2 Pans	3 Gallons 128 Portions 4 Pans	6 Gallons 256 Portions 8 Pans
Water, boiling	1 qt.	2 qt.	1 gal.	2 gal.
Gelatin, lemon	12 oz.	1 lb. 8 oz.	3 lb.	6 lb.
Water, cold	1 qt.	2 qt.	1 gal.	2 gal.
Mayonnaise	1 cup	2 cups	1 qt.	2 qt.

Bananas, sliced,
  EP
	3 cups *or*
	  1 lb.
		1 qt.
		  2 cups *or*
		  2 lb.
			3 qt. *or*
			  4 lb.
				1 gal. 2 qt.
				  or 8 lb.

Orange Sections, drained	1 qt.	2 qt.	1 gal.	2 gal.

1. Add gelatin to boiling water. Stir to dissolve completely.
2. Add cold water and mayonnaise. Mix to combine.
3. Refrigerate until thickened.
4. Put mixture in bowl of beater, add bananas, and whip on high speed in mixer for 5 minutes. Begin to whip on second speed to avoid splashing.
5. Put 3 qts. mixture into each pan.
6. Add 1 qt. orange sections to each pan. Stir to mix.

Note: Mandarin oranges may be used in place of orange sections.

BAN-PINE-GEL

Follow the preceding formula for Ban-Oran-Gel, substituting pineapple (crushed or tidbits) for the orange sections. The salad will be more uniformly colored than when orange sections are used.

MOLDED MEXICAN CABBAGE SLAW

Cut 8 × 4 12 × 20 × 2 Pan	32 Portions 1 Pan	64 Portions 2 Pans	128 Portions 4 Pans	256 Portions 8 Pans
Water, boiling	1 qt. 2 cups	3 qt.	1 gal. 2 qt.	3 gal.
Gelatin, lemon *or* lime	1 lb.	2 lb.	4 lb.	8 lb.
Water, cold	1 qt. 1 cup	2 qt. 2 cups	1 gal. 1 qt.	2 gal. 2 qt.
Vinegar, cider	1 cup	2 cups	1 qt.	2 qt.
Salt	1 tsp.	2 tsp.	1 Tbsp. 1 tsp.	1¼ oz.
Celery, cubed ¼″, EP	2 cups *or* 8 oz.	1 qt. *or* 1 lb.	2 qt. *or* 2 lb.	1 gal. *or* 4 lb.
Cabbage, minced, EP	1 qt. 2 cups *or* 1 lb. 8 oz.	3 qt. *or* 3 lb.	1 gal. 2 qt. *or* 6 lb.	3 gal. *or* 12 lb.
Pimiento, chopped	4 oz.	8 oz.	1 lb.	2 lb.

1. Add gelatin to boiling water. Stir to dissolve completely.
2. Add cold water, vinegar, and salt. Stir to mix.
3. Chill gelatin mixture in pans in refrigerator (3 qt. per pan) until slightly thickened or syrupy.
4. Add 2 cups celery, 1 qt. 2 cups cabbage, and ½ cup pimiento per pan. Stir to mix well and distribute evenly.
5. Chill in refrigerator overnight until set.

Note: Celery and cabbage may be marinated in vinegar before being added to gelatin mixture. Do not marinate more than 15 minutes. This salad is quite tart and the vinegar may be reduced by half.

MOLDED SPRING SALAD

Cut 8 × 4 12 × 20 × 2 Pans	32 Portions 1 Pan	64 Portions 2 Pans	128 Portions 4 Pans	256 Portions 8 Pans
Water, boiling	1 qt. 2 cups	3 qt.	1 gal. 2 qt.	3 gal.
Gelatin, lemon	1 lb.	2 lb.	4 lb.	8 lb.
Water, cold	1 qt.	2 qt.	1 gal.	2 gal.
Cucumber, AP	2	4	8	16
or	*or*	*or*	*or*	*or*
Cucumber, peeled, chopped ⅛″, EP	3 cups	1 qt. 2 cups	3 qt.	1 gal. 2 qt.
Celery, chopped ⅛″, EP	12 oz. *or* 3 cups	1 lb. 8 oz. *or* 1 qt. 2 cups	3 lb. *or* 3 qt.	6 lb. *or* 1 gal. 2 qt.
Green Onions, chopped fine, EP	½ cup	1 cup	2 cups	1 qt.
Radishes, thinly sliced, EP	1½ cups	3 cups	1 qt. 2 cups	3 qt.
Vinegar, cider	½ cup	1 cup	2 cups	1 qt.
Salt	1 oz.	2 oz.	4 oz.	8 oz.

1. Add gelatin to boiling water. Stir until completely dissolved.
2. Add cold water and stir to mix.
3. Put 2 qt. 2 cups gelatin mixture into each 12 × 20 × 2 pan and allow to become syrupy.
4. Combine vegetables, vinegar, and salt and let stand to marinate for not more than 15 minutes. (If allowed to stand longer, more juice is extracted from the vegetables, and salad will not set as it should.)
5. Add 2 qt. combined vegetables to each pan and mix to distribute the vegetables evenly.
6. Chill in refrigerator overnight to set.

MOLDED GARDEN VEGETABLE SALAD

The Molded Spring Salad is particularly attractive with variations in vegetables. Follow the preceding formula, add the following and omit radishes and green onion:

Tomatoes, cubed ½", EP	2½ cups	1 qt. 1 cup	2 qt. 2 cups	1 gal. 1 qt.
Cucumbers, AP, cubed ¼"	2½ cups	1 qt. 1 cup	2 qt. 2 cups	1 gal. 1 qt.
Celery, cubed ¼", EP	3 cups	1 qt. 2 cups	3 qt.	1 gal. 2 qt.

Note: Tomatoes must be firm.

BASIC TOMATO ASPIC

Cut 5 × 3 9 × 13 Pan	30 Portions 2 Pans	60 Portions 4 Pans	120 Portions 8 Pans	240 Portions 16 Pans
Tomato Juice, hot	2 qt. 2 cups	1 gal. 1 qt.	2 gal. 2 qt.	5 gal.
Gelatin, unflavored	1½ oz.	3 oz.	6 oz.	12 oz.
Tomato Juice, cold	2 cups	1 qt.	2 qt.	1 gal.
Pepper, white	¼ tsp.	½ tsp.	1 tsp.	2 tsp.
Celery Salt	½ tsp.	1 tsp.	2 tsp.	1 Tbsp. 1 tsp.
Salt	2 tsp.	1 Tbsp. 1 tsp.	1¼ oz.	2½ oz.
Lemon Juice	½ cup	1 cup	2 cups	1 qt. 2 cups

1. Heat first amount of tomato juice to a boil.
2. Add unflavored gelatin and combined seasonings to cold tomato juice. Allow to hydrate (swell).
3. Add hydrated gelatin mixture to hot tomato juice and stir to dissolve completely.
4. Add lemon juice.
5. Put 1 qt. 2 cups mixture into each 9 × 13 pan. Two 9 × 13 pans equal one 12 × 20 × 2 pan. If using the larger pan, put 3 qt. in each.
6. Chill overnight in refrigerator to set.

TOMATO ASPIC WITH OLIVES

Use the preceding formula for Basic Tomato Aspic, adding the following amounts of olives as the mixture begins to set:

Olives, stuffed, sliced	1 cup	2 cups	1 qt.	2 qt.

1. Sprinkle ½ cup stuffed olives on top of each 9×13 pan.

VEGETABLE ASPIC
(California Aspic)

1. Many canned or frozen vegetables may be added to the Basic Tomato Aspic. Canned and drained green beans or frozen, cooked green peas are two examples. Add 2 cups per 9×13 pan, or 1 qt. per 12×20×2 pan.
2. Many combinations of fresh vegetables may also be added to the Basic Tomato Aspic. Two examples are chopped cabbage and chopped celery. Add 1 cup per 9×13 pan, or 2 cups per 12×20×2 pan.

BASIC TOMATO ASPIC WITH PROTEIN SALAD
(A la Carte Salad)

1. Prepare Basic Tomato Aspic and cut in squares.
2. Top with a scoop of any of the following protein salad mixtures: salmon or seafood salad (crabmeat or shrimp), egg salad, or cottage cheese.
OR
1. Put a scoop of protein mixture on shredded lettuce or on shredded lettuce in a lettuce cup.
2. Surround the scoop of protein mixture with aspic cubes or a combination of aspic and avocado cubes.

TOMATO ASPIC WITH SLICED EGG

1. Prepare Basic Aspic and cut in squares.
2. Slice hard-cooked eggs.
3. Place hard-cooked egg slices on a tomato aspic square in diagonal fashion.
4. Serve with Russian or Combination Dressing (see pp. 145 and 154).
5. Garnish with chicory or watercress.

DEVILED EGGS IN ASPIC

Cut 5 × 3 9 × 13 Pan	30 Portions 2 Pans	60 Portions 4 Pans	120 Portions 8 Pans	240 Portions 16 Pans
Tomato Juice, hot	1 qt. 2 cups	3 qt.	1 gal. 2 qt.	3 gal.
Gelatin, unflavored	1 oz.	2 oz.	4 oz.	8 oz.
Tomato Juice, cold	2 cups	1 qt.	2 qt.	1 gal.
Pepper	⅛ tsp.	¼ tsp.	½ tsp.	1 tsp.
Celery Salt	¼ tsp.	½ tsp.	1 tsp.	2 tsp.
Salt	1 tsp.	2 tsp.	1 Tbsp. 1 tsp.	1¼ oz.
Lemon Juice	¼ cup	½ cup	1 cup	2 cups
Deviled Egg Halves (see p. 312)	30	60	120	240

1. Heat first amount of tomato juice to a boil.
2. Add unflavored gelatin and combined seasonings to cold tomato juice. Allow to hydrate (swell).
3. Add hydrated gelatin mixture to hot tomato juice and stir to dissolve gelatin completely.
4. Add lemon juice and stir to mix.
5. Put 1 qt. mixture in each 9 × 13 pan. Put a deviled egg half in the center of each 5 × 3 square of portion.

Note: Eggs must be ready before aspic is made.

TOMATO ASPIC RIBBON LOAF
(Three-Layer Tomato Aspic Ribbon Salad)

Cut 5 × 3 9 × 13 Pan	30 Portions 2 Pans	60 Portions 4 Pans	120 Portions 8 Pans	240 Portions 16 Pans
Tomato Juice, hot	2 qt.	1 gal.	2 gal.	4 gal.
Gelatin, unflavored	1 oz.	2 oz.	4 oz.	8 oz.
Pepper	⅛ tsp.	¼ tsp.	½ tsp.	1 tsp.
Celery Salt	¼ tsp.	½ tsp.	1 tsp.	2 tsp.
Salt	1 tsp.	2 tsp.	1 Tbsp. 1 tsp.	1¼ oz.
Lemon Juice	¼ cup	½ cup	1 cup	2 cups

1. Heat tomato juice to a boil.
2. Combine gelatin and seasonings. Mix well.
3. Slowly stir gelatin and seasonings into hot tomato juice, using a wire whip.
4. Add lemon juice and stir to mix.
5. Place 2 cups of this mixture into each 9 × 13 pan. Chill until firm. This may require 1 hour in the refrigerator. Reserve remaining aspic mixture.
6. While first portion of mixture is congealing, prepare Cottage Cheese Filling or Egg Salad Filling (see following formulas).
7. Spread 1¾ cups of prepared filling over the congealed bottom layer of aspic in the 9 × 13 pan. Chill until firm. This mixture sets quickly.
8. After the filling has become firm, put 2 cups of aspic on top and chill until firm, preferably overnight, in the refrigerator.

COTTAGE CHEESE FILLING
(Three-Layer Tomato Aspic Ribbon Salad)

Cut 5 × 3 9 × 13 Pan	30 Portions 2 Pans	60 Portions 4 Pans	120 Portions 8 Pans	240 Portions 16 Pans
Gelatin, unflavored	½ oz.	1 oz.	2 oz.	4 oz.
Water, cold	½ cup	1 cup	2 cups	1 qt.
Cottage Cheese	1 lb.	2 lb.	4 lb.	8 lb.
Mayonnaise	1 cup	2 cups	1 qt.	2 qt.

1. Hydrate (soften) the gelatin in cold water.
2. Using flat beater, blend cottage cheese in mixer until smooth and no large curds remain.
3. Add mayonnaise to cottage cheese, and blend.
4. Dissolve softened gelatin over boiling water.
5. Add softened gelatin to cottage cheese mixture.
6. Hold mixture over hot water. This mixture must be liquid enough so that it can be poured over the aspic and spread evenly.
7. Spread 1¾ cups of the cottage cheese mixture over the congealed bottom layer of aspic in the 9 × 13 pan. Chill until firm. This mixture sets quickly.
8. After the cheese mixture has become firm, put 2 cups of the aspic mixture on top of the cottage cheese and chill until firm, preferably overnight, in the refrigerator.
9. Serve 1 portion on a small lettuce cup, chicory, or watercress. Serve with 1 tsp. Mayonnaise or Combination Dressing (see p. 141 or 154).

EGG SALAD FILLING
(Three-Layer Tomato Aspic Ribbon Salad)

Cut 5 × 3 9 × 13 Pan	30 Portions 2 Pans	60 Portions 4 Pans	120 Portions 8 Pans	240 Portions 16 Pans
Gelatin, unflavored	½ oz.	1 oz.	2 oz.	4 oz.
Water, cold	¾ cup	1½ cups	3 cups	1 qt. 2 cups
Worcestershire Sauce	¼ tsp.	½ tsp.	1 tsp.	2 tsp.
Salt	1 tsp.	2 tsp.	1 Tbsp. 1 tsp.	1¼ oz.
Lemon Juice	2 Tbsp.	¼ cup	½ cup	1 cup
Mayonnaise or Salad Dressing	1 cup	2 cups	1 qt.	2 qt.
Celery, finely diced, EP	½ cup	1 cup	2 cups	1 qt.
Green Pepper, finely chopped, EP	¼ cup	½ cup	1 cup	2 cups
Pimiento, chopped	¼ cup	½ cup	1 cup	2 cups
Onion, grated	1½ tsp.	1 Tbsp.	2 Tbsp.	¼ cup
Hard-Cooked Eggs, chopped	3	6	12	24

1. Soften gelatin in cold water.
2. Dissolve gelatin over boiling water. Remove from heat.
3. Add Worcestershire sauce, salt, and lemon juice.
4. Add mayonnaise, onion, celery, green pepper, pimiento, and chopped hard-cooked eggs.
5. Spread 1¾ cups over the bottom layer of aspic in a 9 × 13 pan. Chill.

6. When egg salad is firm, put 2 cups of the aspic mixture on top of the firm egg salad mixture and chill until very firm.
7. Serve in the same manner as Cottage Cheese Filling in preceding formula.

Note: This salad may also be put in 5×9 loaf pans, unmolded, and served on a buffet table. The amounts in the pans may need adjusting.

TOMATO ASPIC RING MOLDS

4-oz. Molds	17 Molds	34 Molds	68 Molds	136 Molds
Tomato Juice, hot	1 qt. 1 cup	2 qt. 2 cups	1 gal. 1 qt.	2 gal. 2 qt.
Gelatin, unflavored	1 oz.	2 oz.	4 oz.	8 oz.
Tomato Juice, cold	1 cup	2 cups	1 qt.	2 qt.
Olives, stuffed, sliced, to garnish				

1. Hydrate (soften) gelatin in cold tomato juice.
2. Add softened gelatin to hot tomato juice and stir to dissolve.
3. Put mixture into 4-oz. ring molds. Chill overnight in refrigerator.
4. When ready to serve, dip mold quickly into very hot water and unmold onto tray. Allow to chill again if possible.
5. Place ring mold on salad plate.
6. Fill with a #50 scoop of cottage cheese or shrimp salad.
7. Top with 1 Tbsp. Russian, Thousand Island, Combination, or Green Goddess Salad Dressing II (see pp. 145, 154, or 149).
8. Top dressing with 2 slices stuffed olives.
9. Garnish with chicory or watercress.

A LA CARTE SALADS

There are five traditional categories of a la carte salad, all of them represented in this section. The categories include: 1) potato salads, 2) macaroni salads, 3) vegetable salads with protein, 4) a la carte protein salads, and 5) a la carte fruit salad.

POTATO SALAD

Although potato salad is a high-labor item, it is commonly prepared in quantity operations. It may be served in a lettuce cup, garnished with tomatoes and hard-cooked eggs or other protein foods, or served as an accompaniment to various types of sandwiches.

Two potato salad formulas have been included in this section. The first has been developed in amounts of up to 200 portions and lends itself to the manual peeling and slicing of cooked potatoes. This formula uses the method of boiling potatoes in their skins and peeling and slicing them by hand after cooking. Although this is an acceptable procedure for small amounts, it requires considerable labor even for 200 portions and should not be considered when more than 200 portions are being prepared.

The second formula has been developed in amounts of up to 800 portions. When preparing such large amounts, potatoes must be mechanically peeled and then sliced with a specially designed machine or on a vegetable slicer plate. After slicing, they should be placed in perforated pans, steamed, cooled, and combined with the other ingredients.

Potatoes should not be cooked a day ahead and held in the refrigerator because they develop a decided off-flavor when held overnight. The flavor does not seem to be affected if potatoes are cooled for only one or two hours in the refrigerator. After cooling, the potatoes should be combined with the dressing to prevent excessive oxidation of tannins. Although the potatoes themselves should not be cooked in advance and stored in the refrigerator, it is acceptable to prepare the salad a day ahead and refrigerate it overnight in shallow pans. It should be kept cold until serving time; chilling in the refrigerator should reduce the interior temperature to 40°F.

Potato salad is highly susceptible to "spoiling" (bacterial growth) because it is made with an egg product in the form of mayonnaise or salad dressing. It is important that the sanitation pro-

GERALINE HARDWICK

Figure 27   A generous serving of potato salad in a lettuce cup, deviled eggs, and tomato slices are combined here for an a la carte salad that may also be used for service with a sandwich or a luncheon entree.

cedures outlined in the formulas be followed during preparation and that these procedures be strictly supervised. If the potatoes are cooked and cooled, combined with cold salad dressing, panned, covered and refrigerated immediately, held at 40°F overnight, and maintained at that temperature until serving time, there should be no problem with control of bacterial growth.

Because potato salad is such a high-labor item, several preparation phases can be completed a day ahead in order to simplify work schedules. The celery may be prepared in advance if treated with an antioxidant, and the onions and green peppers may be cut and held tightly covered in the refrigerator. Polyethylene bags are excellent for the refrigerated storage of onions, celery, and peppers.

As discussed earlier, cooked salad dressings may be made several days in advance and refrigerated in covered stock pots. On the day the salad is prepared, the celery, onions, and peppers may be combined with the cold, cooked salad dressing and added to the cooked potatoes. The salad dressing and vegetables can be combined at a central kitchen and the dressing sent to outlying operations in refrigerated containers, in a manner similar to the one recommended for central kitchen coleslaw preparation. The potatoes may be cooked in the individual operations, cooled, and combined with the dressing on the premises before serving.

The potato salad formulas in this section have been developed with a cooked salad dressing. In some instances, it may be appropriate to combine a cooked salad dressing with mayonnaise on a one-to-one basis or on a one-third (mayonnaise)-to-two-thirds (cooked dressing) basis. A potato salad may be made with mayonnaise only and the product will be completely acceptable, although it will be considerably more expensive to prepare and will lack the tart flavor that results when cooked salad dressing is used.

Hard-cooked eggs are often added to the potato salad mixture. When labor availability and scheduling permit, the use of sliced, hard-cooked eggs or deviled eggs on top of the salad makes a more colorful and appealing salad serving. In operations where limitations of time and labor make such a procedure impossible, the eggs may be coarsely chopped and mixed with the salad. It should be noted that yields in this text have been established without the use of eggs as a part of the basic mixture.

MACARONI SALAD

The procedures involved in the preparation of macaroni salad are similar to those for potato salad. The major difference is the lesser need for concern with discoloration or the development of off-flavors in macaroni. The macaroni may be cooked in the steam kettle and cooled by allowing cold water to run over it. After it has been thoroughly drained, the salad dressing and other ingredients may be added and the salad chilled until serving time. Macaroni salad may be refrigerated overnight in covered, shallow pans.

VEGETABLE SALADS WITH PROTEIN

The third category of a la carte salads includes those vegetable salads with substantial amounts of one or more protein items. These may be tossed salads with added protein—the Shrimp, Egg, and Tomato Salad Bowl, and the Crab Louie are two examples—or vegetable salads with a base of chopped lettuce topped with vegetable and protein items. Some operations feature an additional type of vegetable salad prepared on a large dinner plate with a flat green, such as romaine, as a base. It may be topped with slices of tomato, cucumber, and avocado, along with sliced cheeses or a generous round of cottage cheese as the protein ingredient.

The procedures involved in preparing these salads are the same as those for tossed salads. They include such factors as the importance of serving the salad thoroughly chilled, the preparation of vegetables in advance whenever possible, and the chilling of all ingredients prior to preparation. It is recommended that these salads be served with a French dressing.

A LA CARTE PROTEIN SALADS

The majority of a la carte salads contain a protein item or a combination of protein foods. An a la carte potato salad, for example, is often served with deviled or hard-cooked eggs. A more substantial quantity of protein is included in a la carte protein salads.

Figure 28   The popular a la carte Chef's Salad may be made with any number of ingredients and served with a variety of dressings. Here, the salad has been prepared with turkey strips, cheese strips, green beans, tomato, and sliced egg.

A large scoop (#10 or ½ cup) of a protein mixture is served either in a lettuce cup or on a plate surrounded by greens. The protein mixture may be of poultry, fish, or meat. In some instances, starches, fruits, or vegetables may be combined with the protein mixture; in other salads, the fruit or vegetables may surround the basic ingredient on the plate rather than being combined with it. As an example, a tuna or chicken salad may be surrounded with pineapple spears or other fresh fruit.

A LA CARTE FRUIT SALADS

The instructions for preparing a la carte fruit salads have been written without specific ingredient amounts or portion numbers because it is important, for reasons of economy, to use "in season" fruit whenever possible. So many fruits may be used in these salads that almost limitless substitutions are possible. The partial cans of fruit often leftover in foodservice kitchens may be used in these salads to provide variety and to reduce waste.

There are three basic methods of preparing a la carte fruit salads: 1) in a large lettuce cup with a base of greens or chopped lettuce, if needed, to serve as a foundation for the fruit; 2) as a tossed green salad, placed in a bowl and topped with fruit; and 3) with arrangements of fruit placed on a large salad plate and supported by a few greens or a flat green, such as romaine, for a base.

Although it does add to the cost of a fruit salad, many gourmet restaurants and other quantity operations in which cost is not a basic factor use fresh pineapple, papaya, and other tropical fruits year-round to create more distinctive salads. For added nutritional value, a protein item is often added to a la carte fruit salads. Cottage cheese, cream cheese balls, and nut bread sandwiches with cream cheese are standard favorites.

A LA CARTE SALAD-SANDWICH PLATES

In addition to the more traditional a la carte salad plates or bowls, many restaurants feature a combination salad-sandwich or salad-soup plate. The cold soups or the gourmet cream soups included in Part One could be served in a bowl or soup mug with any of the a la carte salads in this section to provide a nutritional and satisfying meal.

Salad-sandwich plates provide interesting combinations and assortments of foods. Standard sandwich service often includes a small side order of salad to accompany the sandwich. Conversely, in the salad-sandwich plate, the salad is the featured item with the sandwich or bread as an accompaniment. Many salad bars feature assorted breads and/or finger sandwiches as a part of the salad service.

Salad-sandwich plates have been given such intriguing titles as Dutch Plate, Vagabond Plate, Dixie Plate, and New England Plate, to name a few. As one example, the Dutch Plate might include slices of imported sausages, pastrami, smoked cheese, and Gouda cheese arranged on one quarter of a large dinner plate; an arrangement of salad items such as sliced tomatoes, cucumbers, and a dill pickle might fill the second quarter; a serving of crisp coleslaw on a bed of lettuce or in a souffle cup might fill the third quarter; and slices of rye bread or sliced, individual loaves of various breads might complete the salad-sandwich plate. A pat of butter, a jar of mustard and a small serving of mayonnaise, a beverage, and a dessert would provide a hearty and unusual meal.

The a la carte potato salad with tomato wedges or slices and deviled egg may include slices of bread and be called a Vagabond Plate, as it is in one major California operation. Hot or cold chicken could accompany the salad on a Dixie Plate, or fried clams for a Northeastern Plate. One west coast restaurant features a Dilly Beef Cartwheel—a salad-sandwich combination of lettuce, garden fresh vegetables, and cornucopias of roast beef arranged on bread slices. Although it could be described as an open-face sandwich, the preponderance of fresh vegetables with a sour cream dressing make it a salad accompanied by beef and bread. The number of combinations is virtually unlimited. For sandwich shops or restaurants with extended luncheon periods, these salad-sandwich plates are comparatively simple to prepare and add both variety and appeal to menu selections.

Figure 29   Jellied salads may be an important part of any combination meal. This one features navy bean soup, a cheese sandwich, and a jellied vegetable salad.

NUT TREE OF CALIFORNIA

Figure 30   This a la carte Dutch Plate includes slices of sausage, pastrami, smoked cheese, Gouda cheese, tomato, cucumber, dill pickle, crisp coleslaw, and is accompanied by slices from a small loaf of rye bread.

OLD-FASHIONED COUNTRY POTATO SALAD
(Potatoes Boiled, Hand Peeled and Sliced)

½ Cup Portion	24 Portions	48 Portions	96 Portions	192 Portions
Potatoes, AP, whole	7 lb.	14 lb.	28 lb.	56 lb.
Pepper, white	¼ tsp.	½ tsp.	1 tsp.	2 tsp.
Salt	1 Tbsp.	1 oz.	2 oz.	4 oz.
Pimiento, chopped ¼"	¼ cup	½ cup	1 cup	2 cups
Onion, chopped fine, EP	1½ oz.	3 oz.	6 oz.	12 oz.
Green Pepper, chopped fine, EP	2½ oz.	5 oz.	10 oz.	1 lb. 4 oz.
Celery, chopped ¼", EP	8 oz.	1 lb.	2 lb.	4 lb.
Eggs, hard-cooked, optional	6	12	24	48
Cooked Salad Dressing	1 qt.	2 qt.	1 gal.	2 gal.

1. Cook unpeeled potatoes in boiling water for approximately 20 minutes. They should be cooked several hours before salad is to be prepared. Do not cook a day ahead. Potatoes develop an off-flavor when held overnight.
2. Remove skins and slice potatoes approximately ⅛" crosswise. Place in large flat pans and chill in refrigerator.
3. When the potatoes have cooled, add all the ingredients and mix lightly. Allow to marinate in refrigerator for 2 hours.
4. Serve ½ cup in a large lettuce cup or ½ cup surrounded with chicory.
5. Garnish with 2 tomato slices or wedges and 1 sliced hard-cooked egg or other protein item.

COUNTRY POTATO SALAD
(Steamed, Mechanically Peeled and Sliced)

½ Cup Portions	3 Gallons 96 Portions	6 Gallons 192 Portions	12 Gallons 384 Portions	24 Gallons 768 Portions
12 × 20 × 2 Pan	2 Pans	4 Pans	8 Pans	16 Pans
12 × 20 × 4 Pan	1 Pan	2 Pans	4 Pans	8 Pans
Perforated 2″ Pan	2 Pans	4 Pans	8 Pans	16 Pans
Potatoes, peeled, sliced ¼″, EP	20 lb.	40 lb.	80 lb.	160 lb.
Cooked Salad Dressing	2 qt. 2 cups	1 gal. 1 qt.	2 gal. 2 qt.	5 gal.
Celery, chopped ¼″, EP	2 lb.	4 lb.	8 lb.	16 lb.
Green Pepper, chopped ¼″, EP	8 oz.	1 lb.	2 lb.	4 lb.
Onion, chopped ¼″, EP	6 oz.	12 oz.	1 lb. 8 oz.	3 lb.
Pimiento, chopped	4 oz.	8 oz.	1 lb.	2 lb.
Salt	2 oz.	4 oz.	8 oz.	1 lb.
Pepper, white	1 tsp.	2 tsp.	1 Tbsp. 1 tsp.	2 Tbsp. 2 tsp.

1. Peel potatoes in peeler. Slice on machine ¼", or use vegetable slicer plate.
2. Put 10 lb. sliced potatoes in each 2" perforated pan and steam at 5-lb. pressure for 25 minutes. Potatoes may also be cubed, although time for steaming may need to be reduced.
3. Upon removal from steamer, put pans of potatoes on racks. Roll to refrigerator and cool for 2 hours.
4. Empty potatoes into cold steam kettle.
5. Add dressing which has been combined with all vegetables and seasonings.
6. Mix lightly with paddle to prevent breaking up potatoes.
7. Portion 1 gal. 2 qt. in each 12 × 20 × 2 pan. Potato salad may also be put in 4" pans with 100 portions or 3 gal. per pan. Refrigerate immediately. Refrigerate covered overnight.

Note: Potato salad should be prepared a day ahead and refrigerated overnight in shallow pans. It must be kept thoroughly chilled.

Note: Mayonnaise may be substituted for Cooked Salad Dressing, although it is more expensive. Mayonnaise may also be substituted for ½ of the cooked salad dressing.

Note: Celery may be prepared a day ahead of salad. It must be treated with an antioxidant. Green pepper, onion, and pimiento also may be prepared a day ahead and held tightly covered in the refrigerator.

MACARONI SALAD

¾ Cup Portions	1 Gal. 1 Qt. 24 Portions	2 Gal. 2 Qt. 48 Portions	5 Gallons 96 Portions	10 Gallons 192 Portions
Macaroni, elbow	1 lb. 8 oz.	3 lb.	6 lb.	12 lb.
Water, boiling	2 qt.	1 gal.	2 gal.	4 gal.
Salt	1 Tbsp.	1 oz.	2 oz.	4 oz.
Red French Dressing	1 cup	2 cups	1 qt.	2 qt.
Onion, chopped fine, EP	3 oz.	6 oz.	12 oz.	1 lb. 8 oz.
Green Pepper, chopped fine, EP	6 oz.	12 oz.	1 lb. 8 oz.	3 lb.
Pimiento, chopped fine	3 oz.	6 oz.	12 oz.	1 lb. 8 oz.
Celery, cubed ¼″, EP	1 lb.	2 lb.	4 lb.	8 lb.
Pepper, white	½ tsp.	1 tsp.	2 tsp.	1 Tbsp. 1 tsp.
Monosodium Glutamate	1 tsp.	2 tsp.	1 Tbsp. 1 tsp.	2 Tbsp. 2 tsp.
Salt	1 Tbsp. 1½ tsp.	1½ oz.	3 oz.	6 oz.
Salad Dressing, cooked	3 cups	1 qt.	3 qt.	1 gal. 2 qt.

1. Cook macaroni in boiling salted water. Drain. Cool (macaroni may be cooled by running cold water over the cooked macaroni in the kettle).
2. Marinate drained macaroni in Red French Dressing (see p. 161).
3. Combine chopped onion, green pepper, pimiento, and celery. Add to marinated macaroni.
4. Add pepper, monosodium glutamate, salt, and cooked salad dressing.
5. Mix well to combine.

Note: For a different flavor, use half mayonnaise or ⅔ mayonnaise in place of Cooked Salad Dressing.

HAM, MACARONI AND EGG SALAD

Ham, cooked, julienne	1 lb.	2 lb.	4 lb.	8 lb.
Deviled Eggs *or* Egg Halves, hard-cooked	12	24	48	96
Tomatoes, medium, blanched and peeled	5 lb. *or* 15 medium	10 lb. *or* 30 medium	20 lb. *or* 60 medium	40 lb. *or* 120 medium

1. Set up ¾ cup Macaroni Salad in a lettuce cup (see preceding formula).
2. Add the ham by placing 1 oz. on top of the macaroni salad. Ham may be added directly to macaroni salad. Mix to combine.
3. Place ½ deviled egg or ½ hard-cooked egg on top of ham.
4. Place 4 tomato wedges around macaroni salad.

SHRIMP, MACARONI AND EGG SALAD

Follow the preceding formula for Ham, Macaroni, and Egg Salad, substituting an equal amount of shrimp for the ham. Salad shrimp or broken shrimp may be purchased for this salad.

TOSSED SALAD BOWL
WITH
SHRIMP, EGG, AND TOMATO

1. Line each salad bowl with a large lettuce cup.
2. Fill lettuce cup with 1 cup tossed greens (use Garden Green Salad or any other favorite combination of greens).
3. Place 6 to 8 large shrimp on top of greens.
4. Place 1 sliced hard-cooked egg on center top of greens.
5. Garnish with 4 tomato wedges.
6. Serve with Red French or Horseradish French Dressing (see pp. 161 and 162).

Note: This salad may be called Gulf Shrimp Salad Bowl.

SHRIMP LOUIE

1. Follow directions for Tossed Salad Bowl with Shrimp, Egg, and Tomato.
2. Serve with special Crab Louie Dressing (see p. 146).

CRAB LOUIE

1. Follow preceding formula for Shrimp Louie, substituting crabmeat for shrimp.
2. Serve with special Louie Dressing (see p. 146).

Note: Both the Shrimp Louie and Crab Louie may be set up on a large salad plate. The shrimp or crab may be placed on a mound of shredded or chopped lettuce. Salad may be garnished with egg and tomato wedges.

TOSSED SALAD BOWL
WITH
DRIED BEEF, JULIENNE CHEESE, EGG, AND TOMATO

1. Line each salad bowl with a large lettuce cup.
2. Fill lettuce cup with 1 cup tossed greens.
3. Place dried beef, julienne cheese, and sliced, hard-cooked egg on top of tossed salad greens.
4. Garnish with sliced cucumbers, sliced radishes, and tomato wedges, as shown in Figure 31. Center salad with watercress which has been circled by a green pepper ring.
5. Serve with Creamy Red French Dressing (see p. 147).

Note: Julienne beef, turkey, or ham—or cubed turkey or ham—may be substituted for the dried beef.

VOLUME FEEDING MANAGEMENT MAGAZINE

Figure 31   Julienne strips of dried beef and cheese, sliced egg and tomatoes, cucumbers, and sliced radishes top a bed of greens for an a la carte individual chef's salad.

MARINATED MACEDOINE OF VEGETABLES

1. This salad includes an attractive combination of 4 different vegetables, such as lima beans or peas (frozen and cooked), whole baby or sliced carrots (fresh-cooked or canned), shoestring beets (canned), green and wax beans (canned), cauliflowerets (fresh-cooked), or tomato wedges.
2. Marinate any 4 of the vegetables in Red French Dressing (see p. 161) to cover for 2 hours in the refrigerator. Drain.
3. Line a large salad bowl with a large lettuce cup.
4. Place ½ cup shredded or chopped lettuce in center of lettuce cup.
5. Arrange 4 different marinated vegetables (canned, frozen, or fresh-cooked) on top of shredded lettuce. Use approximately ¼ cup of each vegetable.
6. Place a scoop of cottage cheese in center of salad. A hard-cooked sliced egg may be used instead of cottage cheese, or 2 deviled egg halves may be used.

BROCCOLI, DEVILED EGG, AND TOMATO SALAD

¾ Cup Portions	24 Portions	48 Portions	96 Portions	192 Portions
Broccoli, fresh	4 bunches	8 bunches	16 bunches	32 bunches
Lettuce, Iceberg, EP	4 heads	8 heads	16 heads	32 heads
Tomatoes, medium, AP, blanched and peeled	12	24	48	96
Deviled Eggs	24	48	96	192

1. Prepare the broccoli early in the morning by removing the hard outside skin of stems.
2. Soak in salted water for 10 to 15 minutes.
3. Core lettuce heads and remove any dark or brown outer leaves. Wash by soaking in water 10 to 15 minutes. Drain. Separate into lettuce cups. Refrigerate.
4. Cook broccoli in boiling water uncovered only until tender and crisp. Refrigerate until serving time.
5. Blanch and peel tomatoes. Remove cores. Cut tomatoes in wedges, 8 wedges to a tomato. Refrigerate until serving time.
6. At setup time, place a large lettuce cup on a plate. Place approximately ¼ cup chopped lettuce in center of lettuce cup.
7. Place 2 to 3 sprigs of broccoli on top of chopped lettuce.
8. Place 2 halves of deviled egg on top of broccoli.
9. Place 4 tomato wedges around deviled eggs.
10. Serve with 2 Tbsp. Red French Dressing (see p. 161).

Note: Asparagus may be substituted for the broccoli.

DEVILED EGGS

	24 Portions 48 Halves	48 Portions 96 Halves	96 Portions 192 Halves	192 Portions 384 Halves
Eggs, whole, hard-cooked	24	48	96	192
Mustard, dry	1½ tsp.	1 Tbsp.	½ oz.	1 oz.
Salt	1½ tsp.	1 Tbsp.	1 oz.	2 oz.
Pepper, white	⅛ tsp.	¼ tsp.	½ tsp.	1 tsp.
Mayonnaise	½ cup	1 cup	2 cups	1 qt.
Vinegar	¼ cup 2 Tbsp.	¾ cup	1½ cups	3 cups
Pimiento, very finely chopped	2 Tbsp.	¼ cup	½ cup	1 cup
Green Pepper, very finely chopped, EP	2 Tbsp.	¼ cup	½ cup	1 cup

1. Simmer eggs 20 minutes or steam. Do not boil.
2. Immerse eggs in cold water immediately at end of 20-minute period.
3. Peel eggs and cut lengthwise. Put whites on tray. Put yolks in beater bowl of mixer. Use flat beater.
4. Add mustard, salt, and pepper to egg yolks. Beat on #2 speed until yolks are thoroughly broken.
5. Add mayonnaise and vinegar. Beat until very smooth. If necessary, turn machine to #3 speed for a smooth texture.
6. Add very finely chopped pimiento and green pepper by hand. Stir until well-mixed.
7. Put mixture in pastry tube and fill each egg half. Serve 2 halves per portion.

Note: The pimiento and green pepper are optional ingredients. They give the eggs a colorful appearance.

MANDARIN TURKEY OR CHICKEN SALAD

½ Cup Portion	24 Portions	48 Portions	96 Portions	192 Portions
Turkey *or* Chicken, cooked and cubed ½"	3 lb.	6 lb.	12 lb.	24 lb.
Salt	2 tsp.	1 Tbsp. 1 tsp.	1¼ oz.	2½ oz.
Celery, cubed ¼", EP	2 cups *or* 8 oz.	1 qt. *or* 1 lb.	2 qt. *or* 2 lb.	1 gal. *or* 4 lb.
Cooked Salad Dressing	1½ cups	3 cups	1 qt. 2 cups	3 qt.
Mayonnaise	1½ cups	3 cups	1 qt. 2 cups	3 qt.
Mandarin Oranges	½ #10 can	1 #10 can	2 #10 cans	4 #10 cans

1. A day ahead, simmer the turkey or chicken in water until tender. Remove from stock and refrigerate both turkey and stock overnight.
2. Cut turkey or chicken in cubes. Add salt.
3. Cube celery. Add to turkey.
4. Combine Cooked Salad Dressing and mayonnaise (see pp. 152, 141) and add to turkey. Mix to combine.
5. To prepare for service, surround ½ cup turkey salad in lettuce cup with ½ cup Mandarin oranges or use 2 Tbsp. Mandarin oranges and 2 Tbsp. white grapes per salad.

Note: Keep turkey cold at all times. If salad dressing and turkey are mixed together early in the morning, store immediately in the refrigerator until salad setup time. Store in flat pans no deeper than 2". Do not set up a day ahead of time.

Figure 32   A turkey salad with mandarin orange segments served in a lettuce cup with black olives, a souffle cup of cranberry gelatin, and a dark nut bread spread with cream cheese are combined here for an attractive a la carte salad plate.

CHICKEN SALAD WITH MELON SLICES

1. Use any chicken salad formula such as Chicken Vegetable Salad (see p. 318) or Turkey Mandarin Salad (see preceding formula).
2. Put a large scoop (#8, #10, or #12) of chicken salad in center of plate. Garnish with sprigs of watercress or endive. Chicken salad may be put in a lettuce cup if preferred.
3. Surround chicken salad mound with slices of cantaloupe, honeydew, crenshaw, or Casaba melon. Fresh pineapple slices may be used with the melon.
4. Serve with a Fruit French Dressing (see pp. 166–167).

Note: This salad is particularly attractive served on an oval plate with chicken salad in center and melon slices on either side.

SALMON-COTTAGE CHEESE SALAD

½ Cup Portion	24 Portions	48 Portions	96 Portions	192 Portions
Salmon, red, skinned, boned, flaked, and drained	2 lb. 6 oz.	4 lb. 12 oz.	9 lb. 8 oz.	19 lb.
Cottage Cheese	1 lb.	2 lb.	4 lb.	8 lb.
Celery, cubed, EP	4 oz.	8 oz.	1 lb.	2 lb.
Sweet Pickles, chopped	1 cup	2 cups	1 qt.	2 qt.
Cooked Salad Dressing	1 cup	2 cups	1 qt.	2 qt.
Tomatoes, ripe, peeled, cored, and chilled	24	48	96	192

1. Combine flaked red salmon with cottage cheese.
2. Add celery, chopped pickles, and Cooked Salad Dressing (see pp. 152–153).
3. Toss salmon, vegetables, and dressing together lightly.
4. Using a ½-cup measure or #10 scoop, portion salmon salad into tomato cup, which has been formed by partially cutting the tomato into 4 quarters and then spreading open.
5. Garnish with 1 Tbsp. Combination Dressing (see p. 154) and ripe olive or sliced stuffed olive.
6. This salad may also be served by portioning a #10 scoop onto a lettuce cup. Garnish with cucumber slices. Serve with Red French Dressing (see p. 161).

TUNA FISH SALAD

½ Cup Portion	48 Portions	96 Portions	192 Portions	384 Portions
Tuna, light, drained	7 lb.	14 lb.	28 lb.	56 lb.
Pimiento, diced ¼″	½ cup	1 cup	2 cups	1 qt.
Sweet Pickle Relish, drained	2½ cups	1 qt. 1 cup	2 qt. 2 cups	1 gal. 1 qt.
Onion, finely chopped, EP	4 oz.	8 oz.	1 lb.	2 lb.
Celery, cubed ⅛″, EP	2 lb. 8 oz.	5 lb.	10 lb.	20 lb.
Pepper, white	½ tsp.	1 tsp.	2 tsp.	1 Tbsp. 1 tsp.
Salt	2 tsp.	1 Tbsp. 1 tsp.	1¼ oz.	2½ oz.
Lemon Juice	½ cup	1 cup	2 cup	1 qt.
Mayonnaise	1 qt. 1 cup	2 qt. 2 cups	1 gal. 1 qt.	2 gal. 2 qt.

1. Drain tuna fish. If any pieces are large, flake into small chunks. Do not, however, break too fine. Chill tuna fish in refrigerator while preparing other ingredients.
2. Combine all other ingredients with mayonnaise.
3. Add mayonnaise mixture to chilled tuna fish.
4. Toss together lightly but thoroughly.
5. Refrigerate in 2″-deep pans if not using immediately.

HAWAIIAN TUNA SALAD

	48 Portions	56 Portions	192 Portions	384 Portions
Pineapple, sliced, drained, 52 count	2 #10 cans	4 #10 cans	1 case 2 #10 cans	2 cases 4 #10 cans

1. Prepare Tuna Fish Salad as detailed in preceding formula. Refrigerate mixture.
2. Drain pineapple.
3. Put a large lettuce cup on a salad plate.
4. Put 2 drained pineapple slices in center of lettuce.
5. Using a ½-cup measure or a #10 scoop, put tuna mixture onto lettuce cup. (It may be necessary for height to put chopped lettuce or mixed greens into lettuce cup before putting pineapple or salad mixture into cup.)
6. Put 1 Tbsp. Combination Dressing (see p. 154) on top of scoop of salad. Garnish with ripe olives or sliced, stuffed green olives.

CHICKEN VEGETABLE SALAD

½ Cup Portion	24 Portions	48 Portions	96 Portions	192 Portions
Chicken, cooked, diced	14 oz.	1 lb. 12 oz.	3 lb. 8 oz.	7 lb.
Peas, frozen, cooked, drained	1 lb. 2 oz.	2 lb. 4 oz.	4 lb. 8 oz.	9 lb.
Rice, cooked	1 lb. 4 oz.	2 lb. 8 oz.	5 lb.	10 lb.
Celery, finely diced, EP	10 oz.	1 lb. 4 oz.	2 lb. 8 oz.	5 lb.
Pimiento, diced	3 oz.	6 oz.	12 oz.	1 lb. 8 oz.
Mayonnaise	1 lb.	2 lb.	4 lb.	8 lb.
Salt	1½ tsp.	1 Tbsp.	1 oz.	2 oz.
Pepper, white	¼ tsp.	½ tsp.	1 tsp.	2 tsp.
Lemon Juice	1 Tbsp.	2 Tbsp.	¼ cup	½ cup
Lettuce Cups	3 lb.	6 lb.	12 lb.	24 lb.
Tomato Wedges	3 lb.	6 lb.	12 lb.	24 lb.

1. Cut chicken, light and dark meat, into ¼" cubes.
2. Cool rice and drained peas.
3. Combine chicken, peas, rice, diced celery, and pimiento.
4. Blend mayonnaise with seasonings and pour over combined ingredients.
5. Toss together lightly. Taste for salt.
6. Cover and refrigerate at least 30 minutes before serving.
7. Using a #12 scoop, portion 3¼ oz. in a 2-oz. lettuce cup.
8. Cut peeled tomatoes into 4 to 6 wedges (each wedge should weigh 1 oz.). Use 2 wedges per portion, placing one on each side of the salad, as shown in Figure 33. Melon wedges may be substituted for tomatoes.

Note: Chicken, rice, and peas should be salted while cooking.

Note: Cooked macaroni may be substituted for cooked rice. Cubed ham, shrimp, or tuna may be substituted for the chicken; and cubed processed cheese (¼" cubes) may be substituted for ½ of the ham, shrimp, or tuna.

Figure 33   A combination chicken-vegetable salad served on a bed of lettuce with tomato wedges and accompanied by a bread roll provides a hearty luncheon meal.

POLYNESIAN CHICKEN SALAD

½ Cup Portion	1 Gal. 1 Qt. 48 Portions	2 Gal. 2 Qt. 96 Portions	5 Gallons 192 Portions
Chicken or Turkey, cooked, cubed	5 lb.	10 lb.	20 lb.
Celery, cubed ½", EP	12 oz.	1 lb. 8 oz.	3 lb.
Pineapple Tidbits, drained	1 lb.	2 lb.	4 lb.
Pecans, chopped, optional	4 oz.	8 oz.	1 lb.
Monosodium Glutamate	1 oz.	2 oz.	4 oz.
Mayonnaise	1 qt.	2 qt.	1 gal.
Pineapple Syrup, drained from tidbits	½ cup	1 cup	2 cups

1. Toss all ingredients together. Put in shallow pans and refrigerate to chill.
2. Serve a heaping #10 scoop or a heaping ½ cup on a lettuce cup.
3. Garnish with watercress.

Note: Drained, sliced water chestnuts may be used in the same amounts as the pecans.

SEA BREEZE SHRIMP AND MELON BOAT SALAD

	12 Portions	24 Portions	48 Portions
Cottage Cheese	1 qt. 2 cups	3 qt.	1 gal. 2 qt.
Lime Rind, grated	1½ tsp.	1 Tbsp.	2 Tbsp.
Lime Juice	1 Tbsp.	2 Tbsp.	¼ cup
Melon, medium, honeydew *or* cantaloupe	3	6	12
Shrimp, Crabmeat, *and/or* Lobster, cooked and cleaned	1 lb. 8 oz.	3 lb.	6 lb.
French Dressing *or* Oil-Vinegar Dressing, to marinate, optional			
Romaine Leaves	12	24	48
Lime Wedges, to garnish	12	24	48

1. Combine cottage cheese, lime rind, and juice. Blend together and chill.
2. Cut honeydew melon or cantaloupe in quarters. Remove seeds and chill.
3. Marinate seafood in Red French or Oil-Vinegar Dressing if desired (see pp. 161 and 171). Chill. If not marinated, serve dressing on side.
4. Put melon wedge on plate and top with a #10 scoop of cottage cheese.
5. Drain seafood (if marinated) and arrange 2 oz. on 1 leaf of romaine.
6. Sprinkle chopped dill or chives on top of shrimp.
7. Garnish with a lime wedge.

Figure 34   This a la carte salad is a Seabreeze Melon Boat prepared by filling a quarter of a small melon with cottage cheese, placing chilled shrimp on a romaine or lettuce leaf, and adding a wedge of lemon or lime.

GOLDEN FRUIT SALAD
(Peach, Pear, and Pineapple with Grape Garnish)

1. Put a large lettuce cup on a salad plate. Add shredded or chopped lettuce to form a base, if necessary, for added height.
2. Put a peach half, pear half, and pineapple slice in the large lettuce cup.
3. Using deep red grapes, garnish with a grape cluster in center. Add 4 or 5 banana slices. (Dip banana in pineapple juice just before placing on salad in order to prevent discoloration.)
4. Serve with Fruit French Dressing (see pp. 166–167).
5. Serve with cheese roll and butter.

GOLDEN PEACH SALAD
(Peach, Melon, and Blueberries with Cottage Cheese)

1. Set up a lettuce cup according to the preceding formula.
2. Put 3 drained peach halves on a large lettuce cup.
3. Put a small scoop of cottage cheese in the center of each peach half.
4. Surround peach halves with 4 to 6 large cubes of honeydew melon or a combination of honeydew and watermelon.
5. Sprinkle salad with fresh blueberries for garnish.
6. Serve with Fruit French Dressing (see pp. 166–167).

Note: The lime cottage cheese used in the Sea Breeze Shrimp and Melon Boat Salad may be used in place of regular cottage cheese. Pears may be used as a substitute for peaches. Bing cherry halves, red grape halves, strawberries, or red raspberries may be used as a substitute for blueberries.

Figure 35   A chilled fruit salad of fresh bananas and grapes with canned peach slices and orange and grapefruit segments provides a light, attractive, and nutritious lunch when served with buttered hot rolls and a glass of milk.

GOLDEN FRUIT SALAD BOWL
(Assorted Fruit with Parsley-Cream Cheese Balls)
Slices of Nut Bread with Butter

1. Line a salad bowl with a large lettuce cup.
2. Fill salad bowl with 1 cup of assorted greens or chopped lettuce.
3. Put any combination of fruits on top of greens. Use fruits such as peach slices, peach and pear slices, or pineapple chunks; cantaloupe, honeydew, or watermelon cubes (1″ cubes), red grape or Bing cherry halves; green grapes; or banana slices. A combination of 4 fruits will be satisfactory. Two canned fruits and 2 fresh fruits are a good combination.
4. Cut cream cheese into ½″ to ¾″ cubes. Roll cubes to form a small round ball. Roll each ball lightly in chopped parsley. These may be prepared in advance and chilled in the refrigerator.
5. Center 3 to 4 cream cheese balls on top of assorted fruits.
6. Serve with Fruit French Dressing (see pp. 166–167) and slices of banana bread or date nut bread with butter.

Note: A scoop of cottage cheese may be used in place of cream cheese balls. As a variation, cream cheese balls may be rolled in chopped nuts or coconut instead of parsley.

BANANA SUPREME SALAD
(Combination of Assorted Fruits with Sesame Roll)

1. Cut peeled bananas in ¾″ to 1″ chunks.
2. Roll each chunk in mayonnaise so that entire chunk is lightly coated.
3. Roll each banana chunk in chopped nuts. Walnuts, pecans, or peanuts may be used.
4. This salad may be set up in the same manner as any of the Golden Fruit Salads. Top salad with 3 to 4 banana chunks.
5. Serve with Lime Cream Dressing (see p. 157) and a sesame roll.

TROPICAL FRUIT SALAD PLATE

1. For this salad, choose fresh pineapple, avocadoes, bananas, and a papaya, if available. If papaya is not available, cantaloupe may be substituted.
2. Cut all fruits lengthwise, as shown in Figure 36.
3. Using a romaine leaf for each salad, alternate the lengthwise wedges of fruit in a colorful arrangement.
4. Serve with Sesame Lime Dressing (see p. 160) and roll.

Note: If desired, this salad may also be served with a protein item. Use the Lemon-Cheese Mold (see p. 282), a scoop of cottage cheese, or a mound of chicken salad.

WESTERN FRUIT SALAD PLATE
(With Santa Clara Stuffed Prunes)

1. Soften cream cheese with milk until cheese will go through a pastry tube easily. (See the directions for Molded Peach and Stuffed Prune Salad on p. 270.)
2. Chill stuffed prunes in refrigerator until cheese is firm.
3. This salad is very similar to the Tropical Fruit Salad Plate, except that fruits are cut differently and a small iceberg lettuce or escarole cup is used.
4. Put 4 small lettuce cups on a large plate, leaving a space open in the center. In each lettuce cup, put one of the following fruit combinations: drained pear half with a strawberry in its cavity; three stuffed prunes; cantaloupe, honeydew and watermelon cubes; banana or peach slices with a grape cluster.
5. Put a souffle of Fruit French Dressing (see pp. 166–167) in the center of salad.

Note: Any combination of fruits may be used. It is important that the salad be balanced with light and dark fruits and that it also be balanced with canned and fresh fruits. It should be noted that this is a high-labor salad.

Figure 36   A tropical fruit salad of fresh bananas, avocado, papaya slices, and fresh pineapple segments served with a Lime and Sesame Seed Dressing is an excellent prelude to a cheese dessert.

LEMON-CHEESE MOLD
WITH
ASSORTED FRUIT

1. Prepare the Lemon-Cheese Mold on p. 282. Chill overnight and unmold. Chill again.
2. Surround cheese mold with any assorted fruit. For spring, fresh pineapple and whole strawberries are elegant. For winter, grapefruit and orange sections are perfect. Other fruits may be added.
3. Serve with Fruit French Dressing I (see p. 166).

PINEAPPLE-COTTAGE CHEESE MOLD
WITH
ASSORTED FRUITS

1. Prepare the Pineapple Cottage Cheese Ring Mold formula on p. 282.
2. Put the mixture in individual custard cups before allowing to set. Pineapple-Cheese molds, after unmolding, must be firmed again in the refrigerator.
3. Surround cheese mold with assorted fruit.
4. Serve with Fruit French Dressing I (see p. 166).

NOUVELLE CUISINE SALADS

The French *nouvelle cuisine,* sometimes called *naturelle cuisine,* has had a major impact on the foodservice industry in recent years. For generations, French food was noted for its heavy and rich sauces that often masked the original flavor of primary ingredients. Then, in the early 1970s, a few leaders in the French restaurant industry introduced and perfected the new cuisine, which emphasized the natural flavor of fresh food simply prepared and artistically served. Nouvelle cuisine is based on variations of classic cooking methodology and techniques. Because it emphasizes fresh flavor, natural texture, and appearance, considerable care must be taken to protect the natural quality of ingredients. Contemporary food preparation equipment simplifies the processes of slicing, grinding, and pureeing the ingredients that are so important to the success of foods natural in taste and appearance.

In nouvelle cuisine, delicate cream and butter sauces are thickened with vegetable purees rather than unnecessary fats and starches. Fresh, in-season fruit and vegetables, along with other foods containing moderate amounts of fats and protein, are served with creativity and style.

Salads and salad dressings have been influenced by the interest in nouvelle cuisine. In the preparation of salads and salad dressings, the basic principles of simplicity and natural flavor have been combined with an emphasis on contrasts in color and texture. The salads in this section are typical of the nouvelle cuisine, and the dressing formulas to be used with them incorporate the use of light, flavorful ingredients. In some dressing formulas blended cottage cheese replaces the heavier, highly caloric sour cream or mayonnaise. Ingredients and spices are mixed in sometimes unusual combinations. Attention to careful preparation and attractive presentation is the key to the success of each of these salads.

TOMATOES AND CUCUMBERS NOUVELLE

½ Cup Portions	4 Portions	8 Portions	16 Portions	32 Portions
Cucumbers, peeled and cubed ¼″	1 cup	2 cups	1 qt.	2 qt.
Tomatoes, unpeeled and cubed ¼″	1 cup	2 cups	1 qt.	2 qt.
Parsley, minced	1 Tbsp. 1 tsp.	2 Tbsp. 2 tsp.	¼ cup 1 Tbsp. 1 tsp.	½ cup 2 Tbsp. 2 tsp.
Oil, salad	¼ cup	½ cup	1 cup	2 cups
Vinegar, wine	¼ cup	½ cup	1 cup	2 cups
Sugar	1 tsp.	2 tsp.	1 Tbsp. 1 tsp.	2 Tbsp. 2 tsp.
Salt	¼ tsp.	½ tsp.	1 tsp.	2 tsp.
Pepper	¹⁄₁₆ tsp.	⅛ tsp.	¼ tsp.	½ tsp.

1. Combine all ingredients.
2. Mix to combine thoroughly.

Note: Zucchini, unpeeled and cut in ¼″ cubes, may be substituted for the cucumbers.

VEGETABLES NOUVELLE

½ Cup Portions	4 Portions	8 Portions	16 Portions	32 Portions
Cucumbers, peeled and cubed ¼″	½ cup	1 cup	2 cups	1 qt.
Tomatoes, unpeeled and cubed ¼″	½ cup	1 cup	2 cups	1 qt.
Cauliflower, cut in small flowerets	½ cup	1 cup	2 cups	1 qt.
Zucchini, unpeeled and cubed ¼″	½ cup	1 cup	2 cups	1 qt.
Parsley, minced	1 Tbsp. 1 tsp.	2 Tbsp. 2 tsp.	¼ cup 1 Tbsp. 1 tsp.	½ cup 2 Tbsp. 2 tsp.
Oil, salad	¼ cup	½ cup	1 cup	2 cups
Vinegar, wine	¼ cup	½ cup	1 cup	2 cups
Sugar	1 tsp.	2 tsp.	1 Tbsp. 1 tsp.	2 Tbsp. 2 tsp.
Salt	¼ tsp.	½ tsp.	1 tsp.	2 tsp.
Pepper	⅟₁₆ tsp.	⅛ tsp.	¼ tsp.	½ tsp.

1. Combine all ingredients.
2. Mix to combine thoroughly.

Note: Both nouvelle salads are excellent served with steak, lamb chops, or any roast meat. They provide tartness and texture to the meal. These salads are also beautiful served in a transparent glass bowl for buffet tables.

FRESH MUSHROOM SALAD

½ Cup Portions	4 Portions	8 Portions	16 Portions	32 Portions
Mushrooms, small, caps only	8 oz.	1 lb.	2 lb.	4 lb.
Parsley, minced	¼ cup	½ cup	1 cup	2 cups
Green Onions, minced	¼ cup	½ cup	1 cup	2 cups
Oil, salad	½ cup	1 cup	2 cups	1 qt.
Vinegar, white wine	2 Tbsp.	¼ cup	½ cup	1 cup
Salt	¼ tsp.	½ tsp.	1 tsp.	2 tsp.
Pepper, white	¹⁄₁₆ tsp.	⅛ tsp.	¼ tsp.	½ tsp.

1. Wash mushroom caps and allow to dry.
2. Thinly slice mushroom caps.
3. Combine parsley and green onion with sliced mushrooms.
4. Add oil and white wine vinegar.
5. Add salt and pepper. Mix all ingredients to combine.

Note: Replace up to ⅓ of the mushrooms with thinly sliced celery for a variation. Either salad may be garnished with chopped, hard-cooked egg.

AVOCADO AND SHRIMP SALAD

	1 Salad	**2 Salads**	**4 Salads**	**8 Salads**
Iceberg Lettuce Leaves	4 oz.	8 oz.	1 lb.	2 lb.
Iceberg Lettuce, cut into chunks	1 qt.	2 qt.	1 gal.	2 gal.
Shrimp, cooked	3 oz.	6 oz.	12 oz.	1 lb. 8 oz.
Avocado, sliced crosswise	½	1	2	4
Cucumber Slices	4 *or* 5	8 *or* 10	16 *or* 20	32 *or* 40
Vegetables Moreno	1 cup	2 cups	1 qt.	2 qt.
Alfalfa Sprouts, lightly packed	½ cup	1 cup	2 cups	1 qt.
Lemon Wedges	2	4	8	16
Cherry Tomatoes	2	4	8	16

1. Line platter with lettuce leaves; heap with lettuce chunks.
2. Mound shrimp on lettuce.
3. Top with avocado.
4. Arrange cucumber, Vegetables Moreno (formula to follow), sprouts, lemon, and tomatoes around platter.
5. Serve with choice of Oil-Vinegar, Thousand Island, or Easy Blue Cheese Dressing (see pp. 171, 145, and 150).

VEGETABLES MORENO

	2 Gallons	4 Gallons
Vinegar, distilled	2 cups	1 qt.
Oil, salad	1 cup	2 cups
Lemon Juice	½ cup	1 cup
Sugar	½ cup	1 cup
Pickling Spice	¼ cup	½ cup
Tabasco	1½ tsp.	1 Tbsp.
Salt	1½ Tbsp.	3 Tbsp.
Carrots, diagonally cut, EP	2 lb.	4 lb.
Celery, diagonally cut, EP	1 lb.	2 lb.
Zucchini, cut into sticks, EP	1 lb. 8 oz.	3 lb.
Mushrooms, thick-sliced, EP	1 lb. 4 oz.	2 lb. 8 oz.
Onion, large, cut into rings	1½	3
Pickled Cherry Peppers	2 qt.	1 gal.
Garbanzo Beans, drained	½ #10 can	1 #10 can

1. Simmer vinegar, oil, lemon juice, sugar, pickling spice, Tabasco, and salt together 3 to 5 minutes.
2. Cool.
3. Combine vegetables and cooled dressing from above.
4. Refrigerate.

Note: Vegetables may be varied with crookneck squash, artichoke hearts, cauliflower, etc. This formula keeps for days but has the freshest appearance and crispiest texture the first two days after preparation.

FRESH TOMATO STUFFED WITH SCALLOPS AND GRAPEFRUIT

	12 Portions	24 Portions	48 Portions
Tomatoes, large	12	24	48
Scallops	1 lb.	2 lb.	4 lb.
Scallions, sliced, EP	¼ cup	½ cup	1 cup
Green Beans, fresh, julienne	1 lb.	2 lb.	4 lb.
Celery, cut in sticks, EP	2 cups	1 qt.	2 qt.
Grapefruit Sections	2	4	8
Mushrooms, fresh	4 oz.	8 oz.	1 lb.
Apples, cored and diced	2	4	8
Celery Leaves, as needed			
Lettuce Leaves, as needed			

1. Use tomatoes held at room temperature until fully ripe.
2. Cut a thin slice from the top of each tomato; scoop out pulp.
3. Set tomatoes aside with cavities down to drain.
4. Cook scallops in boiling salted water until done, 30 seconds to 1 minute. Place in bowl with scallions and chill.
5. Cook green beans in boiling salted water until barely tender. Drain, place in a bowl or other container and chill.
6. Cook celery sticks in boiling salted water until barely tender. Drain, place in a bowl or other container and chill.
7. Cover and refrigerate vegetables until ready to serve.
8. When ready to serve, fill tomatoes with scallops and scallions. Top with grapefruit sections.
9. Place 1 stuffed tomato on a chilled, lettuce-lined plate.
10. Surround with clusters of celery, green beans, and sliced mushrooms.
11. Sprinkle scallops and vegetables with Salad Dressing Naturelle (see p. 182).
12. Garnish with diced apple and celery leaves.

COBB SALAD

	2 Portions	4 Portions	8 Portions	16 Portions
Lettuce, Iceberg and romaine, chopped	8 oz.	1 lb.	2 lb.	4 lb.
Chicken, white meat, cooked, chopped ¼"	¾ cup	1½ cups	3 cups	1 qt. 2 cups
Green Onions, minced	3	6	12	24
Eggs, hard-cooked, finely chopped	1	2	4	8
Tomatoes, medium, peeled and chopped ¼"	1	2	4	8
Bacon, cooked, crisp and crumbled	4 slices	8 slices	16 slices	32 slices
Blue Cheese, crumbled	1¼ oz.	2½ oz.	5 oz.	10 oz.
Avocado, small, ripe, peeled, seeded, and cubed ¼"	1	2	4	8
Lemon Juice, to coat avocado				

1. Spread chopped greens evenly over bottom of a shallow, medium-large salad bowl.
2. Arrange ingredients in rows over greens with chopped chicken in a narrow strip down center.
3. Put tomato, blue cheese, and avocado in rows to the left of chicken. Coat avocado with lemon juice if not serving immediately.
4. Put green onion, hard-cooked egg, and bacon in rows to the right of chicken.
5. Display the salad at the table before it is tossed.
6. Gently toss at the table and serve on chilled, lettuce-lined plates.
7. Just before serving, add any oil and vinegar salad dressing.

ZUCCHINI SALAD
(Sweet-Sour Salad)

½ Cup Portions	6 Portions	12 Portions	24 Portions	48 Portions
Zucchini, medium, thinly sliced	3	6	12	24
Green Pepper, shredded, EP	½ cup	1 cup	2 cups	1 qt.
Celery, shredded, EP	½ cup	1 cup	2 cups	1 qt.
Yellow Onion, shredded, EP	½ cup	1 cup	2 cups	1 qt.
Sugar	½ cup	1 cup	2 cups	1 qt.
Salt	1 tsp.	2 tsp.	1 Tbsp. 1 tsp.	2 Tbsp. 2 tsp.
Pepper, freshly ground	½ tsp.	1 tsp.	2 tsp.	1 Tbsp. 1 tsp.
Vinegar, cider	⅔ cup	1⅓ cups	2⅔ cups	1 qt. 1⅓ cups
Oil, salad	⅓ cup	⅔ cup	1⅓ cups	2⅔ cups
Wine, burgundy	¼ cup	½ cup	1 cup	2 cups
Vinegar, red wine	2 Tbsp.	¼ cup	½ cup	1 cup

1. Combine all ingredients in a large bowl and mix thoroughly.
2. Cover and refrigerate at least 6 hours before serving.
3. Serve in lettuce cup on salad plate.

Note: Salad will keep up to 2 weeks. Keep refrigerated.

SPINACH SALAD

	6 Salads	12 Salads
Spinach, washed and well-drained	2 qt. 1 cup	1 gal. 2 cups
Mushrooms, large	6	12
Bacon Slices, cooked until crisp	12	24

1. Put 1½ cups spinach in a bowl.
2. Slice 1 large mushroom on top of the spinach.
3. Break 2 crisp bacon slices into large pieces (about ½").
4. Top the salad with ¼ cup Cheddar Cheese Dressing (see p. 178).
5. If a very large salad is desired, use 3 cups of spinach, 2 large mushrooms, 4 slices of bacon, and ½ cup of dressing.

WILTED SPINACH OR LETTUCE
(Sweet-Sour Salad)

Dressing	1½ Cups 9 Portions	3 Cups 18 Portions	1 Qt. 2 Cups 36 Portions	3 Quarts 72 Portions
Bacon Slices, cut in ¼″ squares	4	8	16	32
Bacon Fat, from above				
Vinegar, cider or Tarragon	½ cup	1 cup	2 cups	1 qt.
Sugar	½ cup	1 cup	2 cups	1 qt.
Water	2 Tbsp.	¼ cup	½ cup	1 cup
Salt	¼ tsp.	½ tsp.	1 tsp.	1 Tbsp. 1 tsp.
Pepper	⅟₁₆ tsp.	⅛ tsp.	¼ tsp.	½ tsp.
Eggs	2	4	8	16
Green Onions, chopped, optional	3	6	12	24

Salad

Spinach or Lettuce, washed and dried, EP	12 oz.	1 lb. 8 oz.	3 lb.	6 lb.

Dressing

1. Saute bacon until crisp. To bacon and bacon fat add vinegar, sugar, water, salt, and pepper.
2. Bring to a boil, stirring until sugar is dissolved.
3. Remove from heat and add raw eggs.
4. Stir vigorously with a wire whip.
5. Return to heat and stir until eggs are cooked.
6. For wilted greens, use 1½ cups warm dressing per 12 oz. torn spinach or lettuce.
7. Green onions, chopped, may be added to the dressing just before pouring over greens.

COCONUT SHRIMP SALAD BOWL

1. Put 2 cups of cut romaine and lettuce chunks in a large salad bowl that has been lined with lettuce leaves.
2. Put 6 large, cooked shrimp on top of the greens.
3. Put ¼ cup drained Mandarin orange sections around shrimp in an attractive arrangement.
4. Intersperse 2 thick slices of avocado (cut in small chunks) on top of salad.
5. Arrange 4 tomato wedges around the edge of salad.
6. Sprinkle salad with 1 Tbsp. croutons and 1 Tbsp. coconut.
7. Serve with Orange Blossom Dressing (see p. 170). Serve dressing in an individual china souffle cup or individual glass salad dressing container. Shrimp, oranges, avocado, and greens are dipped into the dressing when eaten.

APPENDIX

FRACTIONAL EQUIVALENTS

The following chart is designed to help you change fractional parts of pounds, gallons, cups, etc., to accurate weights or measures. For example, reading from left to right, the table shows that ⅞ of one pound is 14 ounces; ⅓ of a gallon is 1 quart plus 1⅓ cups; ¹⁄₁₆ of a cup is 1 tablespoon, etc. Using this chart makes it easy to change fractions to weights.

	1 Tbsp.	1 Cup	1 Pint	1 Quart	1 Gal.	1 Lb.
1	3 tsp.	16 Tbsp.	2 cups	2 pints	4 qt.	16 oz.
⅞	2½ tsp.	1 cup less 2 Tbsp.	1¾ cups	3½ cups	3 qt. 1 pt.	14 oz.
¾	2¼ tsp.	12 Tbsp.	1½ cups	3 cups	3 qt.	12 oz.
⅔	2 tsp.	10 Tbsp. 2 tsp.	1⅓ cups	2⅔ cups	2 qt. 2⅔ cups	10⅔ oz.
⅝	2 tsp. (sc)	10 Tbsp.	1¼ cups	2½ cups	2 qt. 1 pt.	10 oz.
½	1½ tsp.	8 Tbsp.	1 cup	2 cups	2 qt.	8 oz.
⅜	1⅛ tsp.	6 Tbsp.	¾ cup	1½ cups	1 qt. 1 pint	6 oz.
⅓	1 tsp.	5 Tbsp. 1 tsp.	⅔ cup	1⅓ cups	1 qt. 1⅓ cups	5⅓ oz.
¼	¾ tsp.	4 Tbsp.	½ cup	1 cup	1 qt.	4 oz.
⅛	½ tsp. (sc)	2 Tbsp.	¼ cup	½ cup	1 pint	2 oz.
¹⁄₁₆	¼ tsp. (sc)	1 Tbsp.	2 Tbsp.	4 Tbsp.	1 cup	1 oz.

sc = scant

COMMON FOOD EQUIVALENTS

Celery Salt, Onion Salt, Granulated Bouillon (Beef Base)

2 Tbsp. = ¾ oz.
¼ cup = 1½ oz.
½ cup = 3 oz.
1 cup = 6 oz.
2 cups = 12 oz.
1 qt.   = 1 lb. 8 oz.

Basil, Oregano, Thyme*

¼ cup = ¼ oz.
½ cup = ½ oz.
1 cup = 1 oz.
2 cups = 2 oz.
1 qt.   = 4 oz.

*If substituting fresh herbs for dried, use approximately 2½ times the amount indicated because dried herbs are more concentrated than fresh.

Parsley, Freshly Chopped

¼ cup = ¼ oz.
½ cup = ½ oz.
1 cup = 1 oz.
2 cups = 2 oz.
1 qt.   = 4 oz.

Bay Leaves

64 Bay Leaves = ¼ oz.
128 Bay Leaves = ½ oz.
250 Bay Leaves = 1 oz.

Garlic, Freshly Chopped*

1 Tbsp.   = ¼ oz. = 8 cloves
2 Tbsp.   = ½ oz. = 16 cloves
¼ cup   = 1 oz. = 32 cloves
½ cup   = 2 oz. = 64 cloves
1 cup   = 4 oz. = 128 cloves
1 bag (AP) = 2 lb. 8 oz., EP (not chopped)

*Garlic cloves vary greatly in size. It is impossible to list garlic in terms of number of cloves, although an attempt has been made.

Garlic Powder, Paprika, Mustard, Parmesan Cheese

1 Tbsp. = ¼ oz.   1 cup = 4 oz.
2 Tbsp. = ½ oz.   2 cups = 8 oz.
¼ cup = 1 oz.   1 qt. = 1 lb.
½ cup = 2 oz.   2 qt. = 2 lb.

Pimiento

½ cup = 4 oz.
1 cup = 8 oz.
2 cups = 1 lb.
1 qt.   = 2 lb.
2 qt.   = 4 lb.

COMMON FOOD EQUIVALENTS (CONT.)

Sugar, Granulated and Brown

2 Tbsp. 2 tsp. = 1 oz.	
½ cup	= 3½ oz.
1 cup	= 7 oz.
2 cups	= 14 oz.
3 cups	= 1 lb. 5 oz.
1 qt.	= 1 lb. 12 oz.
1 gal.	= 7 lb.
2 gal.	= 14 lb.

Sugar, Confectioner's

2 Tbsp. =	½ oz.
¼ cup	= 1 oz.
½ cup	= 2 oz.
1 cup	= 4 oz.
2 cups	= 8 oz.
3 cups	= 12 oz.
1 qt.	= 1 lb.
1 gal.	= 4 lb.

Flour or Nonfat Dry Milk

½ cup	= 2 oz.
1 cup	= 4 oz.
2 cups	= 8 oz.
3 cups	= 12 oz.
1 qt.	= 1 lb.
2 qt.	= 2 lb.
3 qt.	= 3 lb.
1 gal.	= 4 lb.

Nonfat Dry Milk, Reconstituted

8 oz. dry milk + 1 qt. 3½ cups water	= 2 qt. milk
1 lb. dry milk + 3 qt. 3 cups water	= 1 gal. milk
2 lb. dry milk + 1 gal. 3 qt. 2 cups water	= 2 gal. milk
4 lb. dry milk + 3 gal. 3 qt. water	= 4 gal. milk
5 lb. dry milk + 4 gal. 2 qt. 3 cups water	= 5 gal. milk
10 lb. dry milk + 9 gal. 1 qt. 2 cups water	= 10 gal. milk

1. Add lukewarm water to dry milk.

2. Using balloon whip and number 1 speed, mix for 4 minutes.

Butter or Margarine

⅛ cup	= 2 Tbsp.	= 1 oz.
¼ cup	= 4 Tbsp.	= 2 oz.
½ cup	= 9 Tbsp.	= 4 oz.
1 cup	= 16 Tbsp.	= 8 oz.
2 cups		= 1 lb.
1 qt.		= 2 lb.

Salt, Baking Powder, and Soda

2 Tbsp.	= 1 oz.
*2 Tbsp. 2 tsp.	= 1¼ oz.
¼ cup	= 2 oz.
4 Tbsp. 4 tsp.	= 2½ oz.
½ cup	= 4 oz.
1 cup	= 8 oz.
2 cups	= 1 lb.

Cornstarch

½ cup	= 2½ oz.
1 cup	= 5 oz.
2 cups	= 10 oz.
1 qt.	= 1 lb. 4 oz.
1 gal.	= 5 lb.

*This is somewhat under actual weight, but it is best to err on the underside when multiplying salt.

COMMON FOOD EQUIVALENTS (CONT.)

Cornmeal
1 cup   = 5 oz.
2 cups = 10 oz.
3 cups = 15 oz.
1 qt.   = 1 lb. 4 oz.
2 qt.   = 2 lb. 8 oz.
3 qt.   = 3 lb. 12 oz.
1 gal.   = 5 lb.

Cream of Tartar
2 Tbsp. = 1 oz.
¼ cup = 2 oz.
½ cup = 4 oz.
1 cup   = 8 oz.
2 cups = 1 lb.

Rice
1 cup   = 8 oz. = 1 qt. cooked
2 cups = 1 lb. = 2 qt. cooked
1 qt.   = 2 lb. = 1 gal. cooked
2 qt.   = 4 lb. = 2 gal. cooked
1 gal.   = 8 lb. = 4 gal. cooked

Grated Orange or Lemon Rind*
Gelatin (Unflavored)
Allspice—Cloves—Cinnamon—Nutmeg
1 Tbsp. = ¼ oz.
2 Tbsp. = ½ oz.
¼ cup = 1 oz.
½ cup = 2 oz.

1 cup   = 4 oz.
2 cups = 8 oz.
1 qt.   = 1 lb.
2 qt.   = 2 lb.

Grated Cheese
1 cup   = 4 oz.
2 cups = 8 oz.
1 qt.   = 1 lb.
2 qt.   = 2 lb.
1 gal.   = 4 lb.

*It requires 15 minutes to grate 2 oz. orange or lemon rind.

Peanut Butter
¼ cup = 2 oz.
½ cup = 4 oz.
1 cup   = 8 oz.
2 cups = 1 lb.
1 qt.   = 2 lb.

Marshmallows (Miniature)
1 cup   = 2 oz.
2 cups = 4 oz.
1 qt.   = 8 oz.
2 qt.   = 1 lb.
1 gal.   = 2 lb.

Raisins
1 cup   = 6 oz.
2 cups = 12 oz.
1 qt.   = 1 lb. 8 oz.
2 qt.   = 3 lb.
1 gal.   = 6 lb.

COMMON FOOD EQUIVALENTS (CONT.)

Pecan Halves			Nutmeats, Chopped		
1 cup	= 3 oz.		1 cup	= 4 oz.
2 cups	= 6 oz.		2 cups	= 8 oz.
1 qt.	= 12 oz.		1 qt.	= 1 lb.
2 qt.	= 1 lb. 8 oz.		2 qt.	= 2 lb.
1 gal.	= 3 lb.		1 gal.	= 4 lb.

Cocoa and Chocolate

3 Tbsp. Cocoa	= ½ oz. Cocoa	= 1 oz. Chocolate
6 Tbsp. Cocoa	= 1 oz. Cocoa	= 2 oz. Chocolate
¾ cup Cocoa	= 2 oz. Cocoa	= 4 oz. Chocolate
1½ cups Cocoa	= 4 oz. Cocoa	= 8 oz. Chocolate
3 cups Cocoa	= 8 oz. Cocoa	= 1 lb. Chocolate
1 qt. 2 cups Cocoa	= 1 lb. Cocoa	= 2 lb. Chocolate

(1 Tbsp. fat may be added to 3 Tbsp. or ½ oz. Cocoa)

Instant Coffee			Pepper		
2 Tbsp. = ¼ oz.			sc	= scant
¼ cup = ½ oz.			2 Tbsp. = sc ½ oz.
½ cup = 1 oz.			2 Tbsp.
1 cup = 2 oz.			2 tsp. = sc ¾ oz.
2 cups = 4 oz.			¼ cup = sc 1 oz.
1 qt. = 8 oz.			4 Tbsp.
			4 tsp. = sc 1¼ oz.
			½ cup = 2 oz.
			1 cup = 4 oz.
			2 cups = 8 oz.

COMMON FOOD EQUIVALENTS (CONT.)

Fresh Whole Eggs—Medium*		Fresh Whole Eggs—Small*	
5 whole eggs	= 1 cup or 8 oz.	6 whole eggs	= 1 cup or 8 oz.
10 whole eggs	= 2 cups or 1 lb.	12 or 1 dz eggs	= 2 cups or 1 lb.
15 whole eggs	= 3 cups or 1 lb. 8 oz.	18 or 1½ dz eggs	= 3 cups or 1 lb. 8 oz.
20 whole eggs	= 1 qt. or 2 lb.	24 or 2 dz eggs	= 1 qt. or 2 lb.
40 whole eggs	= 2 qt. or 4 lb.	48 or 4 dz eggs	= 2 qt. or 4 lb.
80 whole eggs	= 1 gal. or 8 lb.	96 or 8 dz eggs	= 1 gal. or 8 lb.

Egg Whites**		Egg Yolks**	
8 whites	= 1 cup	10 yolks	= 1 cup
16 whites	= 2 cups	20 yolks	= 2 cups
32 whites	= 1 qt.	40 yolks	= 1 qt.
128 whites	= 1 gal.	160 yolks	= 1 gal.

*Because of the great variation in egg sizes, it is more accurate to weigh eggs. Eggs are a liquid ingredient, however, and the authors find it easier to measure all liquid ingredients instead of weighing them.
**From medium eggs.

STANDARD RATIOS FOR FLAVORED GELATIN SALADS

Gelatin	1 lb. 8 oz. Box	Water	Portions or Molds	Approximate Portions
1 lb. 2 oz.	¾ box	3 qt.	24 ½-cup portions	24
1 lb. 8 oz.	1 box	1 gal.	32 ½-cup portions	32
4 lb. 8 oz.	3 boxes	3 gal.	96 ½-cup portions	100
22 lb. 8 oz.	15 boxes	15 gal.	480 ½-cup portions	500
45 lb.	30 boxes	30 gal.	960 ½-cup portions	1000

STANDARD RATIOS FOR FLAVORED GELATIN SALADS

Gelatin	1 lb. 8 oz. Box	Water	12 × 20 × 2 Pans	Portions Cut 8 × 4	Approximate Portions
1 lb. 8 oz.	1 box	1 gal.	1 pan	32	32
4 lb. 8 oz.	3 boxes	3 gal.	3 pans	96	100
9 lb.	6 boxes	6 gal.	6 pans	192	200
18 lb.	12 boxes	12 gal.	12 pans	384	400
22 lb. 8 oz.	15 boxes	15 gal.	15 pans	480	500
45 lb.	30 boxes	30 gal.	30 pans	960	1000

STANDARD RATIOS FOR GELATIN SALADS
VEGETABLE AND/OR FRUIT ADDED

Gelatin	Liquid Added	Vegetable and/or Fruit	12 × 20 × 2 Pans	Portions— Cut 8 × 4
1 lb.	2 qt. 2 cups*	2 qt. *or* 1 #10 can, drained	1 pan	32

Note: The above amounts provide for ¼ cup fruit and/or vegetable per portion. If gelatin is poor, one may prefer to use 1 lb. 4 oz. or 1 lb. 8 oz. for the above ratio for salad. Some of the salads in this text use the following ratios: 1 lb. gelatin, 3 qt. liquid, and 2 qt. or 1 #10 can drained vegetable and/or fruit per 12 × 20 × 2 pan for 32 portions cut 8 × 4. These salads will set, but an especially good gelatin must be used.

*Two quarts water and up to 2 cups liquid (acid) such as lemon juice, pineapple juice, or canned fruit juice.

STANDARD RATIOS FOR UNFLAVORED GELATIN SALADS

Gelatin	Liquid Added	12 × 20 × 2 Pans	Portions— Cut 8 × 4	Approximate Portions
2 oz.	1 gal.	1 pan	32	32
4 oz.	2 gal.	2 pans	64	64
6 oz.	3 gal.	3 pans	96	100
8 oz.	4 gal.	4 pans	128	125
10 oz.	5 gal.	5 pans	160	150
12 oz.	6 gal.	6 pans	192	200
1 lb.	8 gal.	8 pans	256	250
1 lb. 4 oz.	10 gal.	10 pans	320	300
2 lb.	16 gal.	16 pans	512	500
4 lb.	32 gal.	32 pans	1024	1000

Flavored Gelatin—3 oz. sets 2 cups; 6 oz. sets 1 qt.; 12 oz. sets 2 qt.

Unflavored Gelatin—1 Tbsp. sets 2 cups; 2 Tbsp. sets 1 qt.; 1 oz. sets 2 qt.

VEGETABLE EQUIVALENTS—VOLUME TO EP WEIGHT

All Vegetables, EP	2 Cups	1 Qt.	2 Qt.	1 Gal.	2 Gal.
Cabbage, chopped or shredded	6 oz.	12 oz.	1 lb. 8 oz.	3 lb.	6 lb.
Carrots, shredded	6 oz.	12 oz.	1 lb. 8 oz.	3 lb.	6 lb.
Green Pepper, chopped ¼"	8 oz.	1 lb.	2 lb.	4 lb.	8 lb.
Celery, chopped ¼"	8 oz.	1 lb.	2 lb.	4 lb.	8 lb.
Onion, chopped ¼"	8 oz.	1 lb.	2 lb.	4 lb.	8 lb.

	2 Qt.	1 Gal.	1 Gal. 2 Qt.	2 Gal.	3 Gal.
Potatoes, raw, peeled, cubed ½" (25% waste)	3 lb. 12 oz. (5 lb., AP)	7 lb. 8 oz. (10 lb., AP)	11 lb. 4 oz. (15 lb., AP)	15 lb. (20 lb., AP)	22 lb. 8 oz. (30 lb., AP)
Sweet Potatoes, fresh, cooked, and sliced (20% waste)			8 lb. (10 lb., AP) or 1 12×20×2 pan		16 lb. (20 lb., AP) 2 12×20× pans

VEGETABLE YIELDS
(As Purchased to Edible Portion, or AP to EP)

95% EP 5% Waste	85% EP 15% Waste	75% EP 25% Waste	50% EP 50% Waste
Onions	Green Pepper	Cabbage, Carrots, Celery, Garlic, Lettuce	Potatoes

Note: Potatoes vary from 50% waste to 20% waste. This depends on the human element and/or machine peeling time. It is suggested that the 50% waste figure be used in determining mathematical calculations for cost purposes. One may eliminate onions and green peppers from cost calculations because the waste is nominal. The preceding yields are a simple guide for the common vegetables that are frequently used in a foodservice operation. Actually, the preparation of potatoes is being eliminated in many kitchens. There is a strong trend toward the purchase of potatoes prepeeled.

FROZEN VEGETABLES—AP TO EP (RAW TO COOKED)

1 10-oz. box   = 9 oz. cooked or 1½ cups
2 10-oz. boxes = 1 lb. 2 oz. cooked or 3 cups
4 10-oz. boxes = 2 lb. 4 oz. cooked or 1 qt. 2 cups
1 2½-lb. box   = 2 lb. 4 oz. cooked or 1 qt. 2 cups
2 2½-lb. boxes = 4 lb. 8 oz. cooked or 3 qt.
4 2½-lb. boxes = 9 lb. cooked or 1 gal. 2 qt.
6 2½-lb. boxes = 13 lb. 8 oz. cooked or 2 gal. 1 qt.
8 2½-lb. boxes = 18 lb. cooked or 3 gal.

FRUIT EQUIVALENTS—AP WEIGHT TO EP WEIGHT AND VOLUME

Apples, cubed	1 lb., AP	= 1 qt.
¼″ to ½″	3 lb., AP = 2 lb. 8 oz., EP	= 3 qt.
(20% waste)	(cubed)	
	6 lb., AP = 5 lb., EP (cubed)	= 1 gal. 2 qt.
	12 lb., AP = 10 lb., EP (cubed)	= 3 gal.
	24 lb., AP = 20 lb., EP (cubed)	= 6 gal.
	48 lb., AP = 40 lb., EP (cubed)	= 12 gal.
	96 lb., AP = 80 lb., EP (cubed)	= 24 gal.

FRUIT YIELDS

Note: Figures for all fruits have not been included in this section. Additional yield figures are available in the following bulletin on Fruits: Agricultural Research Service, "Consumer Quality Characteristics, Yield and Preparation Time of Various Market Forms." Available from: Superintendent of Documents, U. S. Government Printing Office, Washington, D.C. 20402.

EQUIVALENTS AND YIELDS

Food Measurement Equivalents

Weights	Measures
1 Tbsp.	3 tsp.
1 cup	16 Tbsp.
1 pint	2 cups
1 qt.	2 pints
1 gal.	4 qt.
1 qt.	32 oz.
1 lb.	16 oz.

Scoop Equivalents

Size	No. to the Qt.	Part of Cup	No. of Tbsp.
6	6	⅔	—
8	8	½	8
10	10	—	—
12	12	⅓	5⅓
16	16	¼	4
20	20	—	—
24	24	—	—
30	30	—	—
40	40	—	—

INDEX